THE UNIVERSITY OF SOUTHERN CALIFORNIA:
1880 TO 2005

THE UNIVERSITY OF SOUTHERN CALIFORNIA:
1880 TO 2005

Written by Sarah Lifton and Annette Moore

Photo research by Annette Moore with Claude Zachary and Susan Hikida

Printed and bound in the United States of America. No part of this publication may be reproduced or transmitted in any form or by any means, electronic or mechanical, including photocopying, recording or any information storage and retrieval system now known or to be invented, without permission in writing from USC Public Relations, 3775 South Hoover Street, H-201, Los Angeles, CA 90089-7790, except by a reviewer who wishes to quote brief passages in connection with a review written for inclusion in a magazine, newspaper or broadcast.

Produced and distributed by Figueroa Press
Los Angeles, California

(Figueroa Press is a division of the USC Trojan Bookstores; Figueroa Press and the USC Trojan Bookstores are trademarks of the University of Southern California.)

Book design by 2B Communications

Printed by Delta Graphics, Los Angeles

Includes bibliographical references

ISBN: 1-932800-19-0

Library of Congress Control Number: 2006930866

Notice of Liability
The information in this book is distributed on an "as-is" basis, without warranty. While every precaution has been taken in the preparation of this book, neither the authors nor Figueroa Press nor the USC Trojan Bookstores nor 2B Communications shall have any liability to any person or entity with respect to any loss or damage caused or alleged to be caused directly or indirectly by any text contained in this book.

First Printing: March 2007

10 9 8 7 6 5 4 3 2 1

Photography

Front cover (below): Photo by Philip Channing, © University of Southern California

Title page and opposite: Photo by Philip Channing, © University of Southern California

Opposite introduction: Photo by Philip Channing, © University of Southern California

Page ix: Photo © John Livzey

Page 214: Photo by Philip Channing, © University of Southern California

Page 229 (top left): Photo courtesy of Thompson Hine, LLP; (top right): photo by Irene Fertik; (middle right and bottom right): photo © John Livzey

Page 230 (top left and bottom left): Photo © John Livzey; (top right): photo © Lee Salem Photography; (bottom right): photo courtesy of Lucasfilm

Back cover (bottom left): Photo © Lee Salem Photography; (bottom center): photo by Philip Channing, © University of Southern California; (bottom right): photo courtesy of USC Public Relations

All other unattributed photographs courtesy of USC University Archives.

Contents

Defining Stories: USC's Three "Myths of Origin"

By Steven B. Sample, President, University of Southern California

The story of USC and the story of Los Angeles are inextricably intertwined, and our university's birth, its purpose and its very character are as unprecedented as are those of the frontier village in which USC was born. One of the most diverse and exciting cities in the history of mankind, Los Angeles is the *de facto* capital of the Pacific Rim, while USC—a latecomer when compared with many Eastern universities—now ranks among a peer group that includes Princeton and Yale. I might add that Princeton and Yale were both past the 125th-anniversary mark when upstart USC opened the front door of its only building to 53 students back in 1880.

I'm reminded of what Winston Churchill once said: "The farther back you can look, the farther forward you are likely to see." The past is indeed prologue. USC would not be what it is today were it not for the genius of those who came before —those founders, trustees, administrators, professors, alumni and supporters who built a small college into a premier research university.

Steven B. Sample, President
University of Southern California
[photo © John Livzey]

To create a context for this book, published to commemorate USC's 125th anniversary, I should like to depict a University of Southern California that foreshadows its future while honoring 125 years of its past. I should like this portrait to be a triptych—a painting in three parts. Each panel of the triptych, as it were, will depict the saga of USC through a corresponding myth from USC's creation story. These three myths reveal three essential components of USC's identity and uniqueness: First, our history of diversity; second, our rootedness in Los Angeles; and third, our relentless quest for academic excellence.

Allow me to explain what I mean when I use the term "myth." Every society has its myths of origin—those stories that are told to define and deepen our self-understanding. In this context the word myth does not mean "something that isn't true." On the contrary, many myths are absolutely true. But whether fact or fiction, myths help us understand who we are, what we believe in and what we want for the future.

The University of Southern California cherishes certain defining myths that serve as creation stories. These "In-the-beginning" stories not only explain USC's uniqueness but also influence its destiny. Our defining myths—the stories of our creation that have helped inform our identity and destiny as an institution thus far—will also serve to guide us in the years ahead.

Story One: Shaped by Diversity

In 1877 the great California naturalist John Muir visited Los Angeles and later recalled his visit with these words: "An hour's ride over stretches of bare, brown plain, and through cornfields and orange groves, brought me to the handsome, conceited little town of Los Angeles, where one finds Spanish adobes and Yankee shingles meeting and overlapping in very curious antagonism."

If he had looked more closely he would have seen an even broader array of residents. At that time about one-fourth of the city was foreign-born, and the populace reflected a wide variety of ethnicities, religions and social classes.

Founded as a Methodist university, USC was in fact created through the efforts of three businessmen from disparate backgrounds—comprising a Jew, a Catholic and an Episcopalian. This ecumenism is a true story, but it has become a defining myth that has taken on a deeper meaning. As a university that welcomed qualified people of all types from its beginning, USC now has a long tradition of educating students no matter what their gender, race, religion or background might be. USC's medical school, when it opened in 1885, also explicitly placed no restrictions based on age, race, religion or sex.

Little did the city's and the university's founders realize the extent to which Los Angeles would become a world city—a true heteropolis. And USC has played, and will continue to play, a major role in shaping this city into the capital of the Pacific Rim.

USC University Professor and historian Kevin Starr has written that "the very DNA code of Los Angeles" is internationalist, and that the City of the Angels is among those great cities known for their *plenum mundi,* or the "fullness of the world." International students began attending USC in 1882, just two years after the university opened. The first two international students arrived from Japan; by 1930, students from more than 30 countries made up 10 percent of USC's growing student population.

The first two international students arrived from Japan; by 1930, students from more than 30 countries made up 10 percent of USC's growing population.

We must remember that most of the nation's prestigious institutions of higher education, at the time of USC's founding, principally enrolled white males, and make no mistake, principally white males of privilege who were almost exclusively Protestant. Most colleges and universities were also segregated by gender: All of the Ivies, for example, admitted only men. By contrast, at USC women were enrolled in our first freshman class, and the university's first valedictorian in 1884 was a woman.

Today, looking around our campus we see the result of this steadfast commitment to open access for all students of merit. As one of the nation's most highly selective universities, we draw a student body that not only exhibits outstanding academic, artistic and athletic accomplishments, but a student body that reflects this country's renowned pluralism, a student body of which 12 percent are the first in their families to attend college; a student body, both graduate and undergraduate, composed of 17 percent international students.

USC's dedication to establishing a global presence hasn't wavered, even with the vicissitudes of recent world events. USC President Rufus von KleinSmid was an avowed internationalist during a period of American isolationism after World War I, and a strong proponent of student exchanges. The nation's first school of diplomacy was created at USC in the 1920s to train students for the foreign service. In the aftermath of the September 11, 2001, terrorist attacks in the U.S., this university continued its strong emphasis on international recruitment, and today enrolls more international students than any other university in the nation. We have alumni clubs around the world, and USC maintains offices in a number of Pacific Rim countries, including our newest one in Mexico City. Faculty research and student exchanges at USC take place every day on every continent.

USC's foundational pluralism is reflected in our long-term ethos of mutual respect, tolerance of difference, and collective commitment to civil discourse. Our trustees have adopted a Code of Ethics that emphasizes the importance that USC places on treating others fairly, honestly and with respect. Our Code of Ethics states that as Trojans we "treat every person with respect and dignity, even when the values, beliefs, behavior or background of a person or group is repugnant to us." But tolerance does not mean that we as Trojans are mute in the face of bigotry and hatred. Indeed our Code of Ethics goes on to say that "because we are responsible not only for ourselves but also for others, we speak out against hatred and bigotry whenever and wherever we find them."

Our Code of Ethics is an outgrowth of our self-perception as a university founded on diversity, mutual respect and academic freedom. As a community of scholars whose oldest

chartered student organization is our debate club, we welcome lively, respectful discussion and debate—including sharply divided opinions

USC's foundational pluralism is reflected in our long-term ethos of mutual respect, tolerance of difference and collective commitment to civil discourse.

and occasional anger—as integral to the intellectual vigor of a university.

Of course what is truly remarkable about our community is what we have in common: We are all members of the Trojan Family. Over the years the Trojan Family has grown to include not only faculty, staff and students, but also parents, friends, supporters, neighbors and alumni—lifelong and worldwide.

Story Two: A City and a University Intertwined

The second component of our creation story has its locus in Los Angeles. The lore surrounding USC's

beginnings includes the fact that an enthusiastic crowd flocked to see the laying of the cornerstone for USC's first building in 1880. One thousand residents of Los Angeles, nearly a tenth of the population, braved the summer heat and thick dust—arriving on foot, on horseback and by horse-drawn trolley or carriage—to witness the birth of the University of Southern California. The nascent USC was a banner-headline, page-one story in this nascent city.

Thus began a rich symbiotic relationship. Los Angeles and USC have literally grown up together. As L.A.'s first and preeminent private university, USC has been inextricably linked to the fortunes of this city, evolving with it, identifying with it, proud of our luster as one of L.A.'s crown jewels, and mindful of how our mutually supportive relationship has helped us navigate the waves of difficulty and prosperity alike.

By 1930—50 years after USC's founding in 1880—Los Angeles had grown from a community of 10,000 to over a million people. Likewise by that year, USC enrolled some 7,000 students, with a burgeoning population of students in our professional schools. Today L.A. is a megacity of 10 million. No other city in history has grown from 10,000 to 10 million in under 100 years. Our student body likewise has exploded in size and complexity, from 53 students in 1880 to more than 30,000 today. Our net worth has gone from a mere $15,000 to more than $3 billion.

Lest we appear vain and trium-phalist, however, we must remember that it has not been a century and a quarter of steady ascent into the golden future. For both L.A. and USC there have been times of self-doubt, fits of confusion and episodes of slack-jawed bewilderment about how to overcome seemingly insurmountable challenges.

When my wife, Kathryn, and I arrived at USC in 1991, I expected to witness, and participate in, something great and historic—the development of this region as the principal global center for trade and communication for the 21st century. Instead I found myself witnessing riots, earthquakes, floods, fires, a major recession and, above all, repeated somber pro-nouncements by experts around the world that "the Southern California dream is now dead."

In the early 1990s, Southern California experienced the greatest downturn in its economy since the Great Depression. The toll was felt

USC has developed a culture of public service— students, faculty and staff voluntarily and generously giving of their time and means to our community ...

keenly at USC where, soon after I arrived, we were forced to eliminate 800 positions, 500 of which were filled with flesh-and-blood human beings.

Amidst all this, the clamor became louder for USC to leave the city in which it was born; to flee L.A. for the greener pastures of the San Fernando Valley or Orange County.

This wasn't the first time a president of USC was enjoined to exchange the rapid pulse of the urban core for the repose of the suburbs or the countryside. As the population of L.A. burgeoned in the early part of the 20th century, many people urged USC President George Finley Bovard to move the university.

Here is what President Bovard had to say to this suggestion: "There are two kinds of institutions, both of which have their place. One is the small college, placed by itself and sufficient to itself, with country surroundings and its campus remote from the city. The other is the city institution—the university which tries to solve the problems of the city." Bovard insisted, and the Board of Trustees agreed, that USC should remain a city uni-versity in both location and in spirit.

USC is profoundly, to our very marrow, committed to the City of Angels. In the past few years we have even redoubled our commit-ment, dedicating considerable resources to the neighborhoods surrounding our two campuses; joining our neighbors in respectful partnerships to create safe streets, good schools and economic vitality; and opening wide the campus for use by neighborhood schoolchildren, churches and other community groups. USC has developed a culture of public service—students, faculty and staff voluntarily and generously giving of their time and means to our community, a strength that was key to USC's being named College of the Year 2000 by *Time* magazine and *The Princeton Review.*

Despite the disasters that hobbled our stride at the start of the 1990s, L.A—resilient, plucky L.A.—recovered. In 1994 we surpassed New York as the nation's busiest trade center. Today our ports of the San Pedro Bay rank third, behind Hong Kong and Singapore, among the world's top container ports.

Likewise, USC has grown stronger. USC is the city's largest private employer, and since its beginning it has provided Los Angeles with the professionals and intellectual capital that have helped Los Angeles prosper. In recent years USC has overhauled its undergraduate curriculum, surpassed both UCLA and Berkeley in average SAT scores for the freshman class and held the most successful fundraising campaign in the history of American higher education. Let me put it in numbers: We now receive 11 applications for each opening in the freshman class, we've quintupled our endowment in the last 14 years and we're in the midst of the largest construction program in our university's history. Along with various public and private partners, we are building the equivalent of an additional

campus by constructing 28 new buildings. This 8.1 million square feet of new space includes additional classrooms, residential halls, research laboratories and patient care facilities.

USC is the city's largest private employer, and since its beginning it has provided Los Angeles with ... professionals and intellectual capital ...

L.A. and USC have come far in just over a century. Each possesses in abundance those qualities that ensure dynamism—restlessness, resilience and ingenuity. These three qualities are the ingredients that constitute our third defining myth.

Story Three: Audacity and Ambition

This part of our creation story has to do with our ability to create something out of nothing, and to then proceed full-throttle to the next opportunity.

USC's founders had the audacity to call a two-story frame building a "university." And not just a university

for the village of Los Angeles. This building in a mustard field on the edge of Los Angeles was a university for all of Southern California.

Was it vision? Was it optimism? Was it prescience? Was it plain old chutzpah on the part of three shrewd real estate speculators and self-styled boosters?

Whatever the motivation, USC grew into its name, far surpassing, I venture to say, what even the most extravagantly farsighted among our founders had imagined.

And we didn't stop.

USC is characterized by a keen desire to do even more tomorrow no matter how much we may have accomplished today. This ambition and distaste for smug self-satisfaction are to me among the most compelling and defining characteristics of the Trojan Family. USC's unappeased nature, its "we-can-do-more" spirit even in the face of naysayers, recurs throughout our history, and it's one of the key factors behind USC's success. Quite simply we never lost that frontier spirit of solving problems ourselves, taking care of each other and venturing down untrodden paths.

In response to a bee plague in Southern California in the 1910s, for instance, USC offered a course in bee culture. In 1912, when it became clear that motorcars were becoming popular, USC offered a course through the Department of Engineering in the automobile, which was taken, incidentally, by both male and female students. This course made a big impression. Both the *L.A. Times* and the *New York Times* announced that USC was the first university in the world to recognize the importance of the automobile by establishing a course on the subject.

As we welcome the 21st century, Southern California is now the world center of both the communications industry, which includes entertainment, and the biomedical industry. Biomedical technology is poised to become the world's leading industry in the decades ahead, and USC is determined to make even greater contributions to these two industries than it has in the past, and thereby to the economic future of Los Angeles and the health and well-being of mankind.

USC's tradition of meeting societal needs and solving societal problems has been incorporated into our new strategic plan, which was adopted by the Board of Trustees in October 2004. The challenges facing the world community include debilitating diseases, ethnic

The overarching goal of the university's strategic plan is to shape USC into ... the touchstone for research universities throughout the world.

hatred, environmental degradation and a population that is quickly overwhelming existing social and technological infrastructures. Simply put, the overarching goal of the strategic plan is to shape USC into an institution that will serve as the touchstone for research universities throughout the world.

From a cornerstone in 1880 to a touchstone for universities in the 21st century, USC is dedicated to strengthening our position as a global research university that is at the forefront of advancing human civilization and of providing an education for our students that is second to none.

How will we accomplish this noble but daunting goal? Boldly. Creatively.

By linking basic and applied research, by spanning disciplinary boundaries, by building additional networks and partnerships with industry and other universities, by being more responsive to lifelong learners, by maintaining our core values and by taking advantage of our location in Los Angeles.

One hundred twenty years ago, seeking to entice students to the newly established USC medical school, President Joseph Widney wrote in the school's first catalog that "because of the cosmopolitan character of the population of Los Angeles, and the constant travel by sea and by land from all parts of the world, disease in all its forms and in almost every race and nationality" was present here for students to study. Today our doctors and medical researchers benefit from the knowledge gained by working in a living laboratory of 10 million people; a living laboratory that, I might add, is expected to have a population of over 14 million by the year 2015.

Looking Ahead

Now I have offered a modest Trojan cosmogony—three components of USC's creation story, three myths that inform our identity and destiny. As we mark the 125th anniversary of our founding, we honor the past and we carry forward a rich legacy articulated in our creation story: our embrace of pluralism; our active role on the global stage, which is guided by an ethos of respect for others; our eagerness to help solve societal problems; our love of Los Angeles; and our unique nature as audacious entrepreneurs.

We as a university and as a community are in the midst of a great social, cultural and economic experiment. Los Angeles—a microcosm of the world —serves as the paradigm for urban regions of the 21st century. Likewise USC is dedicated to becoming the worldwide paradigm for the research university of the 21st century.

In our board room on campus, just above my office, hang portraits of the nine USC presidents who came before me. Sometimes as I sit in that room and look at their faces, I feel a keen desire to have a conversation with them, these men with their solemn, intelligent countenances and their passion for higher education. I want to take them on a tour of the campus, to find out whether, in their most optimistic moments, they could

have envisioned the USC of today.

I imagine them marveling at USC's journey from a small, local college, to the training ground for tens of thousands of professionals keeping

> *As we mark the 125th anniversary of our founding, we honor the past and we carry forward a rich legacy articulated in our creation story ...*

company with the great universities of the world. My predecessors would be pleased to see that USC has remained true to its core values of diversity, free inquiry, ethical behavior and kinship with Los Angeles. They would be inspired to see that these values have remained paramount in the face of stunning changes and myriad challenges. I believe they would wholeheartedly endorse our Code of Ethics, and as well our Role and Mission statement, adopted in 1994, which defines USC's central mission as the "development of human beings and society as a whole

through the cultivation and enrichment of the human mind and spirit."

Yes, I think my predecessors would be inspired and pleased with today's USC, but in true Trojan spirit, they would not be entirely satisfied. They would applaud our successes and then remind me that our task is a never-ending one, and that satisfaction is always over the next hill.

As we work to invent the research university of the 21st century, the worst thing we can do is to be satisfied with the status quo. We cannot afford to slacken our pace or moderate our ambitions. Rather, we must continue to press upward toward increasingly lofty goals. We must fire up the furnaces of ambition to a white heat and take advantage of the extraordinary and exciting opportunities before us.

If those who came before us could transform one little wood-frame building into a premier research university, we owe it to future generations to shape USC into one of the most productive and influential universities in the world.

Los Angeles, California, October 2006 (adapted from a speech to the Newcomen Society of the United States, April 7, 2005)

The University of

Southern California:

1880 to 2005

This 1884 view of "downtown" Los Angeles, showing Main Street north of Temple, would have been a familiar sight to the members of USC's first graduating class [photo courtesy of USC University Archives]

Chapter One

Birth of a University

By Sarah Lifton

At 9 p.m. on Friday, September 3, 1880, a group of men gathered at a large, densely landscaped home on Hill Street in Los Angeles. Their meeting, which included a number of the dusty frontier town's most prominent citizens, was similar to many others that had taken place over the previous 18 months, but this time, there was a special sense of urgency. The order of business—to complete the legal foundation for the region's first full-fledged university—was the culmination of many years of hope, disappointment and perseverance for the evening's host, Judge Robert Maclay Widney. Now, nearly a decade after Widney first began to pursue the idea of establishing a university, his dream was about to assume concrete form: In less than 24 hours, the physical foundation of the institution would become a reality, its cornerstone laid amid considerable publicity and fanfare.

In attendance that evening were most of the fledgling university's board members—S. C. Hubbell, E. F. Spence, Esq., and the reverends A. M. Hough, E. S. Chase, J. A. Van Anda, J. S. Woodcock, and Charles Shelling. Also present were two young Methodist ministers, Marion McKinley Bovard and his brother Freeman D. Bovard, who had been tapped to become the university's first president and vice president.

Unacknowledged but present in spirit was the late Reverend John R. Tansey, presiding elder of the

Although he did not live to see the realization of his dream, the Reverend John R. Tansey took steps to organize a university in Southern California as early as 1875. In 1885, Tansey's widow, Mrs. Sarah E. Tansey, donated 100 acres of land to create USC's first endowed chair, the John R. Tansey Chair in Christian Ethics. [photo courtesy of the California-Pacific Annual Conference Archives of the United Methodist Church]

Los Angeles District of the Methodist Episcopal Conference from 1871 to 1875. Tansey, like Widney, had been a visionary and an optimist who anticipated a great future for Los Angeles, even though the rough little town still lacked paved streets, electric lights, telephones and a reliable fire alarm system. Both men understood that an institution of higher education was essential if Los Angeles was to mature into a city of culture and refinement, and each had made earlier, tentative steps to advance the cause.

In 1871, Widney asked one of his clients, pioneer landowner and civic leader Don Abel Stearns, to donate his 11,000-acre Laguna Rancho, located southeast of Los Angeles, as a building and endowment fund for a university. Stearns, who owned 176,000 acres of some of the choicest lands between San Pedro and San Bernardino, took some time to consider the proposition, but before departing for a business trip to San Francisco, he assured Widney that they would complete the agreement upon his return. Unfortunately, he died in San Francisco, and the project was abandoned. Deteriorating economic conditions, including a financial panic that began to sweep the country in 1873, further under-mined the plans as land values

In 1871, renowned "Yankee Don" Abel Stearns agreed to donate his Laguna Rancho to help create a building and endowment fund for an institution of higher education in Southern California. Unfortunately, Stearns died before the transaction could be completed. [photo courtesy of the Regional History Collection, USC Specialized Libraries and Archival Collections]

plummeted and a depression set in, exacerbated by a severe drought in 1877.

But even those setbacks failed to extinguish the embers of hope within the community. During Tansey's tenure as head of the Los Angeles District, local Methodists held several meetings to discuss the need for educational facilities, and committees were appointed to consider different locations for a university. In 1875, Tansey proposed to donate 200 acres of his own land to the project.

MARION MCKINLEY BOVARD

An Indiana native, Marion McKinley Bovard was the eldest of 12 children, six of whom became Methodist ministers. Bovard, who was born in 1847, arrived at his life's work in a decidedly roundabout way, first teaching school, then studying medicine and working as a physician before turning to the ministry. To enhance his ministry, he returned to college, enrolling in Indiana Asbury University (now DePauw University), where he earned his bachelor's and master's degrees in 1873. It was also there that he met his wife, Jennie. Almost immediately after graduation, he accepted an appointment as a missionary to Kiu Kiang, China. Because his wife was unable to pass the medical examination, however, his appointment was changed to Prescott, Arizona.

The Bovards' route to Arizona—as circuitous as his career path had been—took them to San Francisco by train, then south to Los Angeles by ship before they headed east by stagecoach toward Arizona. When they reached the Colorado River, intending to cross over into Arizona, skirmishes between the Apaches and settlers forced them to turn back to San Bernardino. There, Bovard met the Reverend John Tansey, presiding elder of the Los Angeles District of the Methodist Episcopal Church, who convinced him to stay in Southern California. In 1878, after postings in Riverside and Compton, Bovard became pastor of the Fort Street Methodist Church in Los Angeles. Two years later, he was named the first president of USC.

Bovard was a sincere, scholarly man and an executive of unusual dedication and foresight—a man, who, according to his brother George Finley Bovard, "had the rare gift of making men of wealth and influence sympathize with his work and give nobly to it." He held the USC presidency for 11 years, until his untimely death in 1891, at age 44.

USC's first president, Marion McKinley Bovard, was profoundly dedicated to the new university, whose lofty purpose he spelled out in an inaugural address titled "Education as a Factor in Civilization." [photo courtesy of USC University Archives]

He even approached Marion McKinley Bovard, then pastor of the Methodist church in Riverside, to lead the enterprise. Unfortunately, death again put an end to the plans. Citing his failing health, Tansey stepped down in fall 1875, and he died the following June.

Making Progress

Although a university was not looming on the near horizon, other members of the Methodist Church set their sights on a more attainable goal: secondary education. In May 1875, at Tansey's instigation, a meeting was held at the Fort Street Methodist Church to discuss the feasibility of founding a preparatory school. Those in attendance enthusiastically endorsed the idea, and a committee was appointed to pursue it. Through their efforts, the Los Angeles Academy opened on August 28, 1876, with 15 students. Led by the Reverend O. S. Frambes and his wife, the academy was officially brought under the control of the Methodist Church a month later, becoming its first educational enterprise in Southern California. Despite some initial setbacks, the school's excellent reputation attracted more and more students, and in 1879, the first class, numbering 11, graduated.

ROBERT MACLAY WIDNEY

Robert Maclay Widney
[photo courtesy of USC University Archives]

More than anyone else, real estate promoter, attorney and judge Robert Maclay Widney was responsible for setting into motion the events that led to the founding of USC. A poor Ohio farm boy, Widney left home at 16, arriving in Northern California in 1857. After working at odd jobs, he entered the University of the Pacific, and upon graduation, taught mathematics and geology there, studying law on the side. He was admitted to the California and Nevada bars in 1867 and decided to settle in Los Angeles. He soon found that legal advice was less marketable than real estate in the little town, however, so he diversified, selling land to newcomers, settling land claims and boundary disputes and publishing a monthly newsletter, *Los Angeles Real Estate Advertiser*. Using land he accepted in lieu of fees, he developed such towns as Pacoima, San Fernando, Ontario, Victorville and Long Beach. In 1871, Widney intervened as violent anti-Chinese rioting stormed through town, drawing his pistol and plunging into the mob to escort several immigrants to safety. In December of that year, he was appointed a U.S. district judge.

Widney was instrumental in a number of advances in Southern California. He helped bring the Southern Pacific Railroad to Los Angeles, establish the city's first horse-drawn trolley and organize the first chamber of commerce. He also helped form the Los Angeles County Bar Association and incorporate the city's first light and power company.

When the University of Southern California was founded, largely through his perseverance, he was elected the first president of its Board of Directors and was a member of the original trustees of the endowment fund.

Widney died in 1929, at the age of 93.

The Hill Street home of Robert Maclay Widney was the site of many meetings of USC's founders and early Board of Directors. [photo courtesy of the Regional History Collection, USC Specialized Libraries and Archival Collections]

At the same time the fortunes of the Los Angeles Academy were waxing, circumstances were improving for the university plan. In May 1879, Widney invited the Reverend A. M. Hough, Tansey's successor as presiding elder of the Los Angeles District, to his home to discuss the possibility of resuming the effort to establish a university. Widney was convinced that the long period of real estate depression was about to end, and in the near future, he believed, land values were likely to rise. Now was a suitable time to secure a land endowment for a university, as land owners were eager to sell and would be willing to donate to anything that would make their holdings more saleable. After a lengthy discussion, Hough and Widney decided to proceed. In a series of meetings over the next few evenings, the two invited Marion McKinley Bovard, by then pastor of the Fort Street Methodist Episcopal Church, to join the effort, as well as Widney's brother, Joseph P. Widney; Edward F. Spence, a local businessman who went on to serve as mayor of Los Angeles; and G. D. Compton. All were enthusiastic, and at the last of these meetings, Widney presented a deed of trust he had drawn up with J. S. Griffin, who offered to donate land in East Los Angeles for a university campus and endowment fund. The group—the university's first Board of Trustees—decided to continue soliciting additional donations of land in order to select the most advantageous.

After considering various offers—on Temple Street, in Boyle Heights and in what was then called West Los Angeles—the board accepted the West Los Angeles proposal. In a vote of confidence for the region's future and a display of bravado about their fledgling enterprise, they named the institution, rather grandiosely, the University of Southern California. On July 29, 1879, a deed of trust was executed between land donors Ozro W. Childs, a Protestant; John G. Downey, a Catholic; and Isaias W. Hellman, a Jew; and Methodists A. M. Hough, R. M. and J. P. Widney, E. F. Spence, M. M. Bovard and G. D. Compton as trustees. According to the terms of the document, the trustees were to hold 308 lots. Some were to be reserved for the university campus, while the balance would be sold to create an endowment. The lots were to be sold for a minimum of $100 each, and no encumbrance was to be placed on the endowment fund. The first $5,000 net from the sales was to be used to erect a university building, to be completed within three years. Since the sponsors of the enterprise were all Methodists, the majority of trustees were to be Methodists as well, and control of the university was to fall to the Southern California Conference of the Methodist Episcopal Church.

Gathering Momentum

Childs, Downey and Hellman's gift, which was widely covered in the local newspapers, quickly inspired generosity among the owners of adjacent properties, who made

This early map of "West Los Angeles" shows the location of the original lots donated to provide USC's campus as well those that were intended to be sold to create an endowment for the nascent university.
[image courtesy of USC University Archives]

THE FOUNDING FATHERS

The three men who made the original gift of land to establish the University of Southern California were as diverse as nineteenth-century Los Angeles. They came from three different countries and practiced three different religions, but the civic-mindedness they shared helped direct the course of their young city for decades to come.

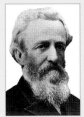

Ozro W. Childs was born in Vermont in 1824, and after paying his own way to gain an education, he became a schoolteacher. A lifelong battle with asthma, however, prompted him to move to Ohio, where he hoped to find a more congenial climate. There he learned tinsmithing, a trade that provided a livelihood when the Gold Rush lured him to California in 1850. Although he prospered, he soon opted for the milder climate of Los Angeles, where he and a partner opened a tin shop, then switched to selling groceries and other provisions—the first of a series of successful ventures. In 1857, he turned to horticulture and founded yet another profitable business, a nursery importing and selling exotic trees and plants. A few years later, the city hired him to construct an irrigation ditch, or *zanja*, for the city. Instead of money, he took land as his payment. The parcel he received was bounded by Main, Figueroa, 6th and 12th streets. When he put the property on the market, his wife named some of the streets after the three Christian graces: Faith Street (which became Flower Street), Hope Street and Charity Street (which became Grand Avenue). A fourth street, called Calle de los Chapules in recognition of its large population of grasshoppers, became Figueroa Street. In 1884, he opened a new theater on Main Street, known as Childs' Opera House.

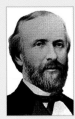

John G. Downey, a native of County Roscommon in Ireland, like Childs was drawn to California by the Gold Rush. He emigrated to America in 1842 and as a young man was apprenticed to a druggist in Washington, D.C. After learning the pharmacy trade, he opened drug stores in Mississippi and Ohio before arriving in California in 1849. In 1850, he opened the second drug store in Los Angeles, becoming a U.S. citizen the following year. Active in his adopted community, he joined its first volunteer police force and was instrumental in bringing the Sisters of Charity to town to provide hospital services and care for orphans. In 1855, he was elected to the state assembly and in 1859, he was elected lieutenant governor, becoming governor of California a year later, when Governor Milton S. Latham was elected to the U.S. Senate. The state prospered under his leadership, but he failed to be reelected and returned to Los Angeles. He entered the banking business; subdivided the Santa Gertrudis Rancho, which gave rise to the town that bears his name; and served as president of the first board of trustees of the Los Angeles Public Library Association. He also helped organize the chamber of commerce and took part in the creation of the Los Angeles Water Company.

Isaias W. Hellman was born in Bavaria and emigrated to Los Angeles in 1859. He began his career in the clothing business, working for his cousins. He soon discovered, however, that since the town had no banks, many people left money in the safekeeping of merchants they trusted. Figuring that he might as well open a bank if he was expected to perform banking services, he established his first financial institution in a corner of the clothing store. By 1865, he was in business for himself, selling dry goods. At the end of the decade, he sold the store and opened a bank, the second organized bank in Los Angeles. In 1871, he opened the Farmers and Merchants Bank, naming Downey as president. Childs served on its board of trustees. When Downey stepped down in 1876, Hellman succeeded him. Hellman also oversaw the establishment of the first synagogue in Los Angeles in 1871 and served as its president.

In 1874, Childs sold Downey and Hellman one half interest in the tract of land he owned in West Los Angeles, at today's Exposition Boulevard and Vermont Avenue. The partners quickly concluded that it held few possibilities for agriculture, and two years later, they decided to subdivide it and sell lots. Unfortunately, in the sluggish economy, sales proved slow. When the partners learned that the Methodists were looking for a location for a new university, they offered a portion of it to be used as the campus and as the basis for an endowment, changing the course of Southern California's history.

additional contributions that expanded the tract by approximately 40 acres. Although the lots were worth about $50 each, Widney felt strongly that they should be priced at $200 apiece—a staggering sum that some of his colleagues opposed.

"There was quite a disagreement as to the price at which we should sell the lots," he wrote some years later. "…The general opinion was that the lots were not saleable at that price." So confident was Widney, however, that he offered to sell the first batch of lots, variously described as 26 or 30, to friends and business acquaintances for $200 each.

"In a short time, I had sold the entire allotment of lots and had the money in the bank to put up the first building," he noted.

Widney's success clearly emboldened his colleagues, for the university's *Prospectus*, published before the campus opened, noted that 243 lots were now offered for sale at $300 each and were expected to generate more than $60,000 for the endowment fund.

Because the progress of the university was of great interest to the burgeoning city, many members of the community came forward to help in different ways. Architects Kyser and Morgan furnished the plans for the building without charge. Lumber dealers and building suppliers provided materials at cost.

In May 1880, the *Evening Express* gushed:

… The college campus has been tastily laid out and most of the trees planted…. [N]ear the center of the campus [plans call for] four college buildings, which are to be erected, one after another as the necessities of the University require…. Along the outer edge of the campus, on the four sides, has been planted a row of eucalyptus, and an inside row of the same, fourteen feet from the first, leaving space for a broad walk…. The endowment of the University by the noble gift of Messrs. Childs, Downey and Hellman is ample… to ultimately afford a steady yearly income sufficient to keep it out of debt and enable the institution to accomplish all that its projectors hope for. The founding of a grand educational institution like this in Los Angeles will not only contribute to the fame of our city as a centre of learning and refinement, but add to our material attractions, which will draw to our locality families of wealth and culture….

The momentum behind the university also led the trustees of the Los Angeles Academy to rethink their enterprise. In June 1880, they voted to close the school and transfer "the assets, patronage, good-will, and

Filed on August 5, 1880, USC's original articles of incorporation established an 11-member Board of Directors and called for the establishment of a university that would be "open in every respect for the equal education of both sexes."
[photo by Steve Schenck]

denominational enthusiasm to the University of Southern California." It became the "academic department" of the new institution, providing a college-preparatory education for young men and women.

On August 5, in accordance with California law, the articles of incorporation for the university were executed and filed. The document established an 11-member Board of Directors (distinct from the Board of Trustees of the endowment fund), including A. M. Hough, Charles Shelling, E. F. Spence, P. Y. Cool, S. C. Hubbell, E. S. Chase, P. M. Green, John G. Downey and R. M. Widney of Los Angeles County, and J. A. Van Anda of Ventura and F. S. Woodcock of Santa Barbara. It also noted that their successors would be elected by the Southern California Methodist Episcopal Conference.

The first meeting of the university's Board of Directors was held September 3, at 4 p.m. in Widney's law office, where a committee on bylaws was appointed. That evening, the meeting continued at Widney's home, where the Bovards presented the terms under which they would accept the positions of president and vice president. After considerable discussion, the parties agreed upon the conditions, and the board ordered a contract to be drawn up and executed. The Bovards were to have complete responsibility for organizing and managing the university and were to select the faculty and set the curriculum. They were to receive all funds from tuition toward an annual salary of $1,500 apiece, with additional moneys from the endowment fund and other sources to make up the difference—unless the funds were inadequate, in which case the deficit would run from year to year. The board would spend all conference educational collections to outfit the university. The term of the contract was one year, renewable on an annual basis for four additional years. Undoubtedly reflecting the limited number of faculty, Marion McKinley Bovard was named president of the university and professor of

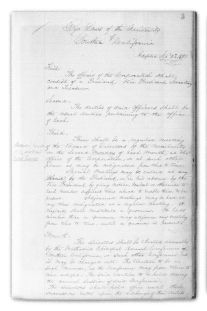
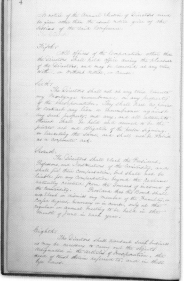

The bylaws of the newly established university were drawn up and adopted on September 3, 1881.
[photo by Steve Schenck]

mental and moral philosophy and natural sciences. Freeman D. Bovard was elected professor of mathematics and ancient languages.

The board also selected officers that long night, electing Widney president. After midnight, the group voted to attend the cornerstone ceremony the following afternoon, and at 1:30 a.m., the meeting was adjourned.

Laying the Foundation

The next day dawned unusually hot, even for late summer Southern California, but the relentless sun, dust and limited transportation did not prevent some 1,000 people—nearly a tenth of the city's population—from converging on the campus, still primarily a field of wild mustard with a partly finished building in its midst. The date was significant beyond the ceremony at hand: 99 years earlier to the day, a band of pioneers had reached the site of the civic center and founded "El Pueblo de Nuestra Señora la Reina de Los Angeles."

According to the September 5 *Daily Herald*, "An immense throng gathered on Wesley Avenue, West Los Angeles, yesterday afternoon, to witness the ceremony of laying the cornerstone of the new building thereafter to be known as the University of Southern California. Nearly two hundred vehicles were on the grounds, while many came on foot, on horseback and by street cars...."

A temporary platform had been erected for the occasion, and the ceremony, which commenced promptly at 2:30 p.m., included hymns, a scripture lesson and prayers, as well as addresses by Hough, Bishop I. W. Wiley, and Senior Bishop Matthew Simpson, a renowned figure in Methodism and a favorite with the audience. Downey was also present and made a brief, cordial speech. Inside the cornerstone, the university's founders placed various documents, including a copy of the deed of trust, the articles of incorporation, a history

The *1880–81 Prospectus of the University of Southern California* (opposite page, left) touted the new institution's solid financial foundation as well as the fact "that the evenness of the climate gives to the studious mind great advantages." It also included an idealized rendering of the university building (above). [images courtesy of USC University Archives]

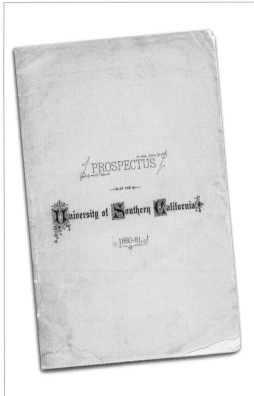

of the enterprise to date, copies of 10 newspapers, copies of deeds and contracts used by the trustees of the endowment fund, a map of West Los Angeles showing the lots sold to date, the invitation to the cornerstone ceremony, the *Prospectus* of the university and business cards, among other items.

"The Board of Directors announce to the public that the organization of the University in all its various departments has been fully consummated," reported the minutes of the Southern California Methodist Episcopal Conference. "The University has been most fortunate in its beginning in securing the services of two of the most thorough and accomplished scholars—Rev. M. M. Bovard and his brother Rev. F. D. Bovard. With these two able instructors, chosen from this Conference, thoroughly imbued with the love and enthusiasm of this work, to head the list of instructors, the University gives good promise of becoming one of the most desirable educational institutions on this Coast. We most heartily recommend it to your fullest confidence, patronage, and financial support."

One month later, the building was completed. Erected at a cost of approximately $5,060, plus $1,200 for furnishings, it was a two-story wood frame structure, with classrooms on the ground floor and an assembly hall and smaller classrooms on the second.

On October 5, the assembly hall saw its first official function. It was there that Marion McKinley Bovard was inaugurated as the first president of the University of Southern California. Widney, as president of the Board of Directors, presided over the ceremony and delivered a speech. At the close of his remarks, he handed Bovard the keys to the university and the future.

The University Park campus was founded on a flat plain covered with mustard plants that, according to legend, had sprung from seeds strewn by Franciscan fathers to mark the missionary trails.
[photo courtesy of USC University Archives]

By 1919, USC had two prominent structures, the College of Liberal Arts building (later known as Old College, pictured here in the foreground) and Bovard Administration Building (to the far left), providing a stately façade for the campus along University Avenue. [photo courtesy of USC University Archives]

Chapter Two

Building a University (1880–1921)

By Sarah Lifton

On October 6, 1880, just days after its building was completed, the University of Southern California opened its doors to its first students. A total of 53 young men and women were enrolled in its two departments, the "academic" or preparatory department, and the college department, with the overwhelming majority of students attending classes in the former.

The academic department, the continuation of the defunct Los Angeles Academy, offered English, literary and classical courses of study, while the college department (later referred to as the College of Liberal Arts) offered three courses of study: the classical, leading to a bachelor of arts; the philosophical, leading to a bachelor of philosophy; and the scientific, which led to a bachelor of science. Coursework for these majors was completely prescribed; students had no room in their academic schedules for electives. In addition, there was a "normal" course for students wishing to become schoolteachers. Tuition was $12 per term for the academic department, and $15 a term for the college department.

Although the university was open to students from all religious and ethnic backgrounds, Methodist doctrine was very much in evidence in day-to-day life. Mandatory services took place each morning in the chapel, and students were required to attend the church services of their choice every Sunday. Early catalogues stipulated that students were "not allowed to use profane or obscene language; to carry concealed weapons; to visit drinking saloons, or places of gambling of any kind; to use spirituous liquors of any kind as a beverage; to use tobacco in any manner in or about the college buildings or campus; to play cards, or permit others to play in their rooms; to mark or deface the buildings or furniture, or to engage in any immoral conduct...." Students who persisted in any of these activities would be dismissed.

The faculty, like the student body, was very small, and their duties often juxtaposed wildly unrelated subjects. President Bovard doubled as "professor of moral, mental and natural sciences," and Vice President Freeman D. Bovard as professor of mathematics and ancient languages.

The president's wife, Jennie Allen Bovard, was professor of English language and literature. Joseph P. Widney, M.D., brother of Robert Maclay Widney, taught English literature, physiology and hygiene. The Bovards' earnings for the first year were a mere pittance, but as time went on, they employed additional teachers to ensure high-quality instruction, even though under the terms of their contract, it meant they would earn less money.

A Growing Enterprise

Only weeks after opening, on October 23, 1880, the university attracted its first eminent visitor. U.S. President Rutherford B. Hayes was visiting Los Angeles. He toured West Los Angeles and, as the *Daily Herald* noted, "In making their trip through the southern suburbs

This is believed to be the earliest photographic view of USC's original building (later renamed Widney Hall). [photo courtesy of USC University Archives]

yesterday the Presidential party stopped at the University of Southern California and Mr. and Mrs. Hayes took a look through the institution. The visit was necessarily brief, but they expressed themselves as pleased with the nucleus which they found and hoped the university would grow into great favor and prosperity."

And for a time it did.

During its first year, the university received a donation of books and periodicals that formed the core of a library and a collection of geological and mineralogical specimens for a museum. In January 1881, it commenced publication of a monthly tabloid periodical, *The University of Southern California*, which reported to the community on developments at the institution, as well as listing odd facts. (The December 1881 issue detailed the number of trees or vines that could be planted on an acre of land when spaced different distances apart, the number of nails and tacks in a pound, and the force of wind per square foot of surface in a breeze vs. a gale.)

The first student organization, the Union Literary Society, was established during the university's inaugural year and met monthly. (The second year, its name was changed to the Platonean Society, but the third year, the faculty decided that the young men and women should meet separately, prompting the organization of the Aristotelian Literary Society, for male students, and the Athena Literary Society, for female students.)

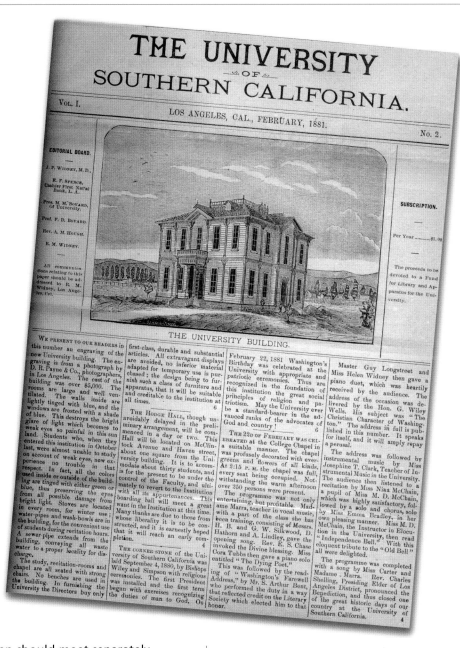

In January 1881, in the interest of "placing university interests before the public," USC began publishing *The University of Southern California*, a tabloid periodical that was issued for some two years. [image courtesy of USC University Archives]

Providing much-needed student housing for the new university, Mr. and Mrs. William Hodge constructed and opened a boarding house in 1881. Hodge Hall served variously as a residence for men and women students before becoming home to USC's music school (1896–1905) and Maclay College of Theology (1907–1919).
[photo courtesy of USC University Archives]

In January 1881, President Bovard presented the Board of Directors with a proposal from Mr. and Mrs. William Hodge, a couple from Denver, that promised to address a nagging issue for the young university. The Hodges had offered to purchase some lots and erect a boarding house for university students. The board, which had been concerned about the dearth of student housing, gratefully accepted, and that spring, Hodge Hall was built on the corner of McClintock Avenue and 35th Street, capable of accommodating

about 25 people. Hodge, a carpenter, did most of the work himself. According to the terms of the agreement, upon the death of the donors, Hodge Hall would belong to the university.

Thanks to solicitations by the Bovards at the Methodist churches, the publication of the university's first catalog, and an improving real estate market that encouraged the sale of lots for the endowment fund, the second year saw the enrollment nearly double, with new students making up 80 percent of the increase. A significant improvement also took place in facilities. In addition to Hodge Hall, which was reserved for female students, a men's dormitory was secured. The faculty also expanded, freeing some of the members from teaching multiple subjects, and significantly, George Finley Bovard, a younger brother of Marion McKinley and Freeman D. Bovard, simultaneously enrolled as a sophomore and was appointed an instructor in English grammar and rhetoric. A graduate of a normal school, he had experience teaching in the Indiana public schools. He had planned to continue his college education at the university his brothers were running, but finding that he would be alone in the class, decided to wait a year before enrolling.

THE STUDENT VOICE

USC students demonstrated their journalistic fervor almost as soon as they began attending classes, although their outlets remained sporadic for many years. The first student publication, *The College Review*, debuted in 1884. It was "a neat monthly of twelve pages on pink tinted book paper with colored cover…published by the Students of the University of Southern California, and conducted by an editorial board chosen from the Arisotelian and Athena literary societies of the University." It was short-lived, however, surviving only the spring semester, and the next publication, *The Sibyl*, did not appear until 1889. *The Sibyl* was more of a yearbook, offering a rundown of the year's activities, and wasn't published on an ongoing basis. It was succeeded in 1891 by *El Rodeo*—not the precursor of today's yearbook, but a magazine.

In 1892, *The University Rostrum* was launched, financed by advertising and subscriptions. It lasted only a year. *The Record* first appeared in 1895 and was followed by a new student paper, the *Cardinal*, which was inaugurated in 1902. Destined to last only three issues, the *Cardinal* was superseded by the *University Advocate*, which was published for nine issues and targeted readers outside the university, especially members of the Methodist Church.

In 1905, the first successful student paper began publication. *The Courier* started out as a literary weekly and was published until June 1912, though its size, editorial policy and format changed yearly. After its staff successfully lobbied for a daily paper, the *Daily Southern Californian* emerged in September 1912, prompting the *Los Angeles Tribune* to note that USC students had "set a new pace on college journalism." It was published four days a week until June 1915, then was replaced by the *Southern California Trojan* the following September. The *Trojan* was published three times a week until 1929, when it became the *Southern California Daily Trojan*. In 1943, its name was shortened to the *Daily Trojan*, the appellation it bears today.

Not all student writings were serious, however. In 1919, the humor magazine *Wampus* debuted. "Our aim is simply to make you laugh; thereby improving digestions and thereby your scholastic standings," the editors wrote in the first issue. And so it did for nearly 40 years, until its demise in spring 1957.

[images courtesy of USC University Archives]

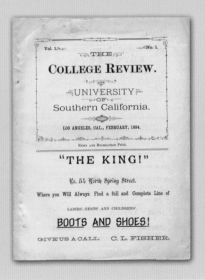

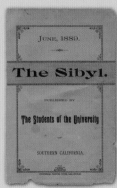

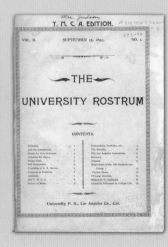

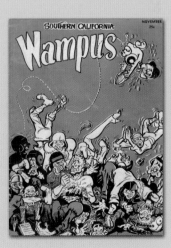

The College of Liberal Arts building, later known as Old College, was dedicated in 1887 and heralded as USC's first "permanent" structure. Ironically, it was deemed seismically unsound and demolished in 1948. [photo courtesy of USC University Archives]

New Facilities

Over the next few years, the enrollment continued to expand rapidly, reaching 154 in the third year and 248 the fourth year. This growth, while welcome, led to an increasingly urgent problem on campus—how to accommodate the larger and larger numbers of students who were enrolling. With the original building operating beyond capacity, new facilities were imperative. Although the university's finances were still touch and go, the Board of Directors decided to move forward with a fundraising effort to generate the resources necessary for the new facilities. They made an appeal for support at the 1883 annual meeting of the Southern California Methodist Episcopal Conference.

"We rejoice that the present building is entirely inadequate to accommodate the school," reported the board. "It is evidence of our prosperity that in these years we have increased so much that new buildings are a necessity, if we meet the promise of future growth and fill the expectations of those to whom we look for patronage. We have decided that a large, commodious, and permanent building should be erected at the earliest possible date, there is need of it; we believe it possible to erect it; we *must* erect it soon."

The board determined that the new structure would cost at least $22,000, and the conference responded enthusiastically to its appeal. By September 1884, more than $28,000 had been raised—enough to warrant laying the cornerstone. Unlike the first building, a modest wood frame structure, the new university building was considered "permanent"—a three-story brick building with clock tower, which included a chapel with a capacity of 500 people, a library, lecture halls, classrooms, music rooms and laboratories. Ultimately built at a cost of $37,000 and dedicated in 1887, it became known as Old College as the campus expanded. (In a twist of irony, the "permanent" building was eventually outlived by the small wood-frame structure; Old College was razed in 1948.)

Milestones

June 1884 saw the graduation exercises for the first class of the University of Southern California. Although the Class of 1884 consisted of only three members, the University Methodist Church, which had been built in 1883, was lavishly decorated for the occasion and was overflowing with spectators. Each member of the class delivered a talk, and following an address by President Bovard, George Finley Bovard, Millie Miltimore and Friend E. Lacey received their bachelor's degrees. Three years later, all were presented with master's degrees for additional study.

On multiple fronts, 1885 was a watershed year. In January, Mrs. Sarah E. Tansey, widow of the Rev. John Tansey, presented the university with a 100-acre tract of land to endow its first chair, the John R. Tansey Chair in Christian Ethics. Freeman D. Bovard resigned in order to resume his ministry, and the Reverend W. S. Matthew was appointed to take his place. President Bovard organized a school of music as a department in the College of Liberal Arts, and in May, eight months after the Board of Directors had given Joseph P. Widney the go-ahead to lay the groundwork, the university officially established a medical school, with Widney appointed dean.

Above: USC's College of Medicine—housed in a former winery building on Aliso Street —welcomed its first students in 1885, with Joseph P. Widney as founding dean.
[image courtesy of USC University Archives].

Left: USC's original seal was created in 1884 for use on the university's first diplomas.
[image courtesy of USC University Archives]

The University System

As spiraling real estate values began to fuel a boom in the economy, a groundswell of enthusiasm surfaced for expanding the university throughout the region. Soon, infected with a limitless sense of possibility, others began to approach the Board of Directors with proposals for new campuses.

These activities were consistent with the vision that Robert M. Widney had held from the outset: With an audacity characteristic of his young adopted city, he foresaw an institution in which the university's College of Liberal Arts in West Los Angeles was the hub of a collection of satellite campuses in outlying areas, which he called the "University System." The system was to encompass everything from grade school through graduate school.

Although the West Los Angeles campus was still very much in its infancy, in 1882, George Chaffey Jr., a Canadian engineer who had installed the first electric street lights in Los Angeles, and his brother, William, offered to give the Board of Directors a tract of land in Ontario to endow and create Chaffey College of Agriculture there as a branch of the university. After due consideration, the board voted to accept the deed of trust and proceed with the campus, even though the venue was even more remote and barren than West Los Angeles had been two years earlier. Under the direction of a separate Board of Trustees, a building was erected and the campus opened in 1885. After two years of financial difficulties, however, the trustees were forced to abandon the agricultural emphasis and focus on the liberal arts. Chaffey College remained affiliated with the university, and by 1888, it had 90 students, mostly enrolled in preparatory courses.

In 1885, Charles Maclay, a Methodist missionary and former California state senator, sold his large ranch in San Fernando and gave $150,000 in stock in the San Fernando Land and Water Company to the university to establish the Maclay College of Theology. Two years later, before its building was complete, the college opened its doors to ten students, who attended classes in small cottages. When the building was finally completed in September 1888,

USC's Chaffey College of Agriculture (left), established in Ontario in 1885, and Maclay College of Theology (right), established in San Fernando in 1887, were part of a vast system of satellite campuses that was envisioned to extend from Baja California to Tulare. [images courtesy of USC University Archives]

enrollment increased to 12 students. The college's first commencement took place June 13, 1889, with a bachelor of divinity degree awarded the sole member of the class.

Between 1886 and 1888, additional branches of the university were founded at Tulare, 150 miles to the north, and in Escondido, near San Diego. A college of fine arts was established in San Diego proper. Other branches were proposed or founded at Ramona, Rialto, Glendora, Elsinore, Montalvo, Inglewood, Whittier and Monrovia. Plans were also made for schools in Ventura, San Luis Obispo, Nordhoff and Santa Maria, as well as Baja California.

A committee on "the best practical method of canvassing the financial yield of Southern California in the interest of the University" reported in 1887 that "the real estate and financial movements in this part of the state [are] so great, and money is being made in such large sums, and is helped with such open hands, that a more opportune time for our work will never occur again…. There are apparent possibilities of securing in our lands and money that which may realize several millions of dollars…. Several more Colleges, quite probably, may be established and endowed in Santa Barbara and Ventura counties."

REACHING FOR THE STARS

Long before Mount Wilson Observatory was opened in 1904, Edward F. Spence, then president of USC's Board of Directors, set in motion plans to create a powerful observatory atop the peak. [photo by Westervelt Studio, courtesy of USC University Archives]

Among the most ambitious projects to emerge from the University System in the 1880s was a proposal to create an observatory on Mount Wilson. In June 1887, E. F. Spence, then president of the university's Board of Directors, pledged a gift of $50,000 in cash to purchase astronomical instruments and identify a location for an observatory in Los Angeles County, to be affiliated with the University of Southern California. An assessment of all the potential sites resulted in the selection of Mount Wilson, near Pasadena. In January 1889, a party of scientists, including President Marion McKinley Bovard, the director of the Harvard Observatory and the superintendent of the University of California's Lick Observatory, hiked to the top of Mount Wilson to mount a 13-inch telescope there to test the peak's atmospheric qualities. The scientists were enthusiastic about the site, declaring it superior to that of the Lick Observatory. Later that month, the trustees of the Spence Observatory placed a preliminary order for a 40-inch telescope and 24-inch photographic telescope, following up with a final contract a month later. The order promised to produce the world's largest telescope ever made up to that time.

The glass disc for the 40-inch telescope was made by a French firm and exhibited at the 1889 Paris Exposition, then shipped to Boston for final finishing. By then, however, the university lacked the funds to complete the project, and during the administration of Joseph P. Widney, the lenses were sold to the University of Chicago. The Spence Observatory was a precursor of the celebrated Mount Wilson Observatory that has stood on the peak since 1904.

Above left: By 1887, the year that the building later known as Old College was completed, Los Angeles roadways were crowded with horse-drawn wagons, buggies and streetcars. This view shows Spring Street, looking north from First. [photo by Dick Whittington Photography, courtesy of USC University Archives]

Right: W. S. Matthew was inaugurated as dean of the College of Liberal Arts in January 1888 and became a university vice president in 1889. From the time of President Bovard's illness in fall 1890 until Joseph Widney's appointment as president in 1892, Matthew assumed responsibility for management of the university. He ultimately resigned as dean and vice president in 1894. [photo courtesy of USC University Archives]

The report, like the University System, proved to be far too optimistic. Just as inflated land values had sparked the development of the University System, so their rapid deflation led to its collapse. By spring 1888, investors were overextended, their profits confined to paper. Without a stable industrial base, the frenzy could not be sustained on the basis of land and congenial climate alone. Desperate to sell at any price, frantic landowners drove down the price of real estate, and Southern California was swept into a depression.

With its assets tied up in property that had lost a significant amount of its value, the university was plunged into a protracted fiscal crisis. Throughout 1889 and 1890, the Board of Directors repeatedly discussed the shortfall and ways to address it through loans, cutting expenses, reducing the faculty and raising tuition, even as enrollment was falling off. Bovard was instructed to concentrate on raising funds for the university. Hodge Hall was closed as a boarding house, and at one point the directors even considered closing the College of Liberal Arts, though ultimately concluded that it was impracticable. There was considerable turnover on the faculty, as well as the Board of Directors.

By late 1890, the strain of trying to maintain the university under the crushing financial burden had destroyed Bovard's health. He was granted a six-month paid leave of absence to recuperate. The Reverend W. S. Matthew, who served as dean of the College of Liberal Arts from 1888 to 1889 and had been vice president of the university since 1889, stepped into the breach. Bovard never regained his vigor, however, and on December 30, 1891, he died, at the age of 44.

Transitions

The city Bovard left behind was a far cry from the one that witnessed the first cornerstone ceremony for the university he carved from a mustard field in 1880. Its population, though down to 50,000 from its peak of 70,000 in 1888, was still nearly five times that at the beginning of the decade. The city was served by two railroads, the Southern Pacific and Santa Fe. Soon a new wave of boosters came to pick over the leavings of the boom and capitalize on what they found.

The university Bovard left behind was in deep trouble, however. Its finances were extremely precarious,

and it was buried in debt. Shortly before Bovard's death, Joseph P. Widney, who became board chair in October 1891, had conducted an audit of its finances and found the records in disarray, largely owing to Bovard's ill health.

"Through the long continued illness of the President of the University, its interests are suffering by lack of constant business supervision," he noted. "It is a great misfortune, as the coming year will be of much importance to our whole University System."

Most likely, Widney had no idea just how important the year would prove. On January 11, 1892, confident of his business acumen, resourcefulness and wisdom, the Board of Directors unanimously elected him the second president of the University of Southern California, a position he accepted reluctantly.

The Presidency of Joseph P. Widney

As president, Widney accepted no salary and paid his own traveling expenses, as well as the postage connected with his office. He was, he later wrote, "willing to do this work for the Lord but not for money."

To begin addressing the debt, he arranged with Childs, Downey and

USC's second president, physician Joseph Pomeroy Widney, took the university's helm in 1892, during a period of severe financial difficulty. After helping facilitate a financial turnaround, he stepped down in 1895.
[photo courtesy of USC University Archives]

THE ORIGINS OF TROJAN FOOTBALL

Beginning a rich tradition of gridiron glory, USC's first football team played two shutout games against the Alliance Athletic Club in 1888. [photo courtesy of USC University Archives]

USC's celebrated football tradition sprang from decidedly modest origins, in the activities of a largely unknown faculty member and the team he organized after seeing the game played once in the East. In 1888, USC Professor E. Suffel sent for a ball and rule book and took on the task of coaching a team made up of male students interested in the sport. According to one account, he was assisted by Dr. Henry Goddard, an instructor in Latin and history. Suffel, Goddard and the athletes learned as they practiced, and the effort was decidedly casual. Their uniforms were made by a quarterback named Arthur Carroll, who later became a tailor in Riverside. Vacancies on the team were sometimes filled by faculty, including Goddard.

Because the team had no opponents to play, they recruited a group of youths from downtown and taught them the basic rules and tactics. Before long, the youths wanted to take on their mentors and organized as a club team called Alliance. The first game was played on November 14, 1888, at the university, and the USC team won, 16-0. The second game was played more than two months later, on January 19, 1889, on a vacant lot bordered by Grand, Hope, Eighth and Ninth streets. By then, the Alliance team had improved considerably: USC won by only 4–0.

Hellman to release the university from the prohibition against encumbering the land. He also reorganized the College of Liberal Arts, which had been under the direct governance of the Board of Directors (including their personal obligation for the debt), and gave it a separate governing body of its own, as the other units in the university had. This body then issued bonds for the campus and buildings to generate capital to pay off the most pressing debts. Finally, he consolidated all the separate endowment funds for the different schools under the Board of Directors, a process that took two years.

To improve the day-to-day operation of the university, Widney revived sagging morale among the faculty by visiting every unit of the University System and taking a keen interest in its educational mission. Thanks to a $5,000 gift from Frederick H. Rindge, owner of the Malibu rancho, the university was able to meet its expenses for the following year and upgrade the campus and buildings, with a surplus left over. New faculty were hired, and in fall 1893, the Board of Directors voted to establish a separate College of Music, to replace the Department of Music within the College of Liberal Arts. The following year, the curriculum of the College of Liberal Arts was revamped, and laboratories and pedagogical methods were modernized. Entrance requirements were tightened; academic standards were raised; and a new emphasis was placed on the sciences. These efforts paid off with a large increase in enrollment and a heightened spirit of hope and possibility. In addition, the Maclay College of Theology was closed and later reopened on the West Los Angeles campus.

With the turnaround in the university's fortunes, Widney considered his work completed, and in April 1895, he resigned as president, as a member of the Board of Directors and as a trustee of the College of Liberal Arts. As he wrote in a letter he presented to the board:

With kindly thanks for the many courtesies of the years during which I have filled the presidency of the University of Southern California, I hereby resign from the presidency and give back into your hands again the trust which you committed to me. This step is not taken hastily. It has been a matter of careful thought and earnest prayer for several months past, and the con- viction is now clear in my mind that it is better so…. [Y]ou all well know that the presidency was unsought by me; that I only consented to

WHAT'S IN A NAME

[image courtesy of USC University Archives]

From the university's inception, its students and athletic teams had been known as the "Methodists," "Wesleyans" or simply "USC"— colorless nicknames that failed to capture the imagination of students or local sportswriters. In 1912, however, *Los Angeles Times* sports editor Owen R. Bird coined a nickname that stuck. Writing about the USC track team in an upcoming meet in the February 23 paper, he said, "The Oxy Tiger will be seen in action … in the clash with Dean Cromwell's U.S.C. Trojans on the Bovard cinder trail. Speculation is running rife as to the outcome of the meet at both colleges." As the *Times* continued to use the nickname, other writers began to adopt it as well.

Recalling his use of the term in the November 1929 issue of *Southern California Alumni Review*, Bird wrote: "Owing to the terrific handicaps under which athletes, coaches, and managers of the university were laboring at this time, and at the same time appreciating their fighting spirit and the ability of the teams to go down under overwhelming odds of bigger and better equipped teams with their colors gloriously nailed to the mast, it seemed to me that the name 'Trojan' fitted their case."

In December 1912, the *Daily Southern Californian* observed that while the rugby team had "lost and lost badly this season, they have gained a reputation of hard fighters, good losers and gentlemen. The name Trojan has been really earned."

And thus the nickname became permanently woven into the fabric of the university.

George Washington White, USC's president from 1895 to 1899, streamlined operations, bolstered finances and promoted academic advances.
[photo courtesy of USC University Archives]

take up the work at the unanimous request of the directors, and this after insisting on a month's delay before taking the vote that it might be well-considered by the board and the church. Coming to me in this manner, I accepted it as a call from God, and abandoned my own business at heavy financial loss to take up this work for the church....I do not see that under existing circumstances I can do any further good by remaining in the Presidency....I request also, as a matter of justice to myself and that your books should contain proper records, that you appoint a committee to examine the official records of my administration and into all financial matters with which I may have been connected in the University work and that their report be entered in full in your minutes. I believe you will find the business interests of the University in a healthy condition and well cared for.

In conclusion, brethren, let me again thank you for the memory of many pleasant hours with you and with the various official boards while we have borne anxious burdens together. It is natural that there should be some slight tinges of sadness in laying down this work with which I have been connected in official capacity from its founding fifteen years ago and to which I have given many of the best years of my life. I believe I am the sole survivor in the University work of the six persons who received and held for the University the original grant of lands for its establishment. Permit me to join with you in the prayer that God may wisely direct the counsel of the University that it may do his work in the years to come.

J. P. Widney
Los Angeles. Apr. 16th, 1895

A Third President

By any standard, the man selected to succeed Widney was indeed a wise choice. Another stalwart of the Methodist Church in Southern California, the Reverend George W. White was no stranger to the university, having served on its Board of Directors since 1890 and become board president in 1893. White had arrived in Los Angeles in 1884 and soon made a name for himself as a scholarly man who preached with authority, yet had excellent business and administrative skills. He held many important pastoral positions in the Southern California Conference

STUDENT TRADITIONS

Although the university's first students filled their leisure time with such sedate activities as literary societies, debates, chapel services and an occasional dance, by the early 20th century, students had developed a campus culture governed by an elaborate set of rules, traditions and intense class rivalries. Seniors enjoyed such privileges as a bench reserved exclusively for their use and the right to don "sombreros," defined as any felt hat with a straight brim. Only juniors and seniors were allowed to wear corduroy trousers on campus.

Freshmen, who bore the brunt of the rules, were supposed to learn verses 1 and 4 of the "Alma Mater" their first week. Men were ordered to wear special hats, while women were forbidden to wear hats on campus and were required to wear green armbands above their left elbows. All were supposed to avoid the walks of Old College, the university's second building, and the administration building, after it was built in 1921. They were banned from wearing any high school jewelry or clothing and from parking their cars on University Avenue. Those who violated the rules risked a dunking in the "duck pond," a large vat filled with water.

Throughout the year, the different classes held athletic contests, some involving conventional sports and some decidedly unorthodox. The Pajamarino, the biggest pep rally held on campus, brought out students clad in pajamas and nightshirts to light a giant bonfire. During Senior Sneak Day, the seniors cut classes and picnicked at the beach while the underclassmen held a mock funeral to commemorate the passing of the graduating class. Ivy Week, named in honor of the seniors' tradition of planting an ivy vine alongside Old College, marked the end of the class rivalries, but included a muddy contest in which the freshman and sophomore classes rushed a greased 25-foot-tall pole set up on the old athletic field and attempted to be the first to plant their class's flag at the top. Afterward, the two class presidents buried a symbolic hatchet and smoked a peace pipe.

By the 1940s, changing mores and the maturation of the university forced most of these traditions into obsolescence.

 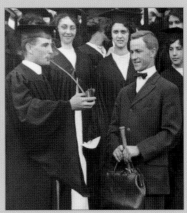

Above left: Junior class president Gene Roberts (center) and senior class president Gordon Pace (class of 1931) carried on a longstanding USC student tradition by burying the hatchet, signifying a halt to rivalry between their two classes.

Above right: Representatives of the senior and junior classes put an end to rivalry during commencement week in 1913 by smoking the pipe of peace.

Below left: From the earliest days, USC upperclassmen punished freshmen for violating an elaborate set of rules by dunking the hapless victims in the "duck pond"—initially an actual pond (as pictured), and later a large vat filled with water.

Below right: USC students produced colorful flyers to publicize the outcomes of athletic contests between classes and also to remind freshmen of their status on campus.

[photos courtesy of USC University Archives]

THE FIRST OLYMPIANS

Sprinter Charles Paddock (class of 1923), nicknamed "The World's Fastest Human," landed on the USC campus in 1918, barely old enough to qualify for the Students' Army Training Corps. Identified as officer material, he was sent to Camp Zachary Taylor in Kentucky and graduated as a second lieutenant, probably the youngest artillery officer in the army. Returning to USC in February, he won a prize for outstanding debate and oratory and later became a member of the varsity debate team. In the meantime, he had been developing a unique, explosive style of running and made a much greater name for himself as an athlete than as an orator. He traveled to Paris that summer for the Inter-Allied Games and to Antwerp in 1920 for the Olympic Games.

During his illustrious athletic career, he set 13 world and U.S. records. At Antwerp, he won two gold medals, for the 100 meters and the relay, and a silver medal for the 200 meters. Four years later, he again won a silver medal for the 200 meters.

Paddock returned to USC in 1930 to pursue a law degree. In 1942, he joined the Marine Corps as a captain and just a year later was killed when the plane he was riding in crashed near Sitka, Alaska.

Paddock was not USC's first Olympian. That honor belongs to Emil Breitkreutz (class of 1906), who competed in the 1904 games and won a bronze medal in the 800 meters. Eight years later, in 1912, freshman Fred Kelly (class of 1916) became USC's first gold medalist for the 110-meter high hurdles, and launched an unprecedented winning streak among American institutions. At least one USC athlete has come home with a gold medal in virtually every Olympiad since, and USC claims more Olympians than any other university in the country.

Left: Emil Breitkreutz became USC's first Olympic champion when he won a bronze medal at the 1904 games.

Above, and below right: Sprinter Charles Paddock set 13 world and U.S. records and took home two gold and two silver medals in the 1920 and 1924 Olympics.

[photos courtesy of USC University Archives]

and in 1892 was appointed the presiding elder of the Los Angeles District. He became president of the university in September 1895.

In his new role, White quickly put his celebrated organizational abilities to work. One of his first acts was to streamline the administration of the university, merging the two corporations known as the "University of Southern California" and the "College of Liberal Arts of the University of Southern California" into a single entity known as the University of Southern California. This new corporation was formed on November 11, 1895, in accordance with California law. Its articles of incorporation stipulated a 21-member Board of Trustees, which replaced the Board of Directors. Eleven were to be members of the Southern California Methodist Episcopal Conference; two were to be alumni of the university. The board was vested with the power "to establish and maintain a University for educational purposes with all the powers necessary to maintain and conduct a University." The articles also noted that the university "shall be open in every respect for the equal education of both sexes." White was once again elected president of the board, a duty he carried out concurrently with his role as president of the university.

To bolster the university's finances, he canvassed the Southern California Conference to secure pledges guaranteeing any deficiency in the university's income for three years. This arrangement meant he could focus less on constantly soliciting funds to meet operating expenses and more on institutional improvements and building the permanent endowment.

The effects of those enhancements were evident almost immediately. The faculty was strengthened, and thanks to recruitment efforts over the summer, enrollment in the college and academic departments increased to 285, more than 100 students higher than it had been the year before; overall the university enrolled more than 500 students. New labs and equipment enhanced the science courses, and a large number of books and magazines were acquired for the library. Numerous specimens were added to the museum. Athletics and physical education assumed greater importance: All students were expected to take part in physical exercise, and athletic facilities were expanded, with croquet and tennis courts, playing fields, a gymnasium and track added. Intercollegiate athletic competition in football, baseball and track and field were added by 1897.

James Harmon Hoose founded USC's pedagogy department and also helped establish a formal graduate program at USC. The north wing of Bovard Administration Building (James Harmon Hoose Hall of Philosophy, opened in 1921) and the library in USC's Mudd Memorial Hall of Philosophy (James Harmon Hoose Library of Philosophy, opened in 1930) are named in his honor. [photo courtesy of USC University Archives]

Left: This postcard shows the original location of the Los Angeles Law School, which affiliated with USC in 1901. [image courtesy of John G. "Tom" Tomlinson Jr., associate dean, USC Gould School of Law]

Ten years after the school's founding, Jamaican-born John Alexander Somerville became the first African-American graduate of the USC College of Dentistry in 1907. In 1918, his wife, Vada Watson Somerville, was the school's first African-American woman graduate, going on to become the first black woman licensed to practice dentistry in California. The Somervilles helped found the Los Angeles chapter of the NAACP, and John Somerville served on the Los Angeles Police Commission and was the second African-American member of the Chamber of Commerce. [photos courtesy of the USC School of Dentistry]

Academically, the university advanced as well. A School of Oratory was established at the beginning of the 1895–96 academic year, as was a College of Commerce, to provide practical business courses. The School of Music was reorganized and its standards raised. In 1896, a Department of Pedagogy was established to meet the needs of students desiring to become teachers. James Harmon Hoose, founder and head of the State Normal Training School in Courtland, New York, for 22 years, was named head of the department. Hoose was an extraordinary teacher and something of a Renaissance man. Endowed with a superhuman intellect and boundless energy, he soon had the title of professor of pedagogy and psychology and was teaching all the courses in history and economics as well. In 1899, as an economy measure for the university, he added philosophy to his course load. He later taught sociology as well. During the following decade, six separate departments with 20 faculty members developed from his original courses.

Accompanying the academic growth of the university was a diversifying social life. A number of new student clubs were formed, including the Pedagogical Round Table, Science Association, Political Science Association and Student Volunteers missionary group.

A nationwide recession caused progress to slow during the last years of the century. Enrollment fell off, and faculty were forced to work for reduced salaries. A school of forestry, established in 1899, operated for one semester before financial constraints caused it to be closed. When the dean of the College of Liberal Arts resigned, to save money, White embraced that responsibility as well, serving as interim dean, along with his presidential duties.

Other enterprises proved more successful. In 1896, 36 law apprentices organized themselves into a study group. Calling themselves the Law Students Association of Los Angeles, they met in Justice Morrison's police court at city hall to pursue their studies together, under the guidance of a prominent attorney. Within a year, they had gained sufficient momentum to incorporate as the "Los Angeles Law School," which in 1901 affiliated with the University of Southern California.

In fall 1897, a College of Dentistry was established at the request of some medical students. Beginning with 20 students in a single room in the medical school building, the school grew so rapidly that by the 1899–90 academic year, it moved into more spacious quarters in the Temple Block, at Main, Spring and Temple, taking up the entire upper floor.

Despite continued debt, things were looking up for the university in 1899. Thanks to White's careful management over the past four years, the deficit was significantly smaller than before, and he had made headway in his efforts to raise an endowment. He was, however, anxious to reenter the ministry, and in September, he submitted his resignation, leaving the university without a leader once again.

Holding Pattern

The trustees did not immediately appoint a new university president. Instead, they placed the institution in a holding pattern until the right candidate materialized—an interregnum that lasted four years. Each of the colleges and departments was left in the hands of its dean, while universitywide decisions were left up to the president of the Board of Trustees, George Finley Bovard, a member of the university's first

graduating class and also the presiding elder of the Los Angeles District of the Southern California Methodist Episcopal Conference. Continuing White's momentum, the trustees made a concerted effort to build the endowment. A campaign was launched in 1899, and by 1903, $230,000 in endowment funds had been raised, $125,000 of which was producing income—the first time in its history that the university had had any significant productive endowment.

Academically, the university also progressed during this period. Enrollment increased, and strong new faculty members were added. In 1901, instruction was terminated at Chaffey College, and the dean and a number of faculty transferred to West Los Angeles, now called University Town or the University section. The campus was upgraded, and two dormitories were built.

In 1903, after the university's financial agent and treasurer, George I. Cochran, submitted a balanced budget, the trustees felt the prospects for the institution were far more encouraging than they had been in a long time. On April 8, 1903, they unanimously elected George F. Bovard president of the university, making official the job he had already been carrying out for four years.

A Pivotal President:
George Finley Bovard

In the annals of the University of Southern California, George Finley Bovard, fully 6 feet 4 inches tall, proved to be a giant in more ways than one. A man of rare graciousness and humility, he was also a skilled and visionary administrator whose steady hand guided the university into a new era of stability and distinction.

Bovard soon announced plans to reorganize and strengthen the university, particularly the College of Liberal Arts. Not surprisingly, one of the greatest challenges facing him was the continued issue of funding, particularly in the face of growing needs on campus. Initially by mortgaging university property, later through fundraising, Bovard managed to scrape together the resources for two important initiatives: increasing the salaries of faculty, who had remained woefully underpaid throughout the difficulties of the 1890s, and expanding campus facilities. In 1908, at a banquet held on Washington's birthday, Bovard launched the Greater University Campaign, an initiative to build up the university physically and academically with the goal of creating a great metropolitan university.

The building program was actually well under way by the time the banquet took place. On April 18, 1904, construction had begun on a gymnasium. In March 1905, work had started on two new wings for the main university building. The additions, which nearly doubled the square footage of the building, were devoted mainly to science and included laboratories comparable to those at the best universities in the country. In May 1907, the trustees authorized a new science building.

Driving the construction—and, indeed, the Greater University Campaign itself—was a rapid growth in enrollment and expansion of the faculty. The student body increased 400 percent between 1900 and 1910. At the same time, the university's academic programs were expanding as well. In 1905, classes in pharmacy were first offered within the College of Medicine. A year later, the university began offering courses leading to degrees in civil and electrical engineering. (The engineering courses were so popular that within two years, 50 students were enrolled in the freshman class.) A summer session was also initiated in 1906, to provide public school teachers with an opportunity to take additional coursework. Enrollment in the law school was skyrocketing, reaching

USC's fourth president, George Finley Bovard, had been a member of the university's first graduating class in 1884, and he also earned a master's degree from USC in 1887. His presidency saw the university expand its academic offerings and physical plant, contribute to the war effort during World War I and redouble its commitment to being "a city institution." [photo courtesy of USC University Archives]

400 in 1910; the school added a Juris Doctor degree in 1914.

At the same time, curricular changes were modernizing and expanding the course of study. By 1909, the university had abandoned the philosophical, classical literary and scientific courses of study in favor of 21 majors. All students were expected to select a major before the end of their sophomore year. In 1911, a Department of Architecture and Drawing was established, distinct from the Department of Art and Design, and the Biology Department added divisions in botany and zoology. Also new was a Department of Oriental Studies. In 1912, the university announced a groundbreaking course in automotive science, the first of its kind in the world. The course, which was open to both men and women, consisted of 16 lectures dealing with the automotive mechanism, lubrication and ignition, as well as driving, rules of the road and use of the automobile. The English department began offering journalism courses in 1914.

To accommodate the mushrooming student population and diversifying curriculum, in 1910 the university hired architects to draw up plans for a new set of buildings, including an administration building, even though it lacked the resources to build them all at once. The same year, Andrew

Carnegie offered $25,000 on the condition that the trustees match it 3 to 1 with an additional $75,000 and liquidate certain debts. They met the terms in a single year, and in 1913, Bovard announced that $1 million had been pledged for new buildings.

With the momentum obviously gathering, a year later, the Reverend Robert J. Coyne, field secretary for the university, declared a previously unthinkable $10 million goal for the Greater University Campaign. By 1916, USC was the second largest denominational university in the country, surpassed only by Northwestern University, and the trustees were thinking even bigger, setting the goal of a student body of 10,000, an endowment of $10 million, an adequate campus with eight to 10 new buildings and a faculty capable of offering every type of instruction.

Above: Old College nearly doubled in size with the addition of two wings in 1905.

Below: Following completion of a new gymnasium in 1904, President G. F. Bovard hired Harvey R. Holmes as USC's baseball, football, and track and field coach. In all probability, Holmes was instrumental in the construction of Bovard Field— located just west of Old College—the following year. Holmes (upper right) is pictured here with President Bovard (wearing the bowler hat) and members of the university's 1907 track team.

[photos courtesy of USC University Archives]

Despite the extraordinary progress, the academic developments weren't without setbacks. In 1910, the College of Fine Arts in Highland Park was destroyed by fire. The same year, Abbot Kinney, developer of Venice, California, and advocate for the defunct school of forestry, donated enough waterfront property to the university to house the Venice Marine Biological Station of Southern California. Construction of the station began in 1911, and the new facility, under the direction of Albert Ulrey, professor of biology, was able to accommodate eight scientists and 40 students. In 1920, however, the building burned and was not rebuilt.

Making Graduate Studies Official

Concurrent with its construction program, the university was making plans to take a monumental step forward. Prior to 1910, the university had conferred a total of 75 graduate degrees, but these had been based on the requirements of the individual departments. In October of that year, the Board of Trustees created the Graduate Department of Arts and Sciences, under the governance of a Graduate Council, made up of senior faculty members appointed by the president. The purpose of the Graduate Council was: "(1) To give

Above: In 1914, the famous African-American political leader, educator and author Booker T. Washington (right) visited USC. Greeting him on campus was the university's reigning track star, Howard Porter Drew (left), class of 1916. Drew, who was deemed the "fastest man in the world" in 1914, 1915 and 1916, was the first African American inducted into USC's Skull and Dagger society. After graduating from USC, he went on to earn a law degree from Drake University in Iowa and led a distinguished career as an attorney, judge and civil rights advocate. [photo courtesy of the USC Black Alumni Association and USC University Archives]

Left: USC's College of Fine Arts building, located in the Garvanza district, along the historic Arroyo Seco in Highland Park, burned down in 1910. [photo courtesy of USC University Archives]

due prominence to the graduate courses of instruction; (2) To insure systematic and efficient administration of this higher work; and (3) To provide instruction for graduate and upper division students." Emphasis was to be placed on the thesis for the master's degree, and "[t]he work of the candidate must show marked excellence." Founding members of the council included such university leaders as Bovard; James Harmon Hoose, professor of philosophy and department chair; Thomas Blanchard Stowell, professor of education; James Main Dixon, professor of English literature; Gilbert E. Bailey, professor of geology; Edgar M. von Fingerlin, professor of modern languages; and Rockwell Dennis Hunt, professor of economics and sociology.

Providing the impetus for the graduate department was a desire, particularly by Stowell, that the university be accredited to grant high school teaching certificates. At that time, UC Berkeley and Stanford University were the only institutions in California authorized to issue secondary credentials. Bovard, Stowell, Hunt and trustee William Bowen applied to the state Board of Education for authorization on behalf of USC in April 1910 but were turned down until the university met a specific set of conditions. The Graduate Council moved

aggressively forward, establishing requirements for admission, credentials and degrees and otherwise seeking to meet the state requirements. In February 1911, the university was accredited to issue secondary teaching credentials, and the same year, the preparatory school was transformed into a model high school (which it remained until its closing in 1928, after the Los Angeles Board of Education gave USC students the right to do their student teaching in the public schools). The university's education department become so strong that in 1917, the state Board

Above: In 1910, USC organized a centrally administered graduate program governed by a Graduate Council composed of senior faculty members. Council members for 1910–11 included (from left) Rockwell Dennis Hunt, Gilbert Ellis Bailey, James Main Dixon, James Harmon Hoose, Edgar Maximilian von Fingerlin, Thomas Blanchard Stowell and George Finley Bovard.

Below: Programs at USC's Venice Marine Biological Station took full advantage of the California coast as a living laboratory for the study of marine biology.

[photos courtesy of USC University Archives]

By then, graduate courses were offered by 26 different departments.

Interrupted by War

The university's forward momentum came to an abrupt halt in April 1917, when the United States entered World War I. Seniors enlisting in the military were given their diplomas, and others were given credit for the balance of the semester. Overall, approximately 300 students left to enter the armed forces.

For those remaining on campus, life changed profoundly.

On December 13, 1917, USC raised a service flag emblazoned with stars—each representing a USC man in the armed forces.
[photo courtesy of USC University Archives]

of Education authorized the university to train teachers in all types of work in California elementary and secondary schools. The following year, the Board of Trustees established a separate School of Education, with Stowell as the first dean, and in January 1920, they created the Graduate School of Arts and Sciences, with Hunt as dean.

Military training was introduced in physical education classes, and Bovard Field was given over to military drills three times a week. A course in international conciliation was added to the curriculum.

Enrollment plummeted, and the proceeds from tuition were so low that the Methodist Episcopal Conference raised its levy on church members to support the university. As prices and operating costs increased, tuition was raised as well. The following year, more than 600 students were absent from the university, making the situation even worse.

A senior division of the Reserve Officers Training Corps was established at the university on April 14, 1918, by order of the Department of War, making USC an official training school for army officers. All able-bodied men were required to take the course for at least two years except those enrolled in the engineering program, who were excused so they could study subjects useful to the war effort. Approximately 1,000 students enrolled in the four-year military course, pitching tents on Bovard Field and living under army regulations while attending classes in uniform. The university's chemistry lab began to produce trinitrotoluene, the base for a new explosive. Female students became active in the Red Cross and hospital work.

Regaining Momentum

The end of the war brought an era of unprecedented growth to the university. Beginning with the 1920–21 academic year, enrollment began to increase by 1,000 students

STATUES ON THE TOWER

George Finley Bovard Administration Building, 1921 [photo courtesy of USC University Archives]

The most prominent feature of the new University of Southern California administration building was its massive central tower, which was surrounded by eight statues of famous and iconic men. The statues were designated by the Board of Trustees in 1919, who intended them to represent the progress of civilization. Although the trustees' choices prompted faculty members and alumni to suggest alternatives they considered more appropriate, the trustees prevailed, and today statues of Abraham Lincoln and Theodore Roosevelt stand on the tower's north-facing facade. On the west, commemorating classical achievement, are Cicero, the orator, and Plato, the philosopher. John Wesley, founder of Methodism, and Bishop Matthew Simpson, renowned preacher and president of De Pauw University, gaze out from the east, and on the south face are statues of Phillips Brooks and Borden P. Bowne, American leaders in religious and philosophic thought.

a year. Fifteen new faculty members were hired, and salaries were increased. Admission requirements were raised.

Plans for the new administration building, which had remained on hold, finally began to move forward. In spring 1919, the trustees authorized its construction; the cornerstone was laid in October. Designed by John Parkinson, whose architectural firm also developed a master plan for the campus, it was a three-story brick building with central tower, in the Romanesque style, erected at a cost of nearly $600,000. Inside its 2,100-seat auditorium was a pipe organ considered one of the finest in the West. Flanking the tower were two wings, one named the James Harmon Hoose Hall of Philosophy, the other the Thomas Blanchard Stowell Hall of Education. Rockwell Dennis Hunt, with the support of the faculty, suggested that the building itself be named in honor of the man who had guided the institution from an unsteady little denominational school to a university of national distinction: President George Finley Bovard.

The post-War years, while promising a new era for the university, proved so demanding for Bovard that in spring 1921, after 18 years of wise and devoted service to the university, he suffered a breakdown in his health. In April, his physicians ordered him to take a six-month rest, and the trustees gladly granted him a leave of absence. He continued to work for several weeks before departing, however, then informed the board that he thought they should find a new president as soon as possible instead.

The building that bore his name was dedicated June 19–23, 1921, and the event marked the end of his tenure as president. Among the many tributes that accompanied his retirement was the one published in the minutes of the October 1921 Methodist Episcopal Conference:

Under the administration of Pres. Bovard our great institution, from small beginnings, has steadily grown in numbers and in influence until it is one of the most notable educational forces of the Republic. He, more than any other man or group of men, has made the University of Southern California what it is today.

Pres. Bovard began his administration in 1903 with 59 students in the College of Liberal Arts, and the total enrollment in the University including about 300 in the academy was 431.

Then the annual income was $21,360—now it is $321,000.

Then the receipts from tuition were $9,997—now they are $220,000.

Then the total assets of the school were $373,000—now they are $1,893,000.

It is obvious that a man who could accomplish such results should be spoken about; it is equally obvious how impossible it is that he should be spoken about adequately.

But the outstanding fact is clear; year after year, under his careful administration and guided by his masterful personality, the University has steadily grown, and carried forward its magnificent work.

Courageous, patient, wise, far-seeing—rarely skilled in administration, undismayed by meager resources, making one dollar do the work of ten, firm when others wavered, courageous when others feared, he has walked bravely up a steep and difficult way....

USC'S FIRST "FIRST LADIES"

From the beginning, the wives of USC's presidents played a significant role in the life of the University of Southern California. In 1880 just as in 2005, the first lady opened her home to all of the university's varied constituencies for events ranging from intimate sit-down dinners to receptions involving 100 or more guests. She had to cope with the stresses and constraints of raising a family while living very much in the public eye and conforming to the highest standards of dress and conduct. She functioned not only as USC's official hostess, but also as special adviser to the president and as the university's unofficial ambassador and fundraiser. Over the past 125 years, each of USC's 10 first ladies has brought her own individual skills, interests, values and styles to bear upon her role—and all have served the university with extraordinary graciousness and dedication.

USC's first "first lady," Jennie Allen Bovard, enrolled at Indiana Asbury University (later named DePauw University) in 1869, just two years after the institution began admitting female students. She graduated in 1873, in the same class as her husband-to-be. At USC, she served as a member of the founding faculty in 1880, although she soon had to forgo this position as her responsibility for coordinating official university entertaining and organizing activities for students took on more prominence.

Mary Bray Widney was educated at the Moravian Seminary for Young Ladies in Bethlehem, Pennsylvania, and married late in life—at the age of 37 in 1882. She was a gifted artist who specialized in painting landscapes, and her artistic talents lent a special touch to the events she hosted in her home. First as a dean's wife (her husband became founding dean of USC's medical college in 1885) and then as USC's first lady, she was lauded as the "moving spirit" behind convivial annual receptions for directors, deans, faculty, students and friends of the university.

Lettie Hutchins White graduated from Cornell College in Mount Vernon, Iowa, in 1883—in the same class as her fiancé—and embarked on a teaching career before marrying and dedicating herself to service as a minister's wife. As first lady of USC, she juggled the responsibilities of raising a newborn son with carrying on the tradition of university entertaining. In 1917, after years of coping with chronic pain resulting from illnesses and a severe back injury, she published a book describing her method for garnering the dual powers of mind and faith to relieve bodily suffering.

The daughter of a prominent California pioneer family, Emma Bradley Bovard was among the first students to enroll at USC. As first lady of the university in 1905, she was instrumental in forming the Women's Club of USC, which had the goal of generating financial support for students and faculty. (The group changed its name to Town and Gown in 1927.) In 1912, at a time when the university had few women faculty members, she helped found the Faculty Wives' Club (renamed the Faculty Women's Club in 1995) to support spouses of university professors. She served as president of this club until 1921. In appreciation for her service to the university, the Faculty Wives' Club established the Emma Josephine Bradley Bovard Award in 1934, which is awarded each year to the graduating senior woman or women with the highest cumulative grade-point average following four years of study at USC.

[Jennie Bovard photo courtesy of USC University Archives; Mary Widney portrait by Tim O'Brien; Lettie White photo courtesy of Patricia White Sprague and Tom Sprague; Emma Bovard photo courtesy of Marjorie Weatherholt]

This aerial view of the University Park campus, shot in 1939, looks southwest toward Exposition Park. [photo courtesy of USC University Archives]

Chapter Three

Coming of Age (1921–1946)

By Sarah Lifton

Bishop Adna W. Leonard, president of the USC Board of Trustees, was presiding over the annual conference of the Methodist Episcopal Church in early October 1921, when he left the podium to speak with his wife, who was in the audience.

"I have a bursting headache," he told her. "Can you get me some tablets to relieve it?"

By the time he returned to retrieve the remedy, however, he had changed his mind. Waving a telegram, he said, "The headache is gone. I have a better cure."

Contained in the telegram was the key to the university's future: "Appreciating confidence expressed in invitation," it read. "I accept presidency of U.S.C. Signed, R. B. von KleinSmid."

Rufus Bernhard von KleinSmid, USC's fifth president, reorganized the university, expanded academic offerings and presided over a building program that transformed the campus. [photo courtesy of USC University Archives]

Transitions

Rufus Bernhard von KleinSmid, president of the University of Arizona, had not been the Board of Trustees' first choice to succeed George F. Bovard. They had originally offered the position to the Reverend Dr. Merle N. Smith, who turned them down, noting that he was temperamentally unsuited to the job and preferred the life of a pastor. But Smith's rejection actually proved to be a rare stroke of luck. Over the next 25 years, von KleinSmid was responsible for an unprecedented period of expansion and advancement for the University of Southern California, transforming it into an institution of national consequence.

Von KleinSmid, who had also received offers from the University of Denver and American University, settled on USC because he recognized its potential.

"The University of Southern California had had a dignified and continuously ambitious program," he said in a 1961 interview. "While it was a small school comparatively, it was located in a large city, or potentially large city, and… it had achieved some very worthy objectives…. The institution was ready, it seemed to me, for both internal reorganization and external expansion…. [T]here was now a likelihood of securing support for a more intensive, as well as extensive, program."

Von KleinSmid was well qualified to orchestrate the expansion he had in mind. In addition to a distinguished appearance, gift for oratory and flamboyance that lent his efforts momentum, he brought a sound background in education, a fresh perspective and boundless energy that meshed perfectly with

FOUNDING OF THE ALUMNI ASSOCIATION

On June 15, 1885, all eight of USC's alumni gathered in the office of the University Building to form an alumni association. They drafted a temporary constitution and bylaws and elected half the membership to office.

George Finley Bovard
Class of 1884

George Finley Bovard, who had been instrumental in convening the group, became its first president. Two days later, they created a permanent organization and resolved to sponsor a reunion every year during commencement week. Although initially the association was little more than a social club for graduates of the College of Liberal Arts, beginning in June 1917, it also began producing *The Alumni Magazine*, a small publication that kept readers abreast of developments at the university and beyond.

In time, informal alumni groups formed in distant cities. By 1923, alumni clubs existed in Boston, Chicago, San Francisco, Pasadena, Glendale, Long Beach, Ventura and San Diego. But, the *USC Alumni News* observed, "There has been one rather serious handicap to alumni work on any large scale. There has been no University Alumni Association." That year, the situation was rectified with the founding of the General Alumni Association.

With Edward L. Doheny Jr. as president, membership climbed to 4,800 in little over a year. The GAA took over publication of the alumni magazine and organized Trojan Clubs in towns and cities around the country.

Edward L. "Ned" Doheny
Class of 1913

In 1924, the association inaugurated an annual Homecoming celebration, and over the next decade and a half, raised funds to create Alumni Park, the Trojan Shrine and the Alumni Memorial Pylon. It continued to sponsor class reunions and raise funds for the university; it also offered job placement services.

Arnold Eddy
Class of 1924

After World War II, under the leadership of executive director Arnold Eddy, the Alumni Association launched many programs that continue today, including women's organizations, an academic open house and SCions, a group made up of the children and younger family members of USC alumni.

Since 1976, the Alumni Association has, fittingly, been headquartered in the university's first building—now called Widney Alumni House—the same building where USC's first alumni association had been founded nearly a century earlier.

[photos courtesy of USC University Archives]

PAN AMERICAN CONFERENCE
AND INAUGURATION OF R. B. VON KLEINSMID
AS PRESIDENT OF U. S. C.

the trajectory of the growing institution. Furthermore, although he was a Methodist, he was a layman, which gave him a secular outlook as president.

A native Midwesterner, von KleinSmid had earned his bachelor's and master's degrees at Northwestern University, then begun his career in education in 1897 as the Illinois superintendent of public schools. After seven years, he transferred to the Northwestern University Academy and then to DePauw University, where he first served as principal of the DePauw Academy and later as professor of education and psychology before leaving to lead the University of Arizona in 1914. During his seven-year tenure in Tucson, he built that institution from a tiny land grant college with 308 students and 18 buildings into a university with 1,368 students and 21 buildings. He

reorganized it into three colleges, established a school of education and launched correspondence courses and night classes. The faculty more than doubled, and the library expanded by 15,000 volumes.

When he arrived at USC in December 1921, von KleinSmid found a growing but undeniably modest institution. Composed of eight schools and colleges, it enrolled 5,635 students, yet the campus consisted of a mere eight buildings, only two of which—the new George Finley Bovard Administration Building and Old College—could be considered permanent. He did not let USC's limitations constrain his ambitions, however.

His inauguration, on April 27–29, 1922, was an audacious spectacle that grabbed attention in the community as well as academia. In conjunction with his formal

investiture as president, the university hosted a Pan-American Conference on Education, the first event of its kind ever held in a U.S. university. Attending the conference were 400 delegates, representing 14 of the 20 Latin American governments, as well as Great Britain and Italy.

"Nothing like this had ever been seen in California," recalled Rockwell Dennis Hunt, emeritus dean of the Graduate School, 40 years later.

Getting Started

Despite the pomp surrounding the inauguration, von KleinSmid realized that the university was facing daunting problems, and he wasted little time in tackling them. Most pressing was the need for facilities to accommodate the rapidly growing student body. In particular, the university needed buildings to house its professional schools, which played an outsize role in the region, as they were the only ones in Southern California, Arizona and New Mexico. Other high priorities included increasing faculty salaries, expanding library collections and enlarging research facilities. The university also urgently needed endowment funds.

Within six months of his inauguration, von KleinSmid announced plans for a $10 million capital campaign to raise funds for several new buildings, as well as for endowment. The university's leadership embraced his bold vision wholeheartedly and lavished praise on his leadership.

"The coming of Rufus B. von Klein Smid [sic] to the Presidency of the University was clearly providential," Merle Smith, chairman of the committee on education, said at the 1922 Methodist Episcopal annual conference. "Highly trained in the science and art of education; skilled in administration; gifted with rare power of persuasive speach [sic]; with a clear vision; contagious enthusiasm and inspiring faith, he is steadily leading our University up a shining way into the new opportunities of the new day. It is a time to support and sustain him. He is doing magnificent work. He has our unwavering confidence, affection and esteem."

Although the campaign ultimately failed to reach its goal, it helped fuel

Opposite and above: This panoramic shot shows participants assembled in front of Old College for the Pan-American Conference on Education in April 1922.

Opposite, below right: An enormous cash register was erected on the lawn of Bovard Administration Building to tally the progress of President von KleinSmid's fundraising drive in 1923.

Below: Constructed in summer 1925 as a temporary facility, USC's old Architecture Building —located on 35th Street off of University Avenue (later renamed Trousdale Parkway)—was hand-decorated by students and faculty.

[photos courtesy of USC University Archives]

Above left: A year before USC's law school gained a permanent home on the University Park campus, the school produced its first Chinese-American graduate. You Chung Hong (LL.B. 1924, LL.M. 1925) achieved a number of other firsts: He was the first person in his family to go to college, and, after passing the bar in 1923, he became the first Chinese American to practice law in California, going on to build a reputation as the country's foremost Chinese civil-rights attorney of his age. [photo courtesy of the USC Gould School of Law]

Right: USC awarded its first doctor of philosophy degree to D. Welty Lefever (pictured here in the 1960s). He went on to pursue an academic career and served on the faculty of USC's School of Education for some 40 years. [photo courtesy of the USC University Archives]

the construction of several much-needed buildings on campus, including Science Hall, which opened in 1923 and housed the College of Pharmacy as well as the science departments; a women's residence hall, dedicated in 1925; a temporary building for the School of Architecture; and a building for the law school, which was dedicated in early 1926. In time, a men's residence hall, Aeneas Hall; student union; and classroom and office building, Bridge Hall, were erected on campus as well.

Extending the University's Reach

In addition to raising money to reconfigure the campus, von KleinSmid was determined to restructure the various academic units of the university. A number of the professional schools were affiliated with USC but governed by their own boards. During the first few years, he worked

tirelessly to integrate the schools of pharmacy, oratory, music and law fully into the university. He also reshaped the Maclay College of Theology into the "School of Religion upon the Maclay Foundation," concentrating all courses in religion within a single unit. The Graduate School of Arts and Sciences was reorganized in 1923, upon recommendation of its dean, Rockwell D. Hunt, its scope broadened to encompass all graduate work at the university. In recognition of its expanded role, it was renamed the Graduate School of the University of Southern California. A year later, plans were made to offer courses leading to the Ph.D. The first USC doctorate was awarded in 1927, to D. Welty Lefever, who went on to become a faculty member in the School of Education.

By December 1922, the university had made such progress that it was added to the approved list of the Association of American Universities, a singular honor that meant that degrees from any department in the university were recognized by other institutions belonging to the AAU, and credits of member institutions were interchangeable. To be included on the AAU list was a public endorsement of USC's academic programs and placed it on a par with other leading institutions in the country. In 1924,

ROCKWELL DENNIS HUNT

[photo courtesy of USC University Archives]

Few faculty members have had as lasting—and far-reaching—an influence on an institution as Rockwell Dennis Hunt did on USC. Raised near Sacramento, the son of pioneers, he earned bachelor's and master's degrees from the "Commercial Department" at Napa College, then taught history at his alma mater for two years before entering the doctoral program in history at Johns Hopkins University. His dissertation was on what was then an unorthodox topic: California history from 1846 to 1850.

After completing his Ph.D. in 1895, Hunt returned to California and took a position as professor of history and economics at University of the Pacific. Unable to make ends meet on his $1,000 annual salary, he became principal of San Jose High School. After six years, at the urging of Freeman D. Bovard and others, he took a substantial salary cut and accepted a position as professor of economics and sociology at USC. He soon found himself teaching an array of subjects, including political science and "Pacific slope history."

"…[A]s the population of Los Angeles maintained its almost dizzying rate of increase, the University administration was under pressure to venture into some new field, establish some new college division, or add to the curriculum new or more specialized courses in keeping with some group demand," he recalled in his autobiography. "I sympathized with a number of plans brought forward for expansion along comparatively untried lines. In more than one field I was even cast in the role of leader."

In 1910, Hunt was named to the newly formed Graduate Council. Ten years later, when the Graduate Department was reorganized into the Graduate School, he was named its dean.

Hunt taught the first courses in government ever offered in Los Angeles and was instrumental in organizing the College of Commerce and Business Administration, serving as its dean from 1921 to 1924 and concurrently as dean of the Graduate School. In 1933, at his instigation, the School of Research was created within the Graduate School.

"It would be impossible to minimize my relationship to the University," he wrote in 1956. "It was my very life from the time I began at age forty until the time of my retirement at the age of seventy-seven."

Hunt retired in 1945 but remained active in civic affairs, becoming, among other things, director of the California History Foundation. He also was a prodigious author, writing at least 17 major works and 169 articles in scholarly journals, popular magazines and newspapers. His contributions to his native state later led to the nickname "Mr. California," bestowed on him by Governor Goodwin J. Knight in 1954, when he was 86. He died 10 years later, in 1964.

Above: From 1924 until 1948, USC held almost all of its commencement ceremonies at historic Los Angeles Memorial Coliseum. Pictured here are the university's 1928 graduates in their caps and gowns.

Left: Housed in the Transportation Building, USC's Metropolitan College served a broad community by offering afternoon and evening classes to working people in Los Angeles.

[photos courtesy of USC University Archives]

Phi Beta Kappa seconded that vote of confidence by establishing a chapter on campus.

Determined to strengthen the university's ties to the community, in 1922, von KleinSmid created the Extension Division, which offered afternoon and evening classes to the community in a variety of locations from Glendale to San Diego. The Extension Division gave way, in 1924, to Metropolitan College, later called University College.

Other schools and colleges came into being at the prodding of different professional groups. In 1923, in response to the growing demand for trained social workers, von KleinSmid separated the university's program in social work from the Department of Sociology and established a dedicated school of social work within the College of Letters, Arts and Sciences. In 1925, at the urging of the Allied Architects Association of Los Angeles, he created a separate school of architecture to house the university's architecture program. Three additional professional schools were created in 1928: the College of Engineering, School of Education and School of Medicine, the latter reopened after an eight-year hiatus, at the instigation of the medical community.

During the same period, several novel programs signaled new directions for the university. In 1927, von KleinSmid was approached by the Academy of Motion Picture Arts and Sciences about establishing courses to educate professionals in the motion picture industry. On February 6, 1929, the first meeting of a course titled "Introduction to Photoplay" took place before a capacity crowd in Bovard Auditorium. It was the first program of its kind in the nation, and some 200 students applied for the 80 places in the first semester's class, which featured such Hollywood notables as D. W. Griffith, Darryl F. Zanuck and Douglas Fairbanks Sr., president of the Academy and von KleinSmid's fencing partner, as faculty. In 1928, von KleinSmid drew on his own interest in international relations to establish the Los Angeles University of International Relations, which was affiliated with USC. A year later, responding to requests from local government officials, von KleinSmid established at USC the first school of public administration west of the Appalachians. Also pioneering were the courses that the university began offering for credit in radio and in journalism.

Other advances that von KleinSmid instituted were designed to lessen the burden on faculty. He introduced sabbatical leaves and a new academic rank—lecturers—for instructors employed less than half-time. To ease his own workload, in 1927, he reorganized the administration to include two vice presidents. Warren Bovard, son of President Emeritus George Finley Bovard and comptroller of the university, became vice president for financial affairs; and Harold J. Stonier, who had been executive secretary of the university, was named vice president in charge of educational contracts and development, with a focus on the interests of the general public.

The University of Southern California

IN COOPERATION WITH

The Academy of Motion Picture Arts and Sciences

OFFERS

INTRODUCTION TO PHOTOPLAY

COURSE BEGINS SPRING SEMESTER

1929

Below left: The brainchild of Rufus von KleinSmid and Douglas Fairbanks Sr., president of the fledgling Academy of Motion Picture Arts and Sciences (founded in 1927), USC's "Introduction to Photoplay" was the first college-level film course in the United States. [photo courtesy of USC University Archives]

Below right: Emory Stephen Bogardus, founder of the Department of Sociology and School of Social Work, joined USC's faculty in 1911. He retired in 1953, although he remained active at the university until shortly before his death in 1973. The "Bogardus Social Distance Scale," which he created in 1925, is still widely used in research on prejudice and cultural and ethnic attitudes. [photo courtesy of USC University Archives]

Alumnus Warren Bradley Bovard (son of USC's fourth president, George F. Bovard) returned to his alma mater following service in World War I to become university comptroller. In 1927, President von KleinSmid appointed him vice president for financial affairs. [photo courtesy of USC University Archives]

Becoming a Secular Institution

More significant than the considerable changes von KleinSmid wrought in the structure of USC, however, was the change he brought about in the course of the university itself.

Determined to see his bold vision for USC reach fruition, he realized that the Southern California Methodist Episcopal Conference, for all its good intentions, was incapable of providing the level of financial support required to transform the institution from a small denominational college into a university of national and even international consequence. Although USC's budget was $1.25 million, the Methodist church provided less than $10,000 annually, and because of its own pressing financial needs, it was in no position to make the individual churches available for university-related solicitations.

Furthermore, USC, now approaching the 50th anniversary of its founding, had grown and diversified in concert with the region and was no longer so closely identified with the church. Students from a multitude of religious backgrounds were now enrolled: In fall 1928, the student body, which numbered more than 15,000 in the various departments (including University College and the Academy), represented 34 separate denominations and religions. Business and professional leaders, many of whom had been educated there, were taking an increasing interest in the university, too.

To mark the university's semi-centennial and provide for its needs, von KleinSmid launched another $10 million campaign. For a number of years, the university had been in dire need of a new, modern library; despite amassing 150,000 volumes, it had never had a freestanding library building. The students had already pledged $150,000 toward the estimated $600,000 that was needed. Also in the plans was a gymnasium.

Like the prior fundraising effort, the campaign quickly fell short of its goals. Donors outside the Methodist community were unwilling to support the university because of the way the board was constituted. Furthermore, under California law, the university could not receive contributions because members of its Board of Trustees were selected by the Methodist Episcopal Conference, rather than self-elected. With the very survival of the institution

In June 1930, USC's 50th-anniversary celebration officially welcomed a number of prominent new additions to Troy, including the campus's most famous landmark—Tommy Trojan, officially known as the Trojan Shrine. [photo courtesy of USC University Archives]

hanging in the balance, in June 1928, von KleinSmid convinced the Board of Trustees to amend the articles of incorporation to conform to California law. Henceforth, the board would be self-perpetuating, and only half its members would be Methodists. The move also freed the church from the crushing responsibility of providing financial support for the university.

Within a year of the decision, the university had raised nearly $2.3 million toward its goal, from students, faculty, alumni, trustees and friends, confirming the wisdom of the decision to secularize the institution. Unfortunately, that momentum came to an abrupt halt when the stock market crashed and effectively ended the campaign.

50 Years and Counting

Although the nation was already caught in the stranglehold of the Great Depression, 1930 was a landmark year for USC. Now 50 years old, it marked its golden anniversary on June 1–7 with an elaborate celebration that included special programs, performances, lectures, luncheons and dinners. State, national and international leaders took part in

the festivities, and the university awarded a phenomenal 56 honorary degrees. Four buildings—Mudd Memorial Hall of Philosophy, Bridge Memorial Hall, the Physical Education Building and Science Hall—were dedicated, as was the Trojan Shrine, a bronze sculpture by Roger Noble Burnham that quickly became better known by its nickname, Tommy Trojan.

Although the anniversary primarily feted the tangible advances the university had made in its first half-century, changes behind the scenes, while less apparent, were equally significant. The enrollment had nearly tripled in the nine years since von KleinSmid had assumed the presidency, and the student body, no longer dominated by Methodists, had become more cosmopolitan and international. USC was, in fact, ranked third in the United States in international enrollment.

And even more changes were on the horizon. On June 6, 1931, ground was broken for the new Edward L. Doheny Jr. Memorial Library, a gift of Edward L. Doheny, oil baron and longtime friend of von KleinSmid, in memory of his son, a USC alumnus and trustee who in 1929 had been murdered in his Beverly Hills mansion. Departing from precedent, the architectural firm selected was not Parkinson and Parkinson, which had

THE ASCENT OF TROJAN FOOTBALL

Elmer C. "Gloomy Gus" Henderson

When USC entered the world of intercollegiate football in the early years of the 20th century, its performance was unremarkable, but the Trojans' luck began to turn in 1919, when Elmer C. "Gloomy Gus" Henderson became football coach. Under his tutelage, the teams began to build a reputation that became the stuff of legends. In 1920, the football team played its first undefeated season. The following year, the Trojans were invited to join the Pacific Coast Conference, giving it equal stature with the University of California, Stanford, Washington, Oregon, Oregon Agriculture College and Washington State. On January 1, 1923, USC played in its first Rose Bowl game, defeating Penn State, 14–3. After Stanford and Berkeley challenged USC's adherence to eligibility rules and publicly severed athletic ties with USC in a humiliating display before 60,000 fans in 1924, however, the administration decided to change coaches, and Henderson was fired.

Taking his place was Howard Harding Jones, who had made a name for himself coaching the University of Iowa. Before his arrival at USC, the Trojans had never won a conference championship, produced an All-American or received national recognition. Jones soon ratcheted up their standing. In his first season at USC, running guard Brice Taylor became the first Trojan All-American. The following year, Jones inaugurated a tradition by scheduling the first USC–Notre Dame game. In 1927, his team tied for the conference title; three years later, his team, now nicknamed the Thundering Herd, won the Rose Bowl game against Pittsburgh, the first of five out of five Rose Bowl games that the Trojans won during his tenure. In all, he produced a total of 11 Trojan All-Americans and four national champion teams during the 16 seasons he coached.

Jones's illustrious career was cut short on July 27, 1941, when he died of a heart attack. The campus was plunged into mourning. As President Rufus von KleinSmid eulogized him:

In the passing of Howard Jones, I have lost one of my most highly prized friends, and from the university has been taken one of her most efficient and loyal faculty members. The nation has suffered the loss of a leader whose influence upon the lives of all who follow athletics has been of incalculable value.

Not only was he a master coach, but he was also a teacher whose first thought was to use athletics as a means of inspiring young men to the highest ideals.

To his own players and to his opponents alike, the name of Howard Jones stood for the highest principles of sportsmanship. Fair play, modesty in victory, courage in defeat, consideration for all—these were elements of his football code which he taught and lived.

His good influence upon the game of football in the nation has been universal and profound. He was a man of whom any institution would be enthusiastically proud. We shall all miss him greatly.

Howard Harding Jones

[photos courtesy of USC University Archives]

USC was engaged in a fundraising drive to construct a new library when the Doheny family came through with a transformative gift made in memory of their late son, who had been founding president of USC's General Alumni Association. Edward L. Doheny Jr. Memorial Library opened with great fanfare on September 12, 1932. At the dedication ceremony, Los Angeles mayor John C. Porter expressed confidence that the splendid new facility would "add to the cultural advancement of all Southern California." [photo courtesy of USC University Archives]

designed most of the new campus buildings, but that of another Los Angeles architect, Samuel Eugene Lunden. Lunden designed the library to be a monumental brick and stone edifice, heavily ornamented with murals, stained glass, carvings and mosaic, which cost the staggering sum of $1.1 million. On September 12, 1932, the first day of school, the members of the Doheny family presented von KleinSmid with the keys to the library. A ceremony to unlock the doors followed, ushering in a new era on campus.

"The formal dedication of the Edward L. Doheny Jr. Memorial Library…was an event of extraordinary interest to me as Dean of the Graduate School," wrote Rockwell Dennis Hunt in his 1956 autobiography. "In the Dean's Annual Report for a number of years I had emphasized the commanding importance of having on the Southern California campus an adequate, fire-proof library building as an imperatively needed feature to support the rapidly developing graduate program of the University. The total inadequacy of library facilities up to this time was fully recognized: accessions to research materials of the library itself could not be expected to keep pace with the demands in the absence of a new, well-equipped building…. Through the munificence of the Edward L. Doheny family the need for the Library Building was handsomely met. The 12th of September, 1932, is therefore a highly important date in the annals of the University of Southern California as a whole, and of the Graduate School in particular…."

With Doheny Memorial Library as the linchpin, the university continued its capital expansion, and from the progress it made, one would scarcely

President von KleinSmid's wife, Elisabeth Patterson Sawyers von KleinSmid (above left), was an ardent and effective advocate for students at USC, particularly women. As president of the university's Women's Club—which changed its name to Town and Gown in 1927—she organized efforts to raise funds for scholarships and student loans as well as a women's residence hall (above right), later renamed John R. Hubbard Hall, and the Town and Gown Foyer (below).

[photos courtesy of USC University Archives]

have known that the Great Depression was ravaging the country. After a long, rancorous battle in the courts with a property owner who refused to sell her parcel, USC used eminent domain to acquire land adjacent to the new library to create Alumni Park, which quickly became a focal point for the campus. In fall 1935, Town and Gown, which had formed in 1904 as the University of Southern California Women's Club, presented a banquet hall, the Foyer of Town and Gown, to the university as a gift.

In 1940, USC's School of Engineering finally moved into its own building. That same year, the architecture and fine arts programs gained a permanent home on campus when Harris Hall, a gift from trustee May Ormerod Harris, was dedicated.

Adjoining the building was a new art gallery, a gift from Elizabeth Holmes Fisher, also a trustee, who included her collection of Old Masters paintings.

Weathering the Great Depression

Despite the outward signs of prosperity on campus, the Depression took a significant toll on the university. By 1932, enrollment had skidded into a decline, and revenues from tuition, athletics and endowment had shrunk considerably; major gifts had essentially disappeared altogether. To make ends meet, von KleinSmid asked the faculty to accept a 10 percent reduction in salary, which they accepted, as institutions across the country had undertaken similar cutbacks.

Despite the lean times, von KleinSmid continued to foster the growth of the university in new and innovative ways. In 1933, as part of USC's commitment to serving the broader community, the University Junior College was founded to cater to students who did not qualify for admission to four-year institutions in California. At the time, junior colleges were scarce, and many offered substandard instruction. USC's boasted a well-qualified faculty, and

Dennis Hunt advanced USC's academic programs. Intent on promoting quality research as vigorously as quality teaching, the Graduate School dean successfully lobbied the president and the trustees to create a school of research within the Graduate School. Hunt was named its director. Declared by Allison Gaw, professor of English literature, to be "the capstone of the entire structure that has been erected by the university administration after fifty-five years of development," it encompassed a selective group of faculty, Ph.D. candidates and other graduate students, visiting scholars and junior faculty who were engaged in research.

In 1936, USC expanded its academic program further by establishing a school of library service, to meet an urgent need within the community. Two years later, the university gained an endowed research foundation. Captain G. Allan Hancock, president of the Board of Trustees, announced a gift creating the Allan Hancock Foundation for Scientific Research, along with a building to support it and an ocean research vessel, the *Velero III*. Although the foundation

the University Junior College helped bolster the university's finances during the Depression. But critics charged that it reflected lax standards overall at USC—a perception that persisted even after the junior college was abolished at the end of von KleinSmid's presidency.

In 1934, USC debuted another innovative educational outreach program, this time broadcast on radio. "University of the Air" aired weekday afternoons on the Columbia–Don Lee network. Four years later, when the Division of Radio-Television launched a series of university-produced telecasts over KHJ's short-wave station, USC became the only university in the country writing and producing TV programs.

On the scholarly end of the spectrum, a brainchild of Rockwell

Left: Dedicated in November 1939, USC's Elizabeth Holmes Fisher Gallery was heralded as the first museum established in Los Angeles devoted exclusively to the exhibition and collection of fine art.

Below: USC's engineering school gained a permanent home in 1940 with the addition of a new building constructed by C. Raimond Johnson. The facility, which was conceived originally by architect John Parkinson and his son, Donald, as part of the Parkinson campus master plan, was named in honor of Philip S. Biegler, USC's first engineering dean, in 1966.

[photos courtesy of USC University Archives]

Above left: During the 1930s, Capt. G. Allan Hancock led 10 expeditions along the Pacific coast in his yacht *Velero III*. The records of these scientific voyages became part of the Hancock Collections and Archives at USC. Hancock is pictured here in 1948, on a press cruise aboard the newly constructed *Velero IV*, which was actively employed as a research vessel for USC from 1948 to 1985.

Above right: Completed in 1940, USC's Hancock Foundation Building is decorated with bas reliefs, designed by sculptor and USC faculty member Merrell Gage, depicting zoological specimens ranging from Pleistocene mammals discovered at La Brea Tar Pits to forms of animal and plant life observed during the cruises of *Velero III*.

[photos courtesy of USC University Archives]

focused on marine biology, the Hancock Foundation Building reflected its donor's broader interests. Hancock was at once an oil tycoon, aviator, musician, marine biologist and explorer, and, in addition to laboratories and a library, the building housed a radio station, auditorium and herbarium as well as four rooms from his family home, which had stood at Vermont Avenue and Wilshire Boulevard. The building was dedicated in January 1941.

Eleven months later, however, everything changed.

World War II

Like the nation, the University of Southern California was immediately transformed by the bombing of Pearl Harbor. Addressing a bewildered but wildly patriotic overflow crowd in Bovard Auditorium on December 8, von KleinSmid advised students and faculty to expect drastic curtailment of athletic and social activities; devote more time to Red Cross, relief and other national aid programs; not hold individual Japanese on the campus responsible for the action of the Japanese nation; continue their work as seriously as before; and dedicate themselves to a program of war but also to a program of peace.

"Let us avoid hysteria and act as men of assurance and of courage," echoed Albert S. Raubenheimer, dean of the College of Letters, Arts and Sciences.

Nonetheless, everyone found it difficult to concentrate on coursework, and every radio available was tuned to news bulletins. At University College, blackouts prevented some classes from holding final exams.

The 120 members of the Trojan Nisei presented von KleinSmid with a poignant letter, dated December 11, which read:

> We, the Americans of Japanese descent of the University of Southern California, are profoundly shocked at the unprovoked aggression by Japan against our country, the United States.

Above: USC's academic enterprise grew significantly in stature when Anton Burg (pictured here in 1954) joined the faculty in 1939. Known as the "father of chemistry" at USC, Burg built a small department into one of the best in the country. He went on to become an internationally acknowledged expert on boron chemistry and continued to conduct research long after his retirement in 1974. [photo courtesy of USC University Archives]

Below: Walt Disney artists designed two insignias for Trojan pilots in service during World War II. The first (below left), showing Tommy Trojan with his shield held high, was created at the request of Donald H. Bootsma (class of 1940), a pilot in the Canadian Air Force. The second (below right), based on the features of a well-known character portrayed in USC windshield stickers and showing "Butch Trojan riding a Block Buster into action," was created for bomber pilot Edward J. Ernst (class of 1940). [images by Walt Disney, originally published in the *Southern California Alumni Review*]

We unreservedly pledge our loyalty one hundred per cent to our country and to our president, Franklin D. Roosevelt.

We will fight for the United States against all enemies, in every possible way.

Everything on campus was soon touched by the war. An all-university committee, the University Organization to Promote Participation in National Defense, was formed to enlist students, faculty and administrators in such activities as Red Cross, air raid, fire, health and sanitation, USO recreation and entertainment, student advisement and morale. By mid-December, USC had been selected as a naval preparatory flight cadet school, and Aeneas Hall was reconfigured to accommodate the influx of servicemen.

Other military programs shortly joined the flight school on campus, including the Marine Corps Reserves, the Army's Specialized Training Unit, the Naval V-12 program and Naval ROTC. By March 1943, there were more than 1,400 military students on campus.

"Until you've actually seen the preponderance of tall forms in sailor suits or khaki garb striding purposefully across the hitherto quiet greensward of campus, no amount of verbiage can convey the reality of Troy preparing manpower for war," reported the September 1943 *Southern California Alumni Review*. By the end of the war, 75 percent of the male student body belonged to some branch of the service.

The university instituted an accelerated program to enable the military students to complete their degrees in record time and adopted a compulsory physical education program to condition all male students under 25 for war. The overall curriculum was reconfigured to emphasize subjects that would benefit the nation in wartime. Programs were created in aerospace sciences, and officers were

trained in photography through the department of cinema. A program in occupational therapy was inaugurated, led by the fine arts department chair, Glen Lukens, a renowned ceramicist. An FM transmitter that the university had installed on the Hancock Foundation Building was requisitioned by the government.

Predictably, enrollment plummeted as students and faculty left to join the armed forces. By March 1942, USC's enrollment was down 10.4 percent, compared with the same semester the previous year; by September, it was down 15 percent, and 75 faculty members had left to join the war effort.

Nonmilitary students enthusiastically embraced the cause and formed the Student War Board in 1942, which sponsored defense and patriotic activities on campus. Female students volunteered in hospitals and donated blood for the Red Cross. In 1944, USC bested the competition in a three-college war bond competition, beating arch-rival UCLA and University of California, Berkeley, by amassing $152,636 in six days.

Carried out in great secrecy was a research program sponsored by the Office of Scientific Research and Development, intended to develop new methods of protecting pilots. Housed in a non-descript building behind Science Hall was an experimental blackout centrifuge. The largest in the country, the centrifuge was designed to conduct physiological experiments concerned with blackout. In the Hancock Foundation Building, experiments in high-altitude reactions were carried out in a high-altitude chamber, part of the aeromedical laboratories of the medical school.

After the War

On September 2, 1945, World War II officially ended, and the university abruptly entered a new era. Before Pearl Harbor, USC had enrolled an average of 6,000 full-time day students. Less than five months after the war ended, returning veterans taking advantage of the GI Bill had swelled enrollment to 8,300 daytime students and 3,500 evening students. The following year, there were 10,500 veterans among the 15,000 day students. And the numbers continued to skyrocket, reaching a peak in 1947–48, when USC's combined day-time and evening enrollment reached 24,000, the overwhelming majority made up of former servicemen.

Left: During World War II, the *Southern California Alumni Review* provided a vivid chronicle of wartime changes at USC.

Above right: Reacting to the terror of the attack on Pearl Harbor in December 1941, USC students rushed to launch an all-campus volunteer defense service.

[images courtesy of USC University Archives]

The challenges attendant on the so-called GI Bulge were enormous. The accelerated program introduced during the war continued, and faculty worked a double shift, from 7 a.m. to 10 p.m., with classes also held on Saturdays in order to accommodate all the students. Because the university also lacked classroom and laboratory space, a wooden annex was built, and old army barracks were brought in from nearby training camps to augment the facilities. Some 111 new faculty members were hired in 1945, many at better pay than those who had toughed out the war years.

Inevitably, the influx of veterans substantially changed the campus culture. As students, they were serious-minded and mature, often demanding, and eager to get an education in order to succeed in life. They placed an added burden on the faculty, which had changed along with the student body. Taking the place of older members who had retired were younger academics less inclined to accept the inflexible, authoritarian style of the president, now over 70 years old. Von KleinSmid, eager to maintain a budget surplus and renovate the dilapidated physical plant out of the increased revenues, dismissed the concerns of the faculty about their appallingly low salaries, even though they were working extra-ordinary hours and lacked such basic considerations as a retirement plan, a faculty senate and research funds and facilities. In 1946, the faculty revolted, reactivating their union, petitioning the Board of Trustees for redress and forcing von KleinSmid to resign.

"Now when 25 years of service is about to be completed, it seems to me that a change in Presidency might well be made..." he said in the statement announcing his retirement. Assuming the title of chancellor, he stepped down from the post he had held for 25 years. In his wake, he left a remarkable legacy: a university transformed from a modest local denominational institution with a scattering of schools and facilities to a consolidated secular institution with 24 schools and colleges, 16 buildings and national standing.

After World War II, University Avenue (later renamed Trousdale Parkway) quickly became the site of daily traffic jams as throngs of veterans took advantage of the educational opportunities provided by the GI Bill. [photo courtesy of USC University Archives]

In 1949, USC purchased a 12-acre parcel of land bordering the county hospital to create its Health Sciences campus. This aerial view shows the new campus (outlined in white) as it appeared in the early 1950s, shortly after construction of its first building (pictured in the lower right-hand corner of the outlined area). [photo courtesy of USC University Archives]

Chapter Four

A Time of Transition (1946–1957)

By Sarah Lifton

President von KleinSmid did not retreat quietly after announcing his retirement. He carried on as acting president for a year until his replacement could be found, serving simultaneously as chancellor.

The problems he had been contending with before his retirement did not retreat either. The post-War enrollment continued to spiral upward; the physical plant remained inadequate and run-down; and the faculty remained underpaid.

Von KleinSmid and his staff were especially resourceful in tackling the problems with the physical plant. The university adapted the existing campus facilities, woefully inadequate for the mushrooming student population, to new uses, converting the Foyer of Town and Gown into a cafeteria, erecting temporary buildings and evicting tenants from cottages owned by the university, among many other strategies. The first of 26 surplus army barracks buildings began arriving in February 1947, and were placed all over campus, where they served as laboratories, classrooms and offices.

In January 1946, the USC chapter of the American Association of University Professors was revived, and it negotiated two increases in faculty salaries, one in March 1946 and another six months later. Although he was a lame duck, von KleinSmid continued to oppose the raises. He did, however, appoint a committee to develop a plan for a University Senate (reorganized as the Faculty Senate in 1973 and renamed the Academic Senate in 1992). When the plan came to fruition in February 1947, Frank C. Baxter, professor of English, was elected president of the group. Even though faculty salaries remained comparatively low, von KleinSmid had little trouble finding the instructors he needed to meet the skyrocketing demand for a university education. During 1946–47 alone, he hired 371 instructors and assistants, many of whom were highly qualified professionals seeking civilian employment after working in war-related industries.

With skyrocketing enrollment in the post-War years, USC's gym overflowed with students during registration week. [photo courtesy of USC University Archives]

In the meantime, the Board of Trustees was working extremely hard to select von KleinSmid's successor. By February 1947, it had winnowed an initial list of 35 candidates down to three or four names. On June 12, the university announced to the world that Fred Dow Fagg Jr., vice president and dean of faculties at Northwestern University, was to be the sixth president of the University of Southern California.

A Fresh Vision

Friendly, personable and eminently qualified, Fagg was an expert in aviation and aviation law, and his arrival in Southern California was something of a homecoming. He had received his bachelor's degree in political science from the University of Redlands in 1920, before earning a master's degree at Harvard a year later and a J.D. at Northwestern in 1927. He had then headed west again, this time to USC, where he served as an associate professor of economics and assistant dean in the College of Commerce, as well as a lecturer in the law school, from 1927 to 1928.

In 1929, Fagg joined the faculty of the Northwestern law school, where he established the Air Law Institute and the *Journal of Air Law,* which he edited. During the mid-1930s, he was a legal adviser to the Federal Aviation Commission and the U.S. Senate subcommittee on aircraft investigation. In 1937, after a succession of plane crashes prompted cries for action, Fagg was summoned to Washington, D.C., to direct the U.S. Bureau of Air Commerce, where he helped write the Air Commerce Act of 1938, which formed the basis for many commercial and private regulations. He held the post for a year before returning to Northwestern, becoming dean of the School of Commerce in 1938 and vice president and dean of faculties a year later. Outside academia, he also served as legal counsel to the Senate

Frederick Dow "Fred" Fagg Jr.—USC's first president with an earned doctoral degree— was no stranger to the university when he took office in 1947. He had served concurrently as a lecturer in the law school, associate professor of economics and assistant dean of the USC College of Commerce during the 1927–28 academic year.
[photo courtesy of USC University Archives]

GEORGE TIREBITER

Around 1940, a mongrel appeared on campus, with a propensity for chasing cars down University Avenue and attacking their tires. This quirky habit won the hearts of students, who dubbed him George Tirebiter. The dog flourished for many years on a diet of hamburgers, bologna sandwiches and vulcanized rubber, and in 1947 the student senate elected him Troy's official mascot. In his new role, George rode around the football field in a convertible and at one Cal game, chased UC Berkeley's mascot, Oskie the bear, and bit his costume nose. Before a USC-UCLA game, he was dognapped and returned with the letters "UCLA" shaved into his fur, making national headlines.

In 1949, George, getting on in years, was retired to an animal shelter in El Centro. The following year, he escaped, and in what was a perhaps inevitable touch of irony, he was killed by a car. In his place, George Tirebiter II was installed as mascot. George II, a terrier, was nervous in front of crowds and barked himself hoarse during football games. After three years, he retired and was succeeded by George III, who lasted one season. The position remained vacant until 1957, when George Tirebiter IV debuted. Another one-season wonder, he was officially ousted as mascot in a spring 1958 student body election, when students cast their votes in favor of a new mascot, the white horse bearing the Trojan Warrior.

Above: George Tirebiter I
Right: George Tirebiter II
[photos courtesy of USC University Archives]

Left: George Tirebiter III with the Victory Bell [photo courtesy of the Regional History Collection, USC Specialized Libraries and Archival Collections]

Right: George Tirebiter IV [photo courtesy of USC University Archives]

Commission on Aircraft Investigation and as consultant to the Civil Air Authority.

When Fagg arrived at USC in September 1947, he found the executive offices rather crowded. Von KleinSmid, as chancellor, had retained the presidential suite in the north wing of the administration building, while a new suite of offices was remodeled for Fagg in the south wing. The chancellor's charge was to assist with public relations, serve on committees and perform other duties specified by the Board of Trustees. Although von KleinSmid asserted that he planned to keep a low profile because "the job is the job of the new president," in reality, he was accustomed to the limelight and reluctant to step aside. His agreement with the trustees stipulated that his name should always be listed first among the university officers and that he remain on the Board of Trustees. Furthermore, on von KleinSmid's recommendation, the trustees had finally filled the position of educational vice president, vacant since 1936, a few months before Fagg had been appointed, preventing the new president from selecting his own candidate for that important post. Von KleinSmid continued to attend every trustee meeting, and he remained on campus into the 1960s.

At President Fagg's inauguration on June 11, 1948, singer Dinah Shore (wearing academic cap and gown) greeted first lady Vera Wilkes Fagg while USC's newly installed sixth president looked on. Mrs. Fagg would go on to become a quiet but capable ambassador and fundraiser for USC, particularly through her dedicated service to the Faculty Wives' Club, Town and Gown, and the university YWCA. [photo courtesy of USC University Archives]

Despite the awkwardness of having his predecessor constantly looking over his shoulder, Fagg plunged into his new position, with a clear sense of the challenges and possibilities before him.

"In looking ahead, we know that we face hard problems," he said at his inauguration dinner. "The first problem we must face pertains to the future size of the university. We know, now, that great demands will be put upon us....We must continue to grow with this great metropolis.... Secondly, we must continue to expand

Above left: Harry J. Deuel Jr., a popular bio-chemistry instructor at USC's medical school and an expert on the role of vitamins and fats in nutrition, became head of the university's Graduate School in 1949.

Above center: Longtime alumni leader and trustee Asa V. Call (class of 1914) became president of the USC Board of Trustees in 1950 and headed the group until 1960. Call's legacy at his alma mater includes the naming of the Asa V. Call Law Library as well as the USC Alumni Association's Asa V. Call Award, established in 1932, which celebrates Trojans whose extraordinary accomplishments have brought honor and recognition to themselves and to USC.

Above right: Joan M. Schaefer—known affectionately by generations of Trojan students simply as "Dean Joan"—joined the university as dean of women in 1955 and continued to serve USC well beyond her retirement in 1992. Since 1993, the Dean Joan Metcalf Schaefer Scholarships have been awarded to students in the USC College of Letters, Arts and Sciences who follow her example of scholarship, leadership, service and love of learning.

[photos courtesy of USC University Archives]

our plant facilities—not only to provide additional classrooms for more students, but because the nature of our educational program itself demands more plant…. Thirdly, we must maintain and strengthen our faculty, for I'm sure we would all agree that no educational institution is stronger than its faculty…. We shall face our problems as frankly and intelligently as we can, and with all the imagination and courage we can muster. But we cannot do the job alone. We must continue to enjoy the helpful counsel and support of our friends. What this community and this state become, the university can become. With your help we shall do our utmost to keep you proud of our attainment in the years which lie ahead."

Fagg moved quickly to implement his vision. He did away with von KleinSmid's dictatorial management framework, in which all expenditures were channeled through a centralized budget within the president's office—an approach that excluded deans and department chairs from discussions of faculty salaries. In its place he established modern business and academic practices, introducing cost accounting and deriving departmental budgets from departmental needs. He created the position of director of development to inaugurate a systematic fundraising program, enhance public relations and produce comprehensive publications.

In multiple ways, he demonstrated his understanding of the university's academic enterprise. He separated the

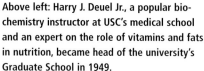

office of educational vice president and dean of the college, and raised the caliber of the deans and directors of the academic units, advancing the role of research on campus. In 1949, he appointed Harry J. Deuel Jr., head of the Department of Biochemistry and Nutrition, to be dean of the Graduate School. Deuel was nationally recognized for his research on vitamin A and the nutritional value of fats in diets; he was a recipient of the Borden Award in Nutrition, the highest honor conferred by the American Institute of Nutrition. Fagg also named James E. Buchanan, a former colleague at Northwestern, director of research for the Allan Hancock Foundation, which started to attract other estab-lished scholars and investigators.

Fagg arranged for deans and faculty members to attend trustees' meetings, where they discussed their programs and needs directly, and he instituted annual retreats in which faculty and administrators met to address university issues. These reforms went a long way toward repairing relations between the president's office and the faculty.

He also cast his reformer's eye on student affairs, creating the positions of chaplain and dean of students. In 1950, he tackled the Board of Trustees itself, spearheading a reorganization in which alumnus Asa V. Call was

Alumni Memorial Pylon and newly completed Founders Hall are clearly visible in this aerial view of the University Park campus in 1951. Bovard Field is just above center and to the right.
[photo by Pioneer/the Flintkote Company, courtesy of USC University Archives]

Deemed seismically unsound, Old College (above) was razed in 1948, making way for Founders Hall (below right), which was later remodeled, expanded and renamed Mark Taper Hall of Humanities. [photos courtesy of USC University Archives]

named president, and new members with diverse skills were elected over the next few years. In 1952, the university's articles of incorporation were amended to eliminate the requirement that a majority of trustees be members of the Methodist Church.

Expanding the Campus

The post-War years, with their double-shift classes, were taking a tremendous toll on USC's already dilapidated physical plant, and Fagg soon turned his attention toward the much-needed renovations and additions to the campus that he had cited in his inaugural dinner speech.

A new women's residence hall, student cafeteria and naval ROTC building were the first facilities to be announced. The next, however, came as something of a shock. Old College had been condemned as a fire and earthquake hazard, and Fagg declared that the old campus icon, with its antiquated classrooms and creaking floors, could not be made sound. As a consequence, it was to be razed. He made the announcement on September 20, 1948, 64 years to the day after the cornerstone was laid for what in 1884 had been billed as USC's first permanent building.

KUSC GOES LIVE

[photo courtesy of USC University Archives]

On October 24, 1946, culminating five years of anticipation, FM radio station KUSC went on the air, making USC the first private educational institution in America to own and operate its own radio station and the first to operate both AM and FM stations. At the time, there were estimated to be only 15,000 FM radios in the greater Los Angeles area, and the station's broadcast range was limited to a 10-mile radius from the USC campus. But the dedication of the station, which took place the following December, attracted the attention of some of the biggest names in broadcasting, who sent their congratulations in a barrage of telegrams.

Initially, KUSC was entirely student-run, confined to a tiny studio and office in the Hancock Foundation Building. The opportunity to work at KUSC was a major draw for students, attracting more than 1,000 applications for admission to the radio department in 1947, some from as far as Miami and New York.

Beyond its educational function, however, KUSC was addressing a need in the community. By 1948, it had an 11–14 percent share of the burgeoning Los Angeles FM audience. The following year, it expanded its programming to 14 hours a day, "thus becoming the only FM station in Los Angeles to run on a full-day operational schedule, and not duplicate AM shows," according to a press release. For the next 25 years, KUSC continued to broadcast on a part-time basis, and its programming remained eclectic, ranging from Jacobean dramas to the USDA agriculture report, from classical music and rock and roll to Trojan sports and talk radio.

KUSC would probably have remained an excellent, but conventional, college station if Congress had not established the Corporation for Public Broadcasting in 1971. At that point, the people responsible for creating National Public Radio began combing the country for noncommercial stations to affiliate with the new public broadcasting service. In Los Angeles, they identified KUSC as the flagship station and offered the university a $15,000 grant to become a member of the new network on the condition that USC hire three full-time employees for the station. Wally Smith, a graduate student finishing his doctorate in communication at the university, became the station's general manager—a move that had far-reaching consequences for him and for KUSC.

Smith quickly recognized an outstanding opportunity, just waiting to be seized.

"As I looked around at the city of Los Angeles," he recalled, "… it was very clear to me that what this city needed and what public radio was uniquely suited to do was a really serious full-time classical music radio station. And that seemed quite compatible with the objectives of the university."

KUSC went all-classical on April 2, 1973, and it set a national standard for classical music radio. Within two years, it was on the air 24 hours a day and had also become a full-fledged production center. By May 1979, it had the largest audience of any public radio station in the country—an audience it eventually augmented by acquiring three additional stations to extend its range. In 2004, under the direction of KUSC president Brenda Barnes, it became one of the first stations in Los Angeles to begin digital broadcasting—reflecting its continuing commitment to remaining at the vanguard of broadcasting.

Above left: In 1952, the USC School of Dentistry gained a new building on 34th Street, providing a 200-chair clinic and a basement accommodating graduate studies and other programs. A three-story addition was added in 1969, when the structure was rededicated as the Eileen and Kenneth T. Norris Dental Science Center.

Above right: In 1950, trustee and Town and Gown president May Ormerod Harris cemented the cornerstone for a new women's residence hall named in honor of USC's fifth first lady, Elisabeth von KleinSmid. Posing with Harris to mark the occasion were Chancellor von KleinSmid (center) and President Fagg (right).

[photos courtesy of USC University Archives]

"Old College, more than any other part of the Trojan campus, has influenced every person who has ever attended the university," observed *Southern California Alumni Review* in an October 1948 article announcing the building's demise. "... It has been—at one time or another—the original home of practically every department, school or college on campus."

But, the article admitted, "every alumnus—fond though his memories may be and great his love for Old College—must honestly admit that the building must go."

In December, after the students had left the campus for the winter holiday, wrecking crews moved in and began to dismantle the aging landmark. In its place, a $1 million, four-story classroom and office building, dubbed Founders Hall, began to rise. A new home for several major departments of the College of Letters, Arts and Sciences, it was dedicated May 20, 1950.

Other new buildings followed in its wake. In March 1951, two women's residence halls were dedicated: Elisabeth von KleinSmid Memorial Hall, named in honor of the chancellor's late wife, who had died in 1947; and University Hall, later renamed in honor of trustee May Ormerod Harris. A new School of Dentistry building, capable of housing the school's entire operation, opened in 1952, and a men's residence hall, David X. Marks Hall, was dedicated in December 1953. Other new facilities included a YWCA building, student clinic and infirmary, as well as an athletic field. An addition to Science Hall was built to house organic chemistry teaching and research activities, while a new art gallery was erected adjoining the Fisher Gallery to house the Florence M. Quinn jade collection. Later, a petroleum and chemical engineering building was constructed, and the law school's building was remodeled.

Fagg also took major steps to create a self-contained campus. In April 1950, the trustees adopted a resolution authorizing the acquisition of the public streets, alleys and rights of way bounded by Exposition Boulevard, McClintock Avenue, Jefferson Boulevard and Figueroa Street. The university began to acquire land almost immediately, and on December 8, 1953, after USC had gained the approval of some 46 public officials, University Avenue was closed to all vehicular traffic. In subsequent years, additional streets were added to the campus and closed to traffic as well. To delineate the

President Fagg (right, in striped suit) beamed as University Avenue was officially closed to vehicular traffic in December 1953—marking a major step toward the creation of a self-contained campus.
[photo courtesy of USC University Archives]

On March 1, 1955, President Fagg (kneeling, second from right) laid the first bricks for the "Walls of Troy." Initially raised along Exposition Boulevard, the block and grillwork walls were not completed until the 1984 summer Olympics. [photo courtesy of USC University Archives]

Above: Raulston Memorial Research Building, opened in 1952 (shown here with Los Angeles County Hospital in the background to the right), remained the only building on USC's Health Sciences campus until the end of the decade. [photo courtesy of USC University Archives]

Below: This 1957 photo of USC's new Organic Chemistry Wing (renamed after Harold E. and Lillian M. Moulton in 1985) highlights the bank of windows on the structure's north façade, which was designed to provide excellent lighting for the laboratories inside. [photo by the USC News Service, courtesy of USC University Archives]

expanded campus, a "Walls of Troy" project was launched to construct block and grillwork walls around the entire perimeter.

A Second Campus

Since 1928, when it reopened, the School of Medicine had held its pre-clinical classes in Science Hall, sharing facilities with the college's science departments for the first two years of instruction. Clinical courses were held in the Los Angeles County Hospital in improvised classrooms, some as makeshift as little-used hallways. The inherent inconvenience of the arrangement was compounded by the geographical separation between the preclinical and clinical faculty.

In 1949, to rectify the situation, the university purchased a 12-acre site bordering the county hospital for a dedicated medical campus.

"The University of Southern California plans to locate its medical school program immediately adjacent to the Los Angeles County Hospital," Fagg wrote in a June 9, 1949, telegram to the director of the National Institutes of Health. "Funds have been allocated by the University to acquire the necessary land and the acquisition thereof is now in progress. Construction of medical school units will begin as soon as sufficient funds are available."

Fortunately, those funds were almost immediately forthcoming. On September 13, 1949, the National Heart Institute announced a $485,000 grant to USC to build a four-story building for cardio-vascular and cancer research. The following year, the National Cancer Institute followed suit, making a $200,000 grant that made it possible to add a fifth floor. The university provided $500,000 for construction and committed an additional $100,000–$200,000 to equip it. Construction began in spring 1950, and the structure, later named the Raulston Memorial Research Building in honor of Burrell O. Raulston, medical school dean from 1943 to 1953, was completed in September 1952. For eight years, it remained the only building on the Health Sciences campus, but a major effort in the 1950s to raise money for new facilities led to the construction of Paul S. McKibben Hall, a classroom and laboratory building, and the Seeley Wintersmith Mudd Memorial Laboratory of the Medical Sciences, a much-needed research facility. Dedicated in 1961, the new buildings made it possible to move all instruction to the new campus, at last consolidating medical school teaching and research in one location.

Left: Created to commemorate USC's first 75 years, the Diamond Jubilee mark showed a sword crossed with a mace.

Below: Looking ahead toward the end of USC's first century, the Century Plan development program aimed to enable the university "to synchronize its educational services with the further development of the city of Los Angeles and the entire Southwest."

[images courtesy of USC University Archives]

The Diamond Jubilee and the Century Plan

In expanding its campuses, the university clearly benefited from the efforts of the new development office. Alumni giving went from $62,000 in 1946–47 to $266,000 in 1955, and corporate contributions rose from $118,000 to $394,000 during the same period. Surprisingly, the university managed to achieve these increases without a coordinated development plan. That changed in 1955, when USC celebrated its 75th anniversary.

The university marked its Diamond Jubilee by sponsoring some 200

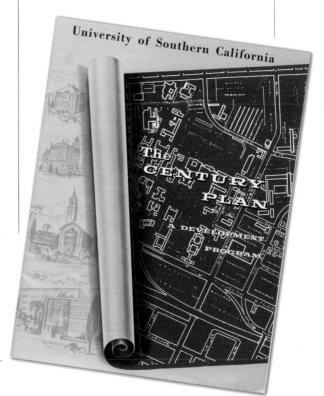

University of Southern California

The CENTURY PLAN

A DEVELOPMENT PROGRAM

President Fagg (second from right) commissioned a model of an expanded University Park campus that was envisioned to extend from Exposition to Jefferson Boulevard and from Figueroa Street to Vermont Avenue by the time of USC's 100th anniversary in 1980. [photo courtesy of USC University Archives]

anniversary events and programs, including a special Founders Day convocation and "Story of Troy" pageant in the Coliseum. The original university building, recently named a state historic landmark, was rededicated and renamed Widney Hall in honor of Robert Maclay Widney. USC also launched Trojan Caravans, "modern Chautauquas" designed to bring the university and its activities, faculty and educational philosophy into major cities across the state. The most important initiative, however, was the capital campaign it rolled out.

"The University of Southern California will embark tomorrow on a campaign to raise $75,000,000 over the next 25 years," reported the Los Angeles Times on December 4, 1955. "The Century Plan is to culminate in 1980, when the university is 100 years old. It encompasses the development of faculty, research, scholarship and new buildings through new endowments in the intervening quarter-century."

The Century Plan sought to generate funds for endowed faculty chairs, research and teaching facilities, scholarships and fellowships as well

as unrestricted endowment. It also presented a campus master plan that proposed increasing campus land-holdings from 60 to 100 acres and adding 30 new buildings.

Unfortunately, it proved only moderately successful. With such a long time frame, the effort had no sense of urgency; by June 1955, only $1 million had been raised. Further-more, the goal was entirely arbitrary, and the objectives had been deter-mined without the input of faculty. Some individual units, such as dentistry, medicine and engineering, did well, enabling them to construct new facilities, but others, like education and religion, foundered.

The campaign did, however, attract the attention of major outside donors, who recognized USC's importance to the region and the nation and were eager to help it make considerable strides. In December 1955, the Ford Foundation, as part of its special $500 million initiative to support private institutions throughout the country, presented USC with a grant of $1,710,900.

"We are thoroughly delighted with the news," Fagg said, in announcing the gift. "With the income from this fund to help us further increase faculty salaries, SC's educational program will now take another significant step forward."

TROY CAMP AND SONGFEST

Above: Since Troy Camp was founded in 1948, thousands of schoolchildren from South Los Angeles have had an opportunity to pack up and leave the city for a week of sports, arts and educational activities in the mountains.

Below: After three years at the Greek Theater, Songfest took its competition to the Hollywood Bowl in 1957 to accommodate an enthusiastic and growing audience.

[photos courtesy of USC University Archives]

In 1948, USC business student Otis M. Healy engaged in a bit of cross-town rivalry that changed many lives. Aware that UCLA had a summer camp for disadvantaged children, he founded Troy Camp because, he later said, he thought USC could do it better. Starting out as a fraternity community project, Troy Camp took children from the surrounding neighborhood to camp in the mountains for a week of fun and learning. It soon expanded to become a universitywide volunteer project—the largest and most diverse philanthropy on campus. In the 1990s, it added monthly events during the school year, including dances, potlucks and sporting events, as well as tutoring and mentoring activities. Thousands of children have taken part in Troy Camp since its inception, and many have gone on to attend college as a result of its influence on their lives.

Six years after the founding of Troy Camp, Robert F. Jani and Robbie Carroll, two USC sophomores seeking to bring together the diverse post-War student body, created Songfest, a campuswide, student-run musical variety show that pitted different student organizations in a competition for the best acts, judged by a panel of celebrities. Twenty-six different groups performed at the first Songfest, which was held at the Greek Theater in 1954. A fundraiser for Troy Camp over the years, Songfest also has been held at the Hollywood Bowl, the Shrine Auditorium and Bovard Auditorium, and became the largest all-student collegiate musicale in the nation.

Above: KUSC-TV, the first university television studio in the West, provided USC students with valuable hands-on studio experience as they prepared for careers in television.

Below right: Arlien Johnson, dean of the USC School of Social Work from 1939 to 1959, built a program that was strong in terms of professional education as well as service to the community.

[photos courtesy of USC University Archives]

Also helping advance the university's educational program was an unrestricted $300,000 grant from the Commonwealth Fund to the School of Medicine.

Although it ultimately fell far short of its goals, the Century Plan did help USC build its endowment. Until the Century Plan, the university's endowment was a mere $2.6 million—smaller than that of either Occidental College or the University of Redlands. By 1958, it had more than doubled, to $6.7 million. While that increase represented important progress, USC's endowment was still only a tenth of that of Stanford, a fifth of that of Caltech and half that of

Pomona College. Even UCLA reported almost twice as much money in contributions in 1956 as USC did.

Without sufficient professional development staff to support the efforts of the trustees and other volunteers, the Century Plan quietly petered out, its potential only partially realized.

Academic Progress

Although the results of the Century Plan were disappointing, USC's academic program continued to expand during Fagg's administration, and the university's reputation was considerably enhanced under his guidance. New programs kept pace with changing technologies and cultural phenomena and added breadth to the course offerings. In 1948, the university began offering courses in television; just three years later, in 1951, it announced that the

television program would expand, thanks to a gift from Capt. G. Allan Hancock to build and equip the first university television studio in the West. By spring 1952, with more than 100 students enrolled in television courses, the Department of Telecommunications began offering a bachelor's degree in television. The same year, USC began offering bachelor's degrees in real estate, making it one of only half a dozen universities in the country to grant degrees in that field. It also initiated the first doctoral program in social work in the Western United States and created the Institute for Safety and Systems Management, the nation's first academic unit to offer degree programs in safety, human factors and systems management. In 1954, USC inaugurated a cross-disciplinary Division of Communication, consisting of the departments of cinema, drama, journalism, speech and telecommunications, which provided an integrated course of study around the concept of human communication.

To support the university's burgeoning academic programs, the library substantially increased its holdings, nearly doubling them during Fagg's tenure. The School of Library Science, under the direction of Fagg appointee Martha T. Boaz,

Above: As part of the hands-on curriculum in USC's Institute for Safety and Systems Management, students enrolled in an accident investigation course examined the wreckage of a downed aircraft.

Right: Dean Martha T. Boaz, pictured here in the 1960s, joined the USC faculty in 1953 and headed the university's School of Library Science from 1955 to 1978.

[photos courtesy of USC University Archives]

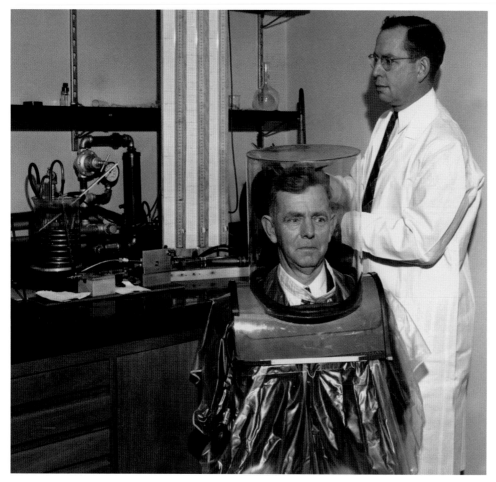

USC responded to Southern California's growing air-pollution problem early on. This 1947 photo, titled "Smog Research," shows USC professors E. A. Swenson (seated, wearing helmet) and H. Roth (standing, right) conducting an experiment. [photo courtesy of USC University Archives]

standard references in the field and boasted alumni at the head of nearly every department in Los Angeles city and county governments, began to reach out to foreign governments, receiving contracts to train civil servants and public administrators from Turkey, Brazil, Iran and Pakistan.

At the same time the academic programs were growing and maturing, USC faculty were expanding their research activities. In 1946, two faculty investigators installed a smog chamber in the Hancock Foundation Building to study air pollution. In the late 1940s, John F. Kessel, head of the medical school's department of bacteriology and parasitology, in collaboration with Charles Pait, assistant professor in the same department, and Los Angeles County Hospital, received grants from the National Foundation of Infantile Paralysis to study the relationship between different polio viruses. In 1949, Daniel C. Pease and Richard F. Baker, both assistant professors in the USC School of Medicine, took the world's first photograph of genes, using an electron microscope. The same year, assistant professor of physics Willard Geer invented a color picture tube for televisions and began conducting experiments with it. Irving Rehman of the School of Medicine, in collaboration with a

strengthened its faculty and added a doctoral program, which raised its ranking to one of the top five library schools in the country.

The law school modernized its curriculum and started offering evening courses to meet the demand from returning GIs. The School of Public Administration, which had already produced a number of

television manufacturer, invented yet another color picture tube in 1951, drawing on his own experience developing the world's first synchronized x-ray motion picture camera a few years earlier. Along with his associates, J. P. Guilford, professor of psychology, developed over 200 tests designed to study reasoning, creative thinking, planning, evaluation and judgment in the performance of scientists, technical personnel and supervisory personnel.

Staff of the Hancock Foundation continued their scientific research into the oceans, equipped with a series of laboratory ships and a benthoscope, a five-foot ball with steel walls and quartz windows, to explore the floor of the Pacific Ocean. One of their members, Otis Barton, renowned inventor of the benthoscope and its predecessor, the bathysphere, set a world record in the device, in 1949 becoming the first person to descend alone to a depth of 2,300 feet, off Santa Cruz Island.

Reaching Out

Accompanying USC's rising academic profile was a concurrent increase in its educational outreach activities. On September 26, 1953, one of the university's most popular faculty members, Frank C. Baxter, debuted a television program that was to revolutionize educational TV. Baxter's "Shakespeare on TV," broadcast by Los Angeles CBS affiliate KNXT, was the first college course to be taught on TV for academic credit in Southern California. Baxter, whose Shakespeare course packed in the students at USC, later admitted that he figured the course would be a "roaring success" if it drew 150 viewers a week. To his astonishment, however, it attracted 400,000, who watched it each Saturday morning from 11:00 to 11:45.

The program received a Sylvania Television Award for "the most

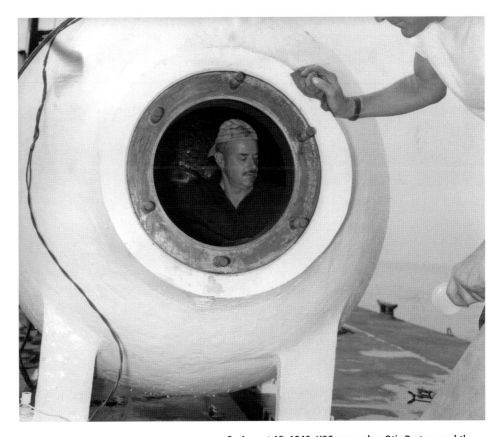

On August 15, 1949, USC researcher Otis Barton used the Hancock Foundation-sponsored benthoscope to become the first human to descend alone to a depth of 2,300 feet.
[photo courtesy of USC University Archives]

USC English professor and distance-learning pioneer Frank C. Baxter, pictured here with a model of the Globe Theatre for his television show "Shakespeare on TV," was named by *Life* magazine as one of America's eight finest college professors in 1950. [photo courtesy of USC University Archives]

outstanding local educational program of the nation for 1953," but neither the course nor the two others that followed stayed local for long. They were offered for credit by Mills College, the University of Hawaii and the University of San Francisco, and in 1955, "Shakespeare on TV" earned Baxter the first George Foster Peabody Award ever presented to an individual for television education. The success of Baxter's lively and erudite presentations also led to a network series, "Then and Now," broadcast on CBS nationally, in which he read and discussed literature as well as a long list of programs that included "Renaissance on TV"; "Harvest"; and the Bell System Science Series titles "Our Mr. Sun," "Hemo the Magnificent," "The Strange Case of the Cosmic Rays" and "The Unchained Goddess," produced and directed by Frank Capra between 1956 and 1958. Baxter won a total of seven Emmy awards between 1953 and 1960 and also hosted ABC's "Telephone Time" and the American airing of the BBC's "Age of Kings." By the time he retired from the university in 1961, he was a national institution, with pages of television credits and awards; he was so prominent that his remarks to his last USC class were quoted in *Life* magazine. Baxter's 1982 obituary in the *Los Angeles Times* noted that "Shakespeare on TV" "brought literature to television, and his flair brought to television a dimension and substance it had not known."

While Baxter was by far the best-known USC professor during that period, others also found ways to reach out to the public. Following World War II, ceramicist Glen Lukens went to Haiti, at the request of the Haitian government, to teach rural populations how to make cooking utensils from clay. He returned to Haiti in 1952, under the auspices of UNESCO, to develop the ceramics program further and establish training and production centers; he was also named an honorary citizen of Haiti and awarded the National Order of Honor and Merit. In 1961, as an emeritus professor, he held a series of workshops at Jackson State College to show rural students ways to convert folk arts into a living.

Merrell Gage, head of USC's sculpture department, parlayed his lifelong fascination with Abraham Lincoln into a half-hour documentary, *The Face of Lincoln,* produced by the USC cinema department. In the film, he transformed a mass of clay into the face of the 16th U.S. president, showing the transformations wrought by the years, while relating anecdotes from Lincoln's life. The film, which

aired on television many times, won an Academy Award for best short documentary in 1956.

The many accomplishments of Fred Fagg's presidency, while significant, belied an unfortunate truth: since 1951, he had been in declining health. By 1957, he no longer had the strength or energy to carry out the growing demands of his office. For the sake of his own health and that of the university, he submitted his resignation on January 11, effective July 1. After 10 years, USC once again found itself in search of a president.

Although he was perhaps best known for his busts of Abraham Lincoln, USC sculptor Robert Merrell Gage also made significant contributions to Southern California's architectural landscape. His handiwork adorns the Southern California Edison Company Building (known as One Bunker Hill), Los Angeles Times Building, Electric Fountain (at the intersection of Santa Monica and Wilshire boulevards) and "Tribute to Motion Picture Celebrities" sculpture (at the corner of Olympic Boulevard and Beverly Drive), as well as USC's own Hancock Foundation Building. [photo courtesy of USC University Archives]

Expanding westward to Vermont Avenue, the University Park campus grew by nearly 60 acres during the 1960s—as can be seen in this aerial view looking southwest. [photo by Rothschild Photo, courtesy of USC University Archives]

Chapter Five

Growth and Maturation (1958–1970)

By Sarah Lifton

USC named its seventh president on May 26, 1958, less than a year after Fred Fagg had left office. Asa V. Call, president of the Board of Trustees, announced that out of 200 candidates, the choice was an alumnus, Norman H. Topping, currently vice president for medical affairs at the University of Pennsylvania.

Topping arrived at USC in September, and his colorful inauguration ceremony, held on October 23, 1958, introduced something new: a silver mace designed by Frank Baxter, USC's renowned Shakespearean scholar, modeled after one Baxter had seen in Cambridge. The mace represented the authority of the president's office, and the inaugural was a fitting occasion for its debut, for both symbol and ceremony signaled a looming sea change at the university. Just as the mace, which would henceforth lead all academic processions at USC, was born of the confluence of old and new, so Topping, who had earned his bachelor's degree and M.D. at USC nearly a quarter-century earlier, would come to embody its future.

Changing of the Guard

Topping assumed the presidency of USC at yet another difficult point in its history. During the months following Fred Fagg's resignation, the university was governed by a committee composed of its three vice presidents. The Board of Trustees had opted not to appoint an acting president, and the arrangement created divisions within the administration.

Adding pressure was the fact that other local institutions, public and private, were growing in resources, strength and standing, eclipsing USC, which remained hobbled by a substandard endowment and uneven academic reputation.

For Topping, who had attended high school in Los Angeles, his return was actually a second homecoming. His first, when he enrolled at USC's medical school, was the terminus of a circuitous and fairly unconventional route. He had completed most of his undergraduate work at the University of Washington, where he played football before knee injuries forced him to abandon the sport, and he racked up a weak academic record, even dropping out of school for a year. During that year, 1929–30, he worked marking board at a stock brokerage; he was on the job when the stock market crashed in October 1929. Later, he and his future brother-in-law opened a music shop. In early September 1930, he got married, and because he had decided to become a doctor, he and his wife, Helen, headed back to Los Angeles, where he intended to enroll in USC's medical school. First, however, he spent a year at

Chancellor von KleinSmid (left) gave a warm welcome to President-elect Norman Hawkins Topping and his wife, Helen Rummens Topping, upon their arrival in Southern California for a series of briefings and conferences in June 1958. [photo from the *Los Angeles Examiner* Collection, courtesy of the Regional History Collection, USC Specialized Libraries and Archival Collections]

UCLA improving his grades. When he entered the USC School of Medicine, he still lacked a bachelor's degree, but he completed it in 1933, concurrent with his medical studies. He earned his M.D. in 1936.

Following medical school and an internship, he joined the Public Health Service, then the National Institutes of Health, where he conducted research into Rocky Mountain spotted fever, developing the first effective treatment for the disease. He also developed the typhus vaccine used in World War II to inoculate U.S., Canadian and British troops and received several prestigious awards for his work. Along the way, he emerged as a skilled administrator, and by the time he left, he had risen to associate director of the NIH. In 1952, he became vice president for medical affairs at the University of Pennsylvania, a post he held for six years before leaving for Los Angeles to assume the presidency of his alma mater.

Topping's inauguration was an impressive affair, with a list of delegates that included University of California president Clark Kerr, Stanford president Wallace Sterling and Caltech president Lee DuBridge as well as elected officials John Anson Ford, representing the Los Angeles County Board of Supervisors, and Los Angeles mayor Norris Poulson.

In his address, before a distinguished crowd, Topping laid out his plan to transform the university.

"I wish to assure you that I shall give of myself unstintingly to help fulfill the desires and ambitions of the family of the University of Southern California," he said in his opening remarks, then went on to detail a plan of action that focused, above all, on attaining excellence in all of USC's endeavors. It was a goal of enormous significance for the institution, the region and the nation, with *Sputnik* casting a large, dark shadow from overhead ever since its launch a year earlier.

"We who set the standards of performance for our youth cannot expect them to aspire to excellence in themselves when they see us willing to accept mediocrity," he said. "We need once again to dedicate ourselves and our university to a constant search for the ways to attain excellence and to a determination to accept no less."

Topping soon proved the depth of his conviction, implementing new measures throughout his first year. He revised the university's bylaws and reorganized the administration to create a new position: vice president for student and alumni affairs, to which he appointed his friend and fellow alumnus Francis Tappaan.

Above: Posing with USC's seventh president (second from right) on the occasion of his inauguration were (from left) Chancellor Rufus B. von KleinSmid, Board of Trustees chairman Asa V. Call and president emeritus Fred Fagg.

Below: At his inauguration in October 1958, President Topping received the university's new silver mace—representing the authority of the president's office—from USC Board of Trustees chairman Asa V. Call, while renowned Shakespeare scholar Frank Baxter, who designed the mace, looked on.

[photos courtesy of USC University Archives]

In keeping with the culture of openness he sought to cultivate, President Topping joined Francis Tappaan (right), USC's newly appointed vice president for student and alumni affairs, on the steps of Bovard Administration Building to talk with students (left to right) Lolita Kennedy, Bunny Levy and Frank Gleberman in 1960. [photo from 1960 *El Rodeo*, courtesy of USC University Archives]

Upon learning that the alumni association was independently incorporated, he persuaded the organization to dissolve its separate corporation and become part of the university, giving USC greater control over alumni involvement in athletic recruitment and covering the association with the university's insurance. This measure was particularly significant because it related to another issue he was contending with: Shortly after his arrival, the NCAA had placed USC on probation for football recruitment violations that had taken place earlier, banning the university from participating in the Rose Bowl. The coaches and alumni had undue influence on admissions, it was felt, and to rectify the situation, Topping placed the entire responsibility for contacting prospective student athletes with the Department of Intercollegiate Athletics. He also ordered that contributions from alumni and friends for support of student athletics should come directly to the university, which would then be responsible for administering the funds. He removed members of the football coaching staff who had been implicated in the affair and replaced the head coach with John McKay, a young assistant coach who would go on to revolutionize the program.

This new culture of openness

(Tappaan resigned and was replaced in 1961 by former alumni association president Mulvey White.) He appointed deans of the Graduate School and the School of Social Work and convened a search committee to find a new dean for the School of Engineering. Law professor Carl M. Franklin became vice president for financial affairs. At Topping's urging, the trustees adopted a tuition exchange plan with other private institutions, and he proposed, and the trustees approved, urgently needed salary increases for faculty as well as construction of a faculty center.

NORMAN TOPPING'S BLUEPRINT FOR ACTION

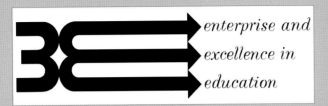

enterprise and
excellence in
education

1. Continuously recognize and emphasize that this university is a community of scholars where academic pursuits are preeminent, where research is fostered to add to our already existing knowledge and where community service is an important and essential element of our overall mission.

2. Do everything within our power and resources to increase the compensation of the faculty, not only to retain those who are here at the present, but also in order to attract other outstanding scholars to the campus.

3. Undertake only those ventures that we can do well, so that there will be no possible dilution or deterioration of the educational program.

4. Steadily upgrade our academic requirements for admission, selecting students with demonstrated abilities, emotional maturity and the greatest potential for further academic development.

5. Provide worthy students with scholarships on the basis of need, with funds obtained for that particular purpose and not diverted from tuition income.

6. Develop loan funds so that educational costs may be amortized over a period of years with low interest rates, and further develop work programs as a form of student assistance for those who wish to defray some of their expenses by part-time employment.

7. Strengthen our alumni relations by providing alumni with an additional voice in policy making, and by giving them

the opportunity to see and discuss the university with the president and the other administrative officers.

8. Keep our excellent educational program and our strong intercollegiate athletic program in the proper balance and perspective so that one supplements the other to the advantage of both.

9. Establish a planning commission, with representation from the trustees, alumni and faculty, to begin the essential studies leading to recommendations concerning the future size and composition of the university.

10. Dedicate ourselves and our university to a constant search for the ways to attain excellence and a determination to accept no less.

[images courtesy of USC University Archives]

In the late 1950s, a high priority for the University Senate (later reorganized as the Academic Senate) was to create a place "where the faculty and staff could … socialize and exchange ideas." President Topping took this idea to heart, and the USC Faculty Center (foreground, later renamed the University Club) opened its doors in 1961. Funds raised through the Faculty Wives' Club by Vera Fagg, USC's sixth first lady, were used to help furnish the new facility. [photo courtesy of USC University Archives]

extended to Topping's interactions with faculty and students as well. He initiated an open-door policy, under which faculty and students could come in and discuss their concerns, and he regularly walked the campus. Every couple of weeks, he would dine in the Faculty Center, sitting down informally with faculty; he would do the same thing in the Student Union, meeting with students over a lunch tray. In the community, he spoke before Kiwanis, Rotary and Lions clubs as well as chambers of commerce, explaining the university's plans.

"My theme everywhere was that the university is part of the community, and that community is very important to the university," he later wrote in his autobiography.

The most significant move of Topping's first year, however, was the university planning commission he created. In February 1959, the group, made up of trustees, administrators, faculty and alumni, began meeting monthly to determine how best to advance the university toward the goal of excellence that Topping was determined it should achieve. For two and a half years, the commission, which had been charged with developing a long-range master plan for the university, pondered USC's future. What emerged from its deliberations would remake the university on every front.

The Master Plan for Enterprise and Excellence in Education

On May 17, 1961, at the second annual dinner of the USC Associates, USC's preeminent support organization, in the Beverly Hilton Hotel, Topping announced the most ambitious and far-reaching fundraising initiative in USC's history: the Master Plan for Enterprise and Excellence in Education. Its goal was nothing less than the transformation of the institution.

"All our faculty, all our trustees, all our administration have agreed that our mission must be, exclusively, to pursue excellence in education— to pursue excellence only with those scholars who show definite promise of attaining it—to pursue excellence *with vigor and without compromise,* as long as we can lead bright young minds along the path to truth," he declared. "We have devoted the past two and one half years to a thorough study of what our task requires.... Together we have formulated precisely the plan we need. With this plan to guide us, our every step will be a stride—our every stride will be sure— and our ascent toward academic excellence will end in triumph." USC must, he added, "continuously recognize and emphasize that this university is a community of scholars where academic pursuits are preeminent, where research is fostered and where community service is an essential element of our mission."

The Master Plan set forth what seemed to many an impossible task: to raise $106,675,000, half designated for academic enrichment and half for new facilities. It was the largest fundraising goal ever set in California, and given the disappointing results of the university's previous capital campaigns, an extremely conservative timeline— 20 years—was projected. A first-phase goal of $30 million by 1964 was set, with the rest to come as soon afterward as possible.

Influential people across the nation quickly took notice of the plan. President John F. Kennedy sent a congratulatory telegram that stated:

...The consequence of higher education to our nation cannot be overstressed, and we must continue to strengthen our universities by every appropriate means.

You are to be congratulated for having so intensively planned your future and for undertaking this important venture.

I am confident that the citizens of the United States as well as the people of California and Los Angeles will give you their untiring support to provide the means whereby your goals

USC trustee and Master Plan Committee national chairman H. Leslie Hoffman (left), President Norman Topping (center) and Board of Trustees chairman Leonard K. Firestone (right) held a press conference on May 17, 1961, to let the media know abut USC's Master Plan for Enterprise and Excellence in Education. [photo courtesy of USC University Archives]

for a new era of enterprise and excellence in education may be attained.

"If he gets the cash," *Time* magazine observed, "Topping's master plan could revolutionize USC."

The Master Plan, however ambitious, was built on a solid foundation. During the months prior to its announcement, the USC Associates had been founded, and USC had set a record for raising money, increasing its endowment by a third. By the time the campaign was announced, the university already had $8 million in hand, thanks to generous commitments by a number of trustees during the planning years as well as grants from foundations and the federal government. H. Leslie Hoffman, chairman of the campaign, and his

wife had given $640,000, which ultimately helped fund construction of the business school's Hoffman Hall. Mr. and Mrs. Frank R. Seaver had contributed $450,000 for a School of Medicine commons and residence hall. Mr. and Mrs. Henry Salvatori made an unrestricted gift of $350,000. Other support came from Frank L. King and Justin Dart. The Ford Foundation gave $660,000 for an experimental teacher-scholar program and $700,000 for a youth studies center. The Firestone Foundation made an unrestricted gift of $500,000. Most noteworthy, the Olin Foundation gave $2.2 million to the School of Engineering to build and equip a new building, which would become the administrative and academic focal point for the school.

"In coming into a new area, we look for those educational institutions that have a future growth potential and whose programs are supported by an outstanding faculty," said Charles L. Horn, president of the Olin Foundation. "Among all the independent colleges and universities on the Pacific Coast, the University of

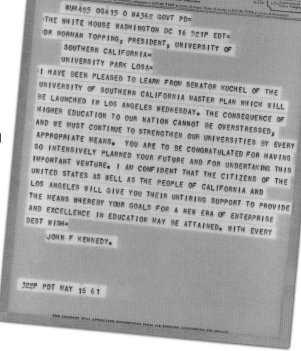

USC President Topping (left) welcomed Democratic presidential contender Senator John Fitzgerald Kennedy (right) to campus for a first-time voter convocation on November 1, 1960. The following May, after hearing about the Master Plan for Enterprise and Excellence in Education, President Kennedy sent Topping a telegram expressing his confidence in USC's success.
[images courtesy of USC University Archives]

Southern California was the one that struck us as the best. We also feel that our gift will provide stimulus for increased support for the University of Southern California from the local community. If we can recognize excellence, looking across this continent from our Eastern headquarters, we feel certain that the people of Los Angeles will also recognize excellence in their midst, and certainly should support it."

The gift, coming from a major foundation, had the desired effect.

"The Olin Foundation gift was the first major grant to the University's Master Plan," wrote Topping in a 1964 letter to Horn, following the dedication of Olin Hall of Engineering. "There have been other gifts and grants since then, but none can rival the inspiration of the first…. There is no question that the Olin gift has provided the great initial impetus needed if we are to fulfill the goals of our Master Plan."

By putting USC on the national philanthropic map, the Olin Foundation gift paved the way for what turned out to be one of the pivotal developments in the campaign: a $6.5 million challenge grant from the Ford Foundation's Special Program in Education, made in December 1962. The Ford Foundation grant, which was intended to help the university

AN ARTFUL GIFT

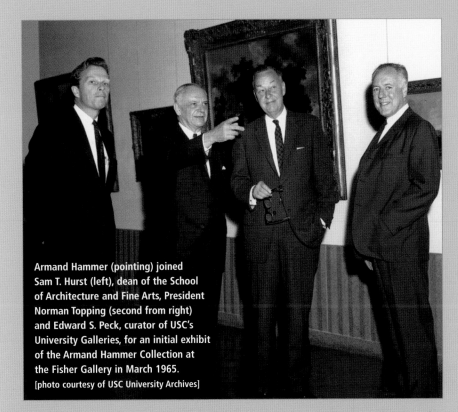

Armand Hammer (pointing) joined Sam T. Hurst (left), dean of the School of Architecture and Fine Arts, President Norman Topping (second from right) and Edward S. Peck, curator of USC's University Galleries, for an initial exhibit of the Armand Hammer Collection at the Fisher Gallery in March 1965.
[photo courtesy of USC University Archives]

In 1965, more than 50 masters took up permanent residence at USC. Originally hailing from England, the Netherlands, Flanders, Germany and Italy, they included some of the top names in European art, including Van Dyck, Hals, Rubens, Veronese, Rembrandt, Breughel the Elder and Younger and Filippo Lippi. All were part of a collection of paintings amassed by noted art collector Armand Hammer, president of Occidental Petroleum, who gave the collection to USC.

"I had made up my mind to give the Hammer Collection to an institution of higher learning located in a city where I have now made my home," Hammer said. "I chose a university instead of a museum because I believe that in doing so, I can best serve both the art lover and the serious student of art. I also elected to give my collection to the university because of my firm belief in the philosophy of private higher education in America and the Master Plan goals."

The collection was valued at more than $1 million.

On December 17, 1962, the Ford Foundation awarded what may well have been USC's single most significant gift to date—a $6.5 million challenge grant. Foundation director James W. Armsey spoke about the grant at the USC Associates' annual dinner in January 1963. Seated with him at the head table were (from left) H. Leslie Hoffman, Leonard K. Firestone, Norman Topping and former U.S. president Dwight D. Eisenhower. [photo courtesy of USC University Archives]

And increase they did. A year later, on January 10, 1963, the *New York Times* reported that "the University of Southern California—rolling along at a $1,000,000-a-month clip—reset its Master Plan fund sights today for this decade, rather than 20 years."

The optimism was clearly warranted; USC had already raised more than $19 million since the Master Plan announcement, and 11 buildings were under construction. Nine months later, by September 1963, USC had achieved its first-phase goal of $30 million, 16 months ahead of schedule. And through the efforts of more than 2,200 volunteers, who obtained nearly 40,000 individual contributions, the university matched the Ford Foundation grant in less than two years.

The foundation was so impressed that in December 1964, it followed up with a second challenge grant, this one for $7.5 million, making USC the only university in the history of the Ford Foundation's Special Program in Education to be awarded a larger grant the second time around. In making the second grant, the foundation noted USC's progress in faculty selection, compensation and awards; curricula; and recruitment and admissions. Under the terms of the grant, USC had to raise a

improve its entire program, was unrestricted but contingent on USC's raising $3 for every $1 from the Ford Foundation—a total of $19.5 million over the next three years. It was one of only two grants the foundation awarded on the West Coast (the other went to Stanford).

"Through the matching requirement—as stiff, I might say, as we felt we could reasonably impose—we hope that the number and amount of gifts from other sources will increase," said James W. Armsey, the Ford Foundation's director.

$22.5 million match in three years from private sources. The momentum the university had gained from the first grant bolstered confidence on campus.

"Having earned our first $6.5 million from the Ford Foundation last September—one year, two months and 15 days ahead of the deadline—we are confident we can succeed again," Topping said.

The second challenge grant was given a boost by the Olin Foundation, which also made a second, larger gift to the university, this time $2.7 million to fund an engineering and materials science center, to be named for Robert Vivian, dean of engineering at USC from 1940 to 1958. Bolstering the Olin gift was a $1 million commitment from the Hoffmans for a research building at the School of Medicine, and three anonymous gifts, totaling $1.37 million, to build and endow a library for the Graduate School of Business Administration as well as to help fund construction of a student activities center and a science lecture hall and auditorium. Five months after the second Ford Foundation grant was announced, the university had raised more than 87 percent of the Master Plan goal—in 20 percent of the time originally allotted. This in turn enabled USC to achieve nearly two-thirds of its academic goals.

"The objectives which we once believed would not be attainable until the 1980s now appear wholly possible in the 1960s," said campaign chairman Hoffman.

And in fact, USC outperformed even that prediction when, in spring 1966, it announced that it had surpassed the Master Plan's original goal, achieving its objectives in just five years. Because the Master Plan had raised the bar so significantly for the university, in November 1966, it officially extended its fundraising efforts by $34 million in order to complete a number of additional projects on its wish list. By the end of the decade, USC had generated more than $160 million, and the trustees decided to build on that success by setting an annual $2.75 million goal during the 1970s—confirmation that the Master Plan had permanently raised expectations and enhanced prospects.

Reshaping the Campus

The changes the Master Plan wrought at USC were profound on every level but were most visible on the campus itself, which was being reconfigured to provide the facilities needed to achieve the excellence that

Dean Emeritus Robert E. Vivian is pictured here in front of his namesake building, Vivian Hall, made possible by a second major gift from the Olin Foundation. [photo courtesy of USC University Archives]

The University Park campus land use plan developed by William L. Pereira and Associates for the Master Plan for Enterprise and Excellence in Education in 1961 called for the acquisition of 57 acres of land from the surrounding community, creating a campus that would be bordered by Exposition Boulevard, Jefferson Boulevard, Figueroa Street and Vermont Avenue by 1981. In this artist's depiction of the proposed campus expansion, a reddish tint identifies existing buildings; lighter buildings are those that were planned. [image courtesy of USC University Archives]

Topping so vehemently sought. As designed by architect William Pereira, the existing 78 acres, which were crisscrossed by city streets, would be replaced by an expanded, 138-acre, pedestrian campus organized into a series of quadrangles, the largest of which would center around the Doheny Library lawn. Others would be related to principal academic fields, such as science, engineering and performing arts, or university functions such as student activities. Contained within an inner ring, the quads would comprise the academic core of the campus, and within that

core, the streets would be closed to traffic. Some, like University Avenue, would be repaved and landscaped as pedestrian malls. Because half the full-time students lived on or near the campus, the outer ring would contain housing. Implementation of the plan was contingent on USC's ability to acquire some 60 additional acres from the surrounding community.

"It was obvious that if we were going to go anywhere, we would have to move well beyond the 78 acres that comprised the campus," Topping recalled in his autobiography.

Shortly after his inauguration,

Topping had visited L.A.'s mayor, Norris Poulson, to discuss the possibility of a community redevelopment plan. The neighborhood surrounding USC was seriously rundown and included a number of houses that were indisputably slums. With the help of the city councilman for the district, Billy Mills, USC hosted a gathering of some of the city's most influential people, including business-people, clergy and representatives of the neighborhood. The group supported USC's campus expansion plan, and its members were instrumental in convincing the City Council to approve it. In April 1961, after two months of hearings, and despite heated opposition from some community members, the City Council endorsed the plan decisively. When the first Ford Foundation grant came in, the university set aside enough money from it to purchase the initial parcels of land. Over the next few years, the broader urban redevelopment plan for the area took shape, but it wasn't until 1966, after many revisions by the Community Redevelopment Agency, that the Hoover Redevelopment Project, as it came to be called, was finally approved by the City Council and put into effect.

Most of the people displaced by the project accepted it. Others, however, blamed the university for aligning itself

THE NORMAN TOPPING STUDENT AID FUND

At a benefit dinner held in November 1975, Chancellor Topping autographed programs for beneficiaries of the Norman Topping Student Aid Fund. [photo by Allan Dean Walker Photography, courtesy of USC University Archives]

The idealism that characterized the 1960s and 1970s was manifest in various ways at USC but none so benevolent as a student-sponsored scholarship fund that was initiated by two African-American students. Ron McDuffie and Dan Smith wanted to help students from low-income families attend USC and came up with a novel proposal: The student body would tax itself a nominal amount each semester, with the proceeds going toward the scholarship fund. As part of the program, recipients were expected to provide 20 hours of volunteer community service each semester.

The student body passed a referendum supporting the measure in April 1970, and the new scholarship fund found a champion in President Topping, who added an endowment of $600,000 in USC Associates funds in order to make it immediately viable. The student council unanimously voted to name the fund in his honor.

From the start, the Norman Topping Student Aid Fund was run by an independent governing board made up of students and administrators from diverse ethnic backgrounds, which set policy and awarded the scholarships. In the intervening years, the structure of the fund has remained essentially unchanged, and the soundness of the concept has been reflected in its ongoing success: In the first three decades of its existence, the fund contributed more than $2 million in scholarships to over 300 USC students.

"Of all the entities that carry my name at the university today," wrote Topping in 1990, "I am most proud of the Topping Student Aid Fund."

On January 22, 1970, astronaut and alumnus Neil
Armstrong (left) spoke at the dedication of Frank
R. Seaver Science Center—the most expensive
complex constructed to date on the University
Park campus. He is pictured here with Blanche
Seaver and President Topping. [photo by Mervyn
Lew, courtesy of USC University Archives]

with the Community Redevelopment
Agency's right of eminent domain.
This caused residual resentment in the
surrounding community that endured
for years to come.

Still, as a 1965 *Los Angeles Times*
article pointed out, "Although the
university could condemn land for
expansion, it has favored the urban
renewal process beause of the aid
forthcoming for displaced residents
and the benefits the neighborhood

would receive through redevelopment." As Topping later recalled,
"It was absolutely essential for us
to move forward as we did in 1961."

At the same time the university
was laying the foundation for the
land acquisition, gifts were coming
in to reshape the campus in the
image of the Master Plan. In 1962,
one of the linchpins of the science
quadrangle was assured when university trustee Howard Ahmanson,
chairman of Home Savings and Loan
Association, National American
Insurance Company and the Ahmanson
Bank and Trust Company of Beverly
Hills, gave $1 million toward con-
struction of a $2 million biosciences
research center, the largest single gift
by any individual to the Master Plan
to date. His gift was matched by a
grant from the National Institutes of
Health. In 1966, Blanche Seaver gave
$1.2 million for another component—
a classroom and laboratory building
dedicated to the solid state sciences,
to be named in honor of her late
husband, Frank. The Stauffer Chemical
Company underwrote much of the
five-story Stauffer Hall of Science, to
house laboratories for physics and
geology. The Olin Foundation gifts
funded the buildings that would
delineate the engineering quadrangle.
Booth Memorial Hall, for the School
of Music, was the first building in the

DAYS OF CONCERN

Throughout the tumultuous 1960s, student protests at USC had been decidedly low-key compared to those at many other institutions. Topping's approach was to meet with students and hear them out, on the theory that an ongoing dialogue would keep the situation from boiling over. It was a strategy that worked well.

"Topping was very good to those kids," observed longtime senior administrator Roger Olson. "He didn't chastise them or try and shout them down or anything like that. He was patient. They, in terms of their relationship with their president, were very fortunate in what kind of a president he was, what kind of a person he was."

When, on April 30, 1970, U.S. president Richard Nixon announced that American troops had invaded Cambodia, the response was fierce and immediate on university campuses across the nation, particularly at Kent State University in Ohio, where National Guardsmen shot and killed four students and wounded nine others. At USC, these events triggered an unprecedented outpouring of emotion. On May 4, a faculty-student coalition called for a strike, to be held on May 7, though the flyer publicizing it hastened to add: "This is a symbolic protest—it is not directed against the Administration of USC. The strike is an effort to coordinate on a national level a symbolic protest which makes visible the outrage that is felt over the escalating war in Cambodia. If faculty and students stand together at USC, we can vocalize our concern as human beings... and insist that President Nixon be responsive to the American People...."

In response to the events, the Faculty Senate went even further. On May 6, it passed a resolution calling on President Topping to close the university for four days "for the purpose of better enabling faculty and students to explore their involvement, role and commitment to the crucial issues which divide the nation."

Topping granted their request, decreeing that no one would be penalized for joining the strike, and as a consequence, the "Days of Concern," which took place from May 7 to 11, were marked by rallies, marches, teach-ins and political canvassing, but none of the violence that marked other campuses.

"These students are activists whose motive is to create a world that is human and sane, where life is precious and neighbors are trusted—a world so improved they can tell their children they did something to elevate rather than lower the human condition," he explained at the June 1970 commencement.

The entire university community was proud of the mature response that had unfolded on campus.

"One expects that USC students would do things a little differently than the rest of the country," wrote Paul Bloland, vice president for student affairs, in the June 1970 *Trojan Family*. "Instead of modeling themselves, as they well might have, after some of the more disruptive kinds of demonstrations of concern, they chose deliberately to make their actions a unique example of how a university community can express itself in a time of crisis without resorting to the cruder, more disruptive kinds of demonstration. This is a source of pride on the part of the people involved, and certainly on the part of the University."

performing arts quadrangle. Gifts from Cecele and Michael Birnkrant and David X. Marks made women's and men's residence halls possible. A bequest of $4.5 million from Waite Phillips gave rise to the 11-story Waite Phillips Hall of Education, at the time the tallest building on campus. Contributions from multiple donors funded the Von KleinSmid Center, which housed the School of Public Administration and the School of Politics and International Relations. Thanks to a similar convergence of donors, Heritage Hall was built to showcase USC's many athletic trophies and memorabilia while providing offices for the coaching faculty and training facilities for the teams.

On the Health Sciences campus, Kenneth T. Norris Sr., chairman of Norris Industries, chaired a committee to generate the funds to build out the campus. Their efforts, coupled with federal matching funds, produced the Elaine Stevely Hoffman Medical Research Center, which was completed in 1968 and was the largest medical structure in Southern California devoted exclusively to research; the Willard Keith Administration and Medical Forum Building; and the Louis B. Mayer Medical Teaching Center. Blanche Seaver funded a residence hall,

Above: Designed by Edward Durell Stone, USC's Von KleinSmid Center for International and Public Affairs (left), Social Sciences Building (center), and Waite Phillips Hall of Education (right) made an architectural statement by combining the simplicity of modernist architecture with the brickwork, arcades and columns characteristic of USC's Romanesque-style buildings. A driving force behind the decision to engage innovative architects such as Stone, I. M. Pei and others to create campus facilities was first lady Helen Topping's vision of the campus as a living museum of the world's finest architecture.

Left: Surrounded by taller structures, the Eileen and Kenneth T. Norris Medical Library— completed in 1968—is a gem on USC's Health Sciences campus.

[photos courtesy of USC University Archives]

and Norris and his wife, Eileen, underwrote the medical library.

On the fifth anniversary of the Master Plan announcement, a crane placed a 5,500-pound finial, representing a globe, atop the 167-foot tower of the new $3 million Von KleinSmid Center. It was a fitting symbol not only of the university's rising place in the world but also of its upward aspirations and the enormous strides it had made toward achieving that vision.

Academic and Faculty Advancement

Even before the Master Plan was announced, USC had been making notable progress toward the academic excellence to which Topping aspired. In 1958, a hypersonic wind tunnel, designed by Raymond Chuan, director of the Engineering Center, was put into operation. The tunnel, capable of testing missile models as though they were flying at 20 times the speed of sound and nearly 60 miles above the earth, was the only one of its kind in the world. Under newly appointed dean Robert Dockson, the College of Commerce was renamed the School of Business in 1959, and a Graduate School of Business Administration was added the following year. In the late 1950s, a linear accelerator came on line, housed in a new nuclear physics laboratory and accompanied by an annual operating grant of $200,000. And Willard Geer, associate professor of physics, followed up his earlier invention of a color television picture tube with a device to track the sun's rays and continually concentrate them on a bank of solar cells to collect solar energy.

To attract top students, honors programs were launched for outstanding undergraduates—a series of intellectually challenging courses for lower-division students, and colloquia for upper-division students. At the same time, the university acquired a remarkable treasure: the 25,000-volume library of the late

Below left: The globe finial was placed atop the Von KleinSmid Center on May 17, 1966—the fifth anniversary of the announcement of the Master Plan.

Right: During the Master Plan era, the university grew in academic stature on many fronts. Pictured here is USC's wind tunnel. Designed by Engineering Center director Raymond Chuan, it was the only one of its kind in the world.

[photos courtesy of USC University Archives]

Marta Feuchtwanger (second from right), widow of celebrated German novelist Lion Feuchtwanger, gave USC her late husband's magnificent book collection following his death in 1958. She is shown here with President and Mrs. Topping (left) and university librarian Lewis F. Stieg (right) at the dedication of the Feuchtwanger Memorial Library. [photo courtesy of USC University Archives]

at USC the nation's first computer center for education and research, making available to faculty and graduate students in business, engineering and the physical and social sciences new electronic, all-transistorized data processing equipment.

If these developments laid the groundwork for the academic advances that followed, the Master Plan served as the principal catalyst. During the five years after the campaign was announced, the university achieved, or came close to achieving, all its goals. Full-time faculty increased by 52 percent and total faculty by 21 percent. Faculty compensation, a longtime stumbling block, was raised sufficiently to earn Topping a faculty resolution commending him for fulfilling his pledge to increase salaries to a B grade rating from the American Association of University Professors. Graduate and professional school enrollment grew to 54 percent of the student body, and full-time graduate enrollment increased 25 percent.

Scholarships and fellowships also multiplied; the Trustee Scholar program was created for 10 outstanding entering freshmen, and the number of graduate students holding fellowships from major national award programs increased fourfold, while financial aid to

novelist Lion Feuchtwanger, which encompassed historical works, biographies and documents and some outstanding works in German, French, Greek and Latin literature, including some extremely rare books published during the first 50 years after the invention of printing—"the last of the great comprehensive collections by an intellectual," according to USC librarian Lewis F. Stieg. And finally, Remington Rand and Minneapolis-Honeywell entered into a $2 million agreement to place

A FOOTBALL POWERHOUSE

[photo courtesy of USC University Archives]

When John McKay took over as USC's head football coach in 1960, he inherited a program in disarray. He spent his first two seasons getting his land legs, but by 1962, his third season, he had hit his stride, and he never broke it, becoming the winningest coach in Trojan football history. That year, his team won USC's first national championship since the 1930s. His teams went on to win three more national titles, in 1967, 1972 and 1974. Under his guidance, his teams had three unbeaten seasons, won nine conference titles and played in eight Rose Bowl games, including four consecutive years from 1967 to 1970.

While McKay, who was as well-known for his acerbic wit as for his signature "I-formation," was indisputably a brilliant coach, it didn't hurt that his teams included some of the best players in university history—a reflection of his uncanny ability to spot and recruit talent. In 1965, tailback Mike Garrett, a two-time All-American, won USC's first Heisman Trophy. He was only the second West Coast player to win the award.

"If I'd wanted to use him as a guard, he'd have been my best guard. If I'd made him a linebacker, he'd have been the best linebacker. If I had taught him to pass, he might have been my best quarterback," McKay said of his star player.

Three years later, USC and McKay chalked up another Heisman when O. J. Simpson won the trophy. Other top players he coached included Clarence Davis, Anthony Davis, Ricky Bell and Pat Haden.

McKay left USC in 1975 to become head coach of the Tampa Bay Buccaneers, but in 1993, his legacy came full circle when Garrett returned to USC to become athletic director.

graduate students, excluding student loans, doubled, to $4 million. Student loan funds grew tenfold, from $250,000 to more than $2.5 million.

USC's additional resources and burgeoning reputation played out in many arenas, most visibly in faculty recruitment. In fall 1961, the university revealed that it was adding to the music faculty three of the world's finest musicians: violinist Jascha Heifetz, cellist Gregor Piatigorsky and violoist William Primrose.

"Jascha Heifetz, Gregor Piatigorsky and William Primrose are just the start of what we hope to bring to campus in many fields," Topping said in announcing the appointments, and the subsequent hiring of other high-profile distinguished scholars bore out his conviction. In 1964, Maurice Pryce, one of the world's leading theoretical physicists and head of England's atomic energy center, joined the physics faculty. Other distinguished faculty who were recruited during the Master Plan included psychologist James E. Birren, systems specialist Solomon Golomb, mathematician Richard Bellman, chemist Otto Schnepp, econometrician Gerhard Tintner and author Irving Stone.

The new facilities, combined with the intensifying intellectual environment, led to a burgeoning of faculty research. A grant from the

World-renowned virtuosos (standing, from left) William Primrose, Jascha Heifetz and Gregor Piatigorsky began teaching master classes at USC in February 1962. [photo courtesy of USC University Archives]

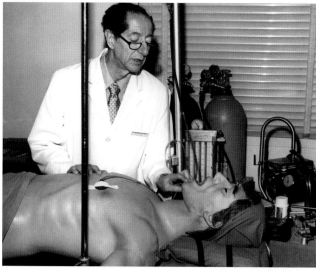

Stephen Abrahamson (standing), chair of USC's Department of Medical Education, led the team that invented Sim One (on table), the world's first computer-controlled, interactive simulated patient. [photo by Joe Friezer, courtesy of USC University Archives]

Headed by Soviet affairs expert Rodger Swearingen (B.A. 1946, M.A. 1948), of the USC School of International Relations, and funded by trustee Henry Salvatori, the university's Research Institute on Communist Strategy and Propaganda was housed in a new building that later became known as the Registration Building. [photo courtesy of USC University Archives]

U.S. Public Health Service funded a long-term study of the public health consequences of air pollution, carried out in the new Laird J. Stabler Memorial Hall. On the Health Sciences campus, the Elaine Stevely Hoffman Medical Research Center housed research projects for 65 faculty investigators in biochemistry, medicine, microbiology, neurology, pathology, psychiatry, public health and surgery. The Raulston Memorial Research Building was remodeled in 1969. A collaboration with Aerojet-General Corporation enabled USC medical researchers to develop a lifelike, computer-controlled manikin named Sim One, which functioned as a simulated patient to train anesthesiologists in endotracheal intubation.

New institutes were established, including the Research Institute on Communist Strategy and Propaganda, housed in the new, rectilinear brick Information Center (which was promptly nicknamed "Red Square"); the Research Institute for Business and Economics; and the Managerial Policy Institute for Business Executives. In 1964, the university created the Rossmoor-Cortese Institute for the Study of Retirement and Aging, which became known as the USC Gerontology Center later in the decade and subsequently the

Ethel Percy Andrus Gerontology Center, in honor of the USC alumna who founded the American Association of Retired Persons (AARP) and the National Retired Teachers Association.

USC's longstanding interest in oceanographic research was advanced in the mid-1960s with the creation of the Marine Science Center at Big Fisherman's Cove on Santa Catalina Island. Launched with a $500,000 grant from the National Science Foundation and land and funding contributed by the Santa Catalina Island Company, the center was administered by the Allan Hancock Foundation, and its facilities were designed by William Pereira as part of a planned 225-acre science center that would also be utilized by Caltech, UCLA, UC Irvine, UC Riverside, California State University, and Pomona and Occidental colleges.

Academic progress was also manifest in the rising quality of the student body. In 1966, senior Jim O'Toole, a humanities major, became the first USC student in 28 years to be named a Rhodes scholar.

Updating the Curriculum

With the momentum gained from the Master Plan, the university revised the curriculum in the college and most of the professional schools and intro-

duced a number of innovative new educational programs, many of them interdisciplinary and, in the spirit of the 1960s, community focused.

"We are convinced that the university's role in relating to urban problems is to provide people with a sound educational background in the troubles of our cities, to conduct definitive research and to identify problems and make recommendations as to their possible solution," Topping commented.

The Urban Semester, launched in February 1968 with the support of the Mary Reynolds Babcock Foundation, thrust students out of the classroom and laboratory and into city streets and the halls of power. Guided by a multidisciplinary faculty representing urban and regional planning, business, sociology, religion, political science, architecture and music, students had a vast array of field experiences, supplemented by readings, lectures and seminars on campus. They then conducted individual research projects on different aspects of the urban landscape to synthesize their findings.

The Biology Semester, funded initially by a grant from the Esso Foundation and designed for students who were not life science majors, took a similar interdisciplinary tack with the biological aspects of

With support from the National Science Foundation and the Santa Catalina Island Company, USC launched a new Marine Science Center located near Big Fisherman's Cove on Catalina Island. The facility was renamed the Philip K. Wrigley Marine Science Center in 1990. [photo by Allan Dean Walker, courtesy of USC University Archives]

urban problems, drawing on faculty from medicine, law, architecture, engineering and public administration. A new Center for Urban Affairs was established in 1969, offering under-graduate and graduate degrees in urban studies and putting USC on the cutting edge of institutions offering interdisciplinary degrees in the field. An undergraduate major in ethnic studies was also launched, one of less than a half-dozen similar programs in American universities.

Other programs combined learning and community service. The School of Education's Rural Migrant Teacher Corps trained bilingual teachers for the children of migrant farmworkers, while other programs produced

teachers for inner-city schools and those on Indian reservations. The Dental Ambassadors, a group of School of Dentistry faculty, students and staff, gave free dental care to impoverished children and adults on Indian reservations, in migrant farm-worker camps and in remote areas of Mexico. The School of Medicine's "Community Medicine" program took sophomore medical students into the field to work in clinics in underserved areas.

Collaborations were also forged with other institutions. At the request of the Pakistani government, the Graduate School of Business Administration helped establish programs for a business school in

Karachi. It also took part in a five-university consortium, funded by private industry, that began preparing members of minority groups for careers as business executives in retail and industrial fields. A 1965 agreement with Hebrew Union College, the oldest school for Jewish studies in the world, provided for the mutual exchange of academic credits, use of shared facilities and faculty supervision of students involved in jointly sponsored programs.

National Recognition

While USC had been making enormous advances academically, Topping was lobbying behind the scenes to help the university achieve another milestone, one that would signal to the rest of the world its maturation and ascent into the top ranks of U.S. research institutions: membership in the Association of American Universities, the most esteemed organization of academic institutions. The association had been founded in 1900, an outgrowth of an effort by deans of American graduate schools to improve graduate education. Its purpose was to advance the international standing of American institutions, and it was made up of a highly select group of universities.

With the progress USC had made

Founded in 1968, USC's Urban Semester gave students the opportunity to use the city as a laboratory for study in fields ranging from urban and regional planning to architecture and music. [images courtesy of USC University Archives]

through the Master Plan, Topping felt that it was developing into a major research university, and he believed its accomplishments deserved recognition through membership in the AAU.

For a time, however, not everyone agreed. Lee DuBridge, the president of Caltech, had initially opposed USC's election to the association, believing it was not of high enough caliber to warrant membership. By the late 1960s, however, much had changed. One day in late 1969, while Topping was attending a meeting of the council of deans, he was interrupted by an urgent phone call. On the line was the president of the AAU, who informed him that USC had been elected to membership. When he returned to the meeting and shared the good news, the deans stood and applauded.

"It immediately transformed a lot of things for us because all of a sudden, doors that took us six months to get into, we could get into next week," recalled Roger F. Olson, a fundraiser who joined USC during the Topping years and later served as senior vice president for university relations from 1983 to 1993. "And it began to change the nature of the federal view of us, and once research money started to flow, then faculty began to increase and improve. It created an upward trajectory, and Topping did that single-handedly."

THE GAMBLE HOUSE

Discussing the transfer of the Gamble House (above left) to USC and the City of Pasadena in 1966 were (above right, clockwise from left): Pasadena vice mayor Boyd P. Welin, USC vice president for financial affairs Carl M. Franklin, Pasadena city manager Elder Gunter and James H. Gamble. [photos courtesy of USC University Archives]

Designed in 1908 by renowned architects Charles and Henry Greene as a retirement residence for the heirs to the Procter & Gamble legacy, the Gamble House in Pasadena is the material realization of the philosophy of the Arts & Crafts Movement that that which was made to be useful—whether a chair, a cupboard or even a rafter tail—should also be beautiful. With its open spaces, hand-sculpted woodwork, simple lines and quiet beauty, the house is a monument to the lifestyles and architectural innovations of turn-of-the-century Southern California.

In the interest of historic preservation, the Gamble family deeded the house to the City of Pasadena in a joint agreement with the USC School of Architecture in 1966. Since that time, the house has been designated as a National Historic Landmark and emerged as an international center for architectural and cultural education. Several courses are taught at the house, and each year the school offers two scholars-in-residence fellowships that enable advanced architecture students to live and study in the home. The house is also a case study for the school's historic preservation program. Operated by the USC School of Architecture, the home also is open for tours, welcoming more than 30,000 scholars, tourists and students each year.

As the Gamble House approaches its centennial in 2008, significant steps are being taken to preserve the home for future generations. A meticulous restoration of the building's exterior was completed in 2004, and the next phases focus on landscaping, interior decoration and furnishings. The hope is to ensure that countless future generations will have the opportunity to visit this fine example of 20th-century architecture and experience, if only for a while, the warmth and tranquility that beckoned Pasadena's earliest settlers.

Chancellor Topping beamed as he read a 1979 *Trojan Family* retrospective commemorating USC's election to the Association of American Universities, "the nation's premier academic group," 10 years earlier.
[photo courtesy of USC University Archives]

Topping, however, distributed the credit more generously.

"That we have qualified for this honor is the result of the splendid effort of the university family," he said. "We thank the faculty who give of their knowledge and intellect so productively in research and teaching. We thank the students who work with profound interest and ability to make their own education meaningful and to develop ideas which enrich the education of students who follow. We thank the alumni who recognize the university's need for growth and development and who contribute generously to the university in both time and money. And we thank the administrators and trustees who strive so diligently in pursuit of learning at USC. The university family is entitled to be proud."

Another Transition

The tremendous success of Topping's vision had wrought immense changes in his alma mater, but it had also had a profound and less beneficial influence on him. In 1969, his cardiologist, concerned about the constant pressure of his job, advised him to retire, and Topping, who at 62 had had two heart attacks, accepted his recommendation. At the annual trustees' conference in Palm Springs in spring 1970, the man who had put USC on the national map formally announced his retirement, which took place in August.

"I have decided, in fairness to my wife, Helen, and to myself, that after nearly two decades in educational administration, the time to retire is now while my health is still reasonably good," he said.

With great reluctance, the board accepted his request and named him chancellor. "USC has flourished under Norman Topping these past 12 years," said Justin Dart, who had become chairman of the board in 1967. "Men of his leadership and academic stature are most rare."

Topping's contributions to the university as president and later as chancellor quickly became the stuff of legends. "I don't know what would have happened if somebody else had been president," Roger Olson speculated 35 years later. "I am sure that some of these same things might have happened, but somebody else wasn't president; he was. They happened on his watch. He was great."

BIRTH OF THE WARRIOR

[photo courtesy of USC University Archives]

It's a familiar spectacle and a beloved tradition: A Trojan warrior riding a splendid white horse galloping through the Los Angeles Memorial Coliseum, to stir up the Trojan Spirit during football games.

Their antecedents, however, were considerably less grand than today's dynamic duo. The earliest equestrian to make an appearance at a USC football game was a costumed warrior on a palomino, who carried the colors for the 1948 Trojan Marching Band, wearing cowboy boots and rolled-up pants. Six years later, in September 1954, the Trojan Knights' spirit committee recruited a rider and rented a horse and costume for an appearance at the Pittsburgh game. The designated rider backed out at the last minute, and the only committee member with any experience on horseback was a tall, skinny student barely able to keep his mount on track. Horse and rider were laughed off the field.

Dismayed by the spectacle, alumnus Bob Caswell descended from the stands to volunteer his services and offer his own horse, Rockazor. Caswell and Rockazor made their debut at the following game and soon made the image of the noble Trojan warrior and white horse famous across the country. When they retired in the late 1950s, it was several years before replacements could be found. In 1961, however, USC special events director Bob Jani (class of 1956) spotted Richard Saukko and his horse, Traveler, in the Rose Parade and asked them to assume the role. Saukko agreed, and they began a 27-year run the following season. Initially, Saukko wore a costume from the movie *Ben Hur*, but he soon replaced it with a more comfortable leather outfit that he made himself. Saukko and a total of four Travelers entertained football fans until 1988. Saukko died in 1992, but the tradition lives on with their successors.

In 2004, Bill Tilley (class of 1961) and his wife, Nadine, gave $2 million to endow the Traveler Mascot Program, ensuring that Traveler's appearances would always be a vital part of the Trojan Family.

USC's new performing arts complex takes center stage in this 1977 aerial view looking southeast across the University Park campus.
[photo courtesy of USC University Archives]

Chapter Six

Holding the Course (1970–1980)

By Annette Moore

Choosing a new president to succeed Norman Topping was no easy task, but after screening about 100 candidates for the job, a 16-member search committee composed of trustees, deans, faculty members, students and alumni eventually identified—and unanimously elected—a successor from within USC's own ranks. That person was John Randolph "Jack" Hubbard, a self-professed "tough Texan with a heart" who had served as the university's provost and vice president for academic affairs for the past year. Prior to that, he had spent four years in India as chief education adviser for the U.S. Agency for International Development. Hubbard's previous academic experience included 12 years as dean of H. Sophie Newcomb Memorial College at Tulane University in New Orleans as well as teaching posts at Yale University, Louisiana State University and the University of Texas, where he also earned three history degrees.

News of the appointment of John Randolph "Jack" Hubbard (right) as USC's eighth president was announced at a press conference. Breaking the news were outgoing president Norman Topping (left) and Justin W. Dart (not pictured), chairman of the USC Board of Trustees. [photo by Nurettin Erturk, courtesy of USC University Archives]

expressed unqualified optimism:

> *Dr. Hubbard has made a great impact on the faculty, students, alumni and trustees since he joined USC last summer. His administrative ability, his wise decisions, his emphasis on excellence in education, and his dedication to undergraduate study in the humanities and social sciences have won him many loyal supporters on the campus.*
>
> *We are confident that we have chosen a man who will keep USC moving forward to even greater achievements in the decade culminating in the university's 100th year in 1980.*

Meeting that charge would prove a challenge indeed.

The "Steady State"

Not only did Hubbard inherit what he characterized as "commodious shoes" to fill, but he also took the university's helm during a period of mounting uncertainty for colleges and universities across the United States. Compounding the effects of what *Time* magazine called a "nation-wide student strike," inflation was pushing up the costs of higher education, creating ever-higher differentials between public and private tuition rates. Federal support for many

With campuses nationwide still reeling from the horror of the May 4 Kent State shootings, university officials opted to forgo a formal inauguration ceremony for USC's eighth president. Instead, Hubbard's appointment was made public at a press conference held on August 3, 1970.

The USC community received the news with enthusiastic support, and in making the announcement to the media, board chairman Justin Dart

academic research programs was on the decline. The overall population of college-age students was beginning to level off, and, what is more, many young people had become disillusioned by the perception of poor job opportunities for individuals with liberal arts degrees.

While these developments heralded the rapid approach of what he later termed the "steady state"—that is, the need to sustain vitality in the face of limited funds and constricted growth potential—Hubbard asserted his intention to consolidate the gains made during the Master Plan era, and to keep the momentum going for the future. "Universities simply now have to demonstrate greater imagination and follow good management practices," he explained in an interview for a short-lived annual publication called *USC Aspects* in 1972, "if they are to achieve their previously established goals or even to maintain their present status."

A series of energy-conservation policies was among the more practical measures implemented during the Hubbard administration to keep what then executive director of university facilities Arnold F. Shafer called an "inflation-riddled" budget under control. These ranged from the consolidation of evening classes into fewer buildings to the installation of clock controls to regulate air-conditioning and heating systems and the shutting down of ornamental fountains and "aesthetic lighting."

To ensure that the university's adjustment to steady state would not be arbitrary, but rather "fair and reasoned and responsible," Hubbard placed a high value on maintaining open channels of communication. Toward that end, in fall 1974 he welcomed the launch of a new internal newsletter, *Chronicle*, as "an additional means of increasing the flow of information about the life of the university primarily to those who spend their working lives involved with the institution and its community."

Another key element of Hubbard's management strategy—reflecting a national movement among universities to create more responsive governance structures—was the establishment of the President's Advisory Council, or PAC, which was convened as a formal mechanism for giving various constituencies within the university organization a voice in administration. Bringing together elected representatives of USC's faculty, deans, students and staff to make policy

Above: President Hubbard (center) had been in office just under three months when several trustees agreed to take questions from students as part of a "student forum" held on the Von KleinSmid Center steps. Participating in this event were student leader Sam Hurst (left) and board chairman Justin Dart (right). [photo courtesy of USC University Archives]

Below: In late 1971, Frances Lomas Feldman (left) brought two Eskimos to Los Angeles to report on a four-year project she had directed to improve life for Eskimos in Alaska. A social work pioneer who joined USC in 1954, Feldman was instrumental in founding the first credit counseling service, the first industrial social work curriculum in the West, and USC's staff and faculty counseling center—which became a model throughout California. She became the first chair of USC's newly reorganized Faculty Senate in 1973–74. [photo by Mervyn Lew, courtesy of USC University Archives]

One of President Hubbard's first orders of business was to appoint the university's engineering dean, Zohrab A. Kaprielian (right), to head the newly created Office of Academic Planning and Research. [photo courtesy of USC University Archives]

A Faculty of Distinction

From his initial days in office, Hubbard voiced his priorities of continuing to improve the college and the graduate school, and strengthening the faculty. As he said in an exclusive interview with *USC Trojan Family* in December 1970:

We can never be a really distinguished institution without a really distinguished college and graduate school to go along with our fine professional schools. The liberal arts, as intellectual disciplines, are as important to our survival as human beings as is quantum mechanics.

Nothing, however, qualifies a university for greatness more surely or visibly than the people who teach and conduct research. Nothing surpasses a faculty of quality as a determinator of institutional merit.

In keeping with these stated objectives, one of the first moves Hubbard made was to create the USC Office of Academic Planning and Research, and to appoint the university's high-powered engineering dean, Zohrab A. Kaprielian, to head it. Charged with defining institutional goals and building upon "the considerable and diversified competence" of the university's faculty,

recommendations to the president, PAC—originally called the University Council—was formed in 1973. Its first chair was law professor Martin Levine, who was succeeded by social work professor Frances Lomas Feldman in 1974. PAC remained in operation until May 1982, when it was formally disbanded. Among the council's most enduring achievements was the establishment of USC's Staff Assembly and Student Senate organizations, which carried forward PAC's legacy of staff and student participation in university governance at USC.

ZOHRAB A. KAPRIELIAN

A pivotal figure in USC's emergence as a major research university, Zohrab A. Kaprielian wielded considerable influence throughout the Hubbard administration.

Born in Syria to Armenian refugees, the young Kaprielian was single-mindedly dedicated to his studies, earning bachelor's and master's degrees in physics from the American University of Beirut, Lebanon, and a doctorate in electrical engineering from the University of California, Berkeley. After spending three years as a research fellow at the California Institute of Technology, he joined USC's electrical engineering department in 1957.

Zohrab A. Kaprielian
[photo courtesy of USC
University Archives]

USC soon became Kaprielian's life. In 1962, he was promoted to department chair, and President Topping appointed him head of the USC Science Development Program in 1965. Shortly after becoming engineering dean in 1970, Kaprielian was drafted by President Hubbard to serve, concurrently, as vice president for academic planning and research. That title was changed to vice president for academic administration and research in 1972, when Kaprielian's duties were expanded to include budgetary as well as administrative responsibilities. In fall 1975, Hubbard named Kaprielian executive vice president. In this new capacity, Kaprielian was in effect the university's chief operating officer, responsible for overall administration of academic affairs, research, resource management and long-range planning.

Ambitious and fervently dedicated to securing USC's status as an elite institution, Kaprielian set himself to the task of building faculty and research strength. He obtained a number of major government grants, including a coveted Joint Services Electronics Program from the U.S. Department of Defense, and also was instrumental in the creation of the Lord Foundation of California, which was established in 1977 by technology innovator Thomas Lord, chairman of the board of the Lord Corporation, to support USC's engineering and business

schools. Among the numerous distinguished scholars Kaprielian helped recruit were Solomon Golomb, who in 1976 became USC's first faculty member to be elected to the National Academy of Engineering, and Irving S. Reed, who is known for helping create the Reed-Solomon Codes, which became the standard error-correction method used in compact discs, fax machines and other devices.

George A. Olah—another Kaprielian recruit— characterized Kaprielian as a modest man who had vision and "a nose for good people," and who basically tried to let those people do their best. "Without any question, we have made remarkable progress during the 29 years I have been here," Olah reflected in 2005. "But it's a slow process. It's like an apple orchard. You plant the trees, but they don't bear fruit immediately. Kaprielian was one of the men who started planting the seeds. And we are benefiting from that now."

Despite his successes, however, Kaprielian's methods were not universally applauded. In budgetary matters, he maintained such tight controls that deans and directors had to apply to him directly for program funding, and a lack of transparency surrounding the outcomes of these requests on occasion gave rise to mistrust among academic units.

Kaprielian died in December 1982, only a year after stepping down as executive vice president. At the memorial service held in his honor, Paul Hadley, former vice president for academic affairs, reflected: "Zohrab was a tough manager. I'm sure I had as many proposals vetoed as anyone. His management style was idiosyncratic, unorthodox and certainly not derived from any textbook. But it worked."

In remembrance of Kaprielian's contributions and steadfast dedication to USC, the university's Kaprielian Hall, opened in 1990, bears his name.

Gerald R. Ford, 38th president of the United States (right), made a campaign visit to the University Park campus in 1976. Following his defeat to Jimmy Carter, Ford returned to USC on two separate occasions to lecture to a variety of classes. He is pictured above with President Hubbard. [photo courtesy of USC University Archives]

Kaprielian—who would be named executive vice president in 1975—set himself to the task of advancing USC's faculty and research enterprise.

Fortunately, even in the face of federal funding cutbacks for university-based research and development, USC found itself in a relatively strong position to attract top-flight scholars, particularly in engineering and the sciences. According to Hubbard, unlike many institutions that had amassed large numbers of government-sponsored research programs in the post-World War II, post-*Sputnik* era and now were being forced to scale back, USC had not over-capacitated itself. As a consequence, Hubbard believed, USC was poised to recruit distinguished teachers and investigators who, through no fault of their own, now found themselves looking for jobs. "This was the milieu in which I found myself," he recollected in 2005. "An annual high point was the president's faculty breakfast, when I would introduce our new faculty members."

In a 2005 interview, William Spitzer, professor emeritus of electrical engi-neering, materials science and physics (and the first person in USC's history to have served at every level of academic administration), recalled that Kaprielian effectively leveraged faculty quality by recruiting new faculty members who had strong reputations in areas that bridged two or more disciplines (e.g., engineering and chemistry) and giving them joint appointments, thereby strengthening more than one department or school through a single hire. Another strategy, first put into operation during the Topping administration, was to consciously target areas in which other local universities (especially Caltech and UCLA) were less developed. This yielded particular success in fields such as electrical engineering, where USC built up impressive strength in emerging disciplines such as solid-state electronics, communications, signal processing and computer engineering. Where the approach was not as successful—and where in subsequent years USC had to exert considerable effort to catch up—was in areas such as physics and biology.

Just a few of the many acclaimed scholars who joined USC's faculty during the Hubbard administration were campaign finance expert Herbert Alexander; sociologist and demographer Kingsley Davis (who coined the terms "population explosion" and "zero population growth); former state controller and gubernatorial candidate Houston I. Flournoy; American literature specialist and violence expert Ronald Gottesman; Charles Heidelberger, developer of the widely used cancer drug 5-fluorouracil; Martin D. Kamen, discoverer of carbon 14; hydrocarbon chemist George A. Olah (who went on to win the 1994 Nobel Prize in chemistry); planning and transportation authority Harry Richardson; and geographer John Weaver, former president of the University of Wisconsin System. In addition, a variety of prominent figures came to USC to serve as distinguished visiting lecturers during this time, including former U.S. president Gerald R. Ford, the Rev. Jesse Jackson and statesman Henry Kissinger.

Transcending Disciplinary Boundaries

Accelerating the development of interdisciplinary programs was another high priority for USC during the 1970s. Consistent with the times, as Hubbard stated in his address at the 1971 faculty-staff breakfast, part of the rationale was to "maximize faculty knowledge and skills while minimizing effort and proliferation of equipment." But cost-savings was

by no means the only motivation. USC remained intent on bolstering its research and educational enterprise, and capitalizing on its location as well as its strong tradition of innovation and entrepreneurialism. Hubbard affirmed this in an interview that was published in *USC Aspects* upon completion of his first two years in office:

> USC does not have to be bound by traditional guidelines and definitions. ... [O]ur development will be characterized by problem-oriented academic programs.... And our development will surely be characterized by the constant use to best advantage of the manifold, complex urban area of Southern California as an educational and research resource.

Among the first interdisciplinary centers that had their origins during this period was the Annenberg School of Communications (later the USC Annenberg School for Communication). Named for its principal benefactor, Ambassador Walter Hubert Annenberg, the school was dedicated to "the art and science of communication." According to the April 1972 issue of *Trojan Family*, Annenberg cited the emergence of Los Angeles as a

The Annenberg School of Communications (later renamed the USC Annenberg School for Communication) was established in 1971 through the support of Ambassador Walter H. Annenberg, pictured here in front of his namesake building. [photo courtesy of USC University Archives]

national center for the communications and entertainment industries,
together with USC's strong existing
programs in telecommunications,
journalism, speech communication,
performing arts and related fields,
as underpinning his decision to create
the school.

Cross-disciplinary work in gerontology also shifted into high gear
with the dedication of USC's Andrus
Gerontology Center building in
February 1973. "The Ethel Percy
Andrus Gerontology Center will be a
dramatic step forward in providing
a comprehensive research-educational
program in pursuit of understanding
the basic processes of aging and the
development of experts in the field,"
said James E. Birren, center director
and a noted researcher into the
psychological processes of aging. "[It]

will be an innovation for universities,
in that there is no other comparable
example of such a university-based,
interdisciplinary facility. It is hoped
that the Ethel Percy Andrus
Gerontology Center will become a
model for research facilities at other
universities throughout the nation
and the world." Two years later, USC
became home to the world's first
professional school dedicated to
gerontological study. The USC Leonard
Davis School of Gerontology had
the goal of integrating research and
education regarding the biological,
behavioral and societal processes of
aging with services for older adults
and their families. The venerable
cellist and USC faculty member Gregor
Piatigorsky offered sage counsel as
well as musical entertainment at the
opening ceremonies for both the

center and the school, gently reminding his listeners that, after all, "An
old fiddle sounds the best."

Based on the growing importance
of USC's health sciences programs and
the increasing demand for interdisciplinary collaboration in health-related
fields, the position of vice president
for health affairs was created in 1972,
representing dentistry, medicine and
pharmacy in the university's top-level
administration. Edmund F. Ackell Jr.
was brought in to fill this position in
1974, and was succeeded by Joseph P.
Van Der Meulen in 1977.

Additionally, building on basic
and clinical research under way by
investigators at the USC School of
Medicine, the National Cancer
Institute designated the USC–Los
Angeles County cancer program as
one of eight newly established

When USC's Andrus Gerontology Center was dedicated in 1973, a time capsule
was formally placed in a steel vault under a plaque on the building's patio.
Participating in the ceremony were (from left) USC vice president for university
affairs Thomas P. Nickell Jr., Los Angeles mayor Tom Bradley and James E. Birren,
center director. The capsule—which was opened on February 12, 2000—
contained letters from some two dozen people, including Harry Belafonte,
R. Buckminster Fuller, Richard Nixon, Ronald Reagan and John Wayne, expressing
their predictions about the role and status of older persons in 2000.
[photo courtesy of USC University Archives]

comprehensive regional cancer centers in 1973, providing funds for interdisciplinary work in areas spanning biochemistry, immuno-therapy, microbiology, pharmacology, radiology and virology.

Another pace-setting operation, conceived in the aftermath of the 1973 energy crisis, was the USC Hydrocarbon Research Institute (renamed the Donald P. and Katherine B. Loker Hydrocarbon Research Institute in 1984). The institute was established in 1977, and ground was broken for a building to house it in February of the following year. Under the leadership of founding director George A. Olah, Loker Institute researchers have produced findings with practical implications ranging from fuel cells to pharmaceuticals and telecommunication devices.

Grounded in USC's enduring commitment to urban issues, Hubbard established the Task Force on the Urban University in 1974, with the goal of bringing various academic units with urban interests closer together. In part based on the recom-mendations of this task force, USC's Center for Urban Affairs and Graduate Program in Urban and Regional Planning—the latter of which was a joint effort of the schools of architec-ture and public administration—were merged into a new unit, the School of

A BASEBALL LEGEND

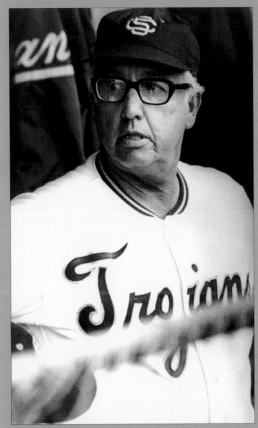

Raoul "Rod" Dedeaux in 1973
[photo courtesy of USC University Archives]

March 30, 1974, was an auspicious day for baseball at USC. Dedeaux Field opened its gates, and that very afternoon, Russ McQueen threw a no-hitter in a 7–0 victory against California. The Trojans went on to win the national champion-ship that year—their fifth straight championship since 1970—setting a record no other team has come even close to matching. (No other school has won more than two in a row.)

Of course, nothing less could have been expected on a field named for legendary USC baseball head coach Raoul "Rod" Dedeaux. During his 44-year tenure at USC (1942–86), Dedeaux led the Trojans to a record 11 national champion-ships and 28 conference titles. He was also an incomparable mentor, as exemplified in 1979, when four former Trojans he had coached at USC played in the Major League All-Star Game. By the time of his retirement, Dedeaux had helped develop more than 200 pro players, coached nearly 60 future major leaguers and racked up more wins than any other college baseball coach in history at that time.

Dedeaux, who died at the age of 91 in January 2006, was named "Coach of the Year" six times by the College Baseball Coaches Association and was inducted into the organization's Hall of Fame in 1970. In 1999, both Baseball America and *Collegiate Baseball* magazine named him "Coach of the Century."

The Donald P. and Katherine B. Loker Hydrocarbon Research Institute building opened its doors in September 1979. [photo courtesy of USC University Archives]

Administration to form the USC School of Policy, Planning, and Development in 1998.)

Although it lacked the longevity of the programs described above, another notable outgrowth of the university's focus on interdisciplinary scholarship in the 1970s was the USC Center for the Humanities, which was founded in 1975 and eventually disbanded in 1984. Sylvia Manning, who arrived at USC in 1975 to help start the center, described it as having been conceived as a strategic means of reaching out from the humanities to the professional schools in order to build relationships and programs. Despite the fact that it never achieved real financial viability, according to Manning, the center did spawn some significant innovations. These included an internship program for humanities majors and universitywide "theme years," which provided a focus for education, teaching and research centered on such broad subjects as "The Medieval World" and "Gender and Scholarship." The center also sponsored a variety of high-visibility conferences addressing topics such as "Jazz, Painting and Literature," "Anti-Semitism: A Map of Prejudice" and "Vietnam Reconsidered." The center provided a nexus for truly trail-blazing work on the part of several faculty members as well, such

Planning and Urban Studies. Alan Kreditor was appointed to direct the new school, which drew upon fields as diverse as architecture, business administration, economics, engineering and sociology, and was heralded as the first independent planning program in the United States. (The school underwent two subsequent name changes, to the School of Urban and Regional Planning and the School of Urban Planning and Development, and ultimately merged with the university's School of Public

as that of popular religion professor J. Wesley Robb (for whom the university's J. Wesley Robb Endowed Scholarship in Human Values was named). Robb's initial classes in biomedical ethics ultimately led to required ethics courses for second- and third-year medical students at USC.

At the same time the university was investing in schools, institutes and centers, it also took measures to ensure that undergraduates would reap the greatest possible benefit from their experience at a major research institution. Implemented in 1977 and established as an independent unit in 1978, USC's Freshman Writing Program provided a mechanism for ensuring that

incoming students developed the critical thinking, reading and writing skills that are the foundation for success in all university work. Additionally, the success of USC's Urban Semester and Biology Semester course offerings (inaugurated in 1968 and 1971) prompted other concentrated single-semester programs in which a limited number of undergraduates took an in-depth look at complex clusters of issues. The Semester of the Arts, for example, integrated studies in architecture, fine arts, cinema, drama, literature, dance, music and aesthetics. By the mid-1970s, there were nine such programs, including a German Semester (encompassing disciplines ranging

from German language, literature and arts to science, philosophy and psychology), a Sacramento Semester and a Washington, D.C., semester, which continues to this day.

The USC Information Sciences Institute

One of the most celebrated academic units launched during the Hubbard administration was USC's Information Sciences Institute (ISI). In early 1972, Keith Uncapher, then director of the Santa Monica-based Rand Corporation's computer science division, was leading a project on "packet-switching" technology, which breaks down digital messages into parts that can be sent

A member of the faculty since 1954, religion professor J. Wesley Robb was one of USC's most memorable instructors. He was among the eight faculty honored for excellence in teaching at the USC Associates' first annual dinner in 1960, going on to teach courses in human values that would inspire generations of students at USC. [photo courtesy of USC University Archives]

A major contributor to the country's information technology knowledge base, the USC Information Sciences Institute was opened in 1972. It is housed in a high-rise in Marina del Ray.
[photos by Marti Cole, courtesy of USC University Archives]

over a network and reassembled at their destination. This effort—and the possibilities it presented for communication networks—caught the attention of officials at the Department of Defense Advanced Research Projects Agency, who were eager to support Uncapher in rapidly expanding the scope of his research. The management team at Rand demonstrated little enthusiasm for moving forward with this work, however, and Uncapher began casting about for a new home base. He first approached UCLA, but became discouraged when he was told that it would take well over a year to solidify an agreement. Upon hearing about Uncapher's nego-

tiations with UCLA, Kaprielian, with his customary firm resolve, stepped in with a much more persuasive offer. The two men shook hands, and ISI was officially founded on April 24, 1972.

Housed in a 12-story office tower overlooking the harbor of Marina del Rey, the new institute attracted some of the most creative minds in computer science, and within three years it evolved into one of the country's leading information technology research centers. ISI is acknowledged as one of the birthplaces of the ARPAnet (a precursor to the Internet) and provided key support for the development of the Internet into a national and international system. It was ISI researchers Jon Postel and Paul Mockapetris, for example, who invented the domain name system—what we know as ".com" and ".edu"—in 1983. Under Uncapher's watch, ISI also made early forays into the fields of artificial intelligence, computer security and human/machine communication.

Uncapher stayed on as ISI's executive director until 1987. His successor, Herbert Schorr, took over in 1988 and set to work broadening the institute's funding base, increasing the scope of its graduate education program and expanding expertise in strategic areas such as cyber-security, educational technology and chip design.

Beyond Greek Life

While fraternities and sororities—which had declined in popularity during the 1960s—experienced a resurgence of student interest in the 1970s, there was a recognition during the Hubbard administration that USC was under-programmed in terms of student services. When he arrived as the university's newly appointed vice president for student affairs in 1972, James Appleton found an institution that was much more a commuter school than a residential college. "Even though there were lots of students in residence," he recalled some 33 years later, "they tended to vacate on the weekends, unless there was an athletic event, and go home." He also noted that USC's professional schools were functioning largely as disparate units, with the result that there was little coordination across campus with respect to student life.

Based on these observations, and intent on enriching the out-of-class environment, Appleton decided to bring campus services closer to the academic programs. After consulting extensively with the deans, he and his staff implemented what they termed a "hub-spoke" arrangement, whereby the major academic units identified internal student affairs personnel who worked within the schools, but

whose activities were coordinated by the Office of Student Affairs. Under this arrangement, the individual priorities and challenges of the various schools and units—such as dental students' need for financial aid and counseling services, and liberal arts students' need for career counseling—could be accommodated within a coordinated, universitywide framework.

As needs were identified and

As part of a broad effort to beef up student programming in the 1970s, Addie Klotz (left), associate vice president and health center director, gave USC students the opportunity to meet with campus "big shots" and get acquainted with available services and activities. The program was organized under the auspices of USC's student affairs office, directed by James Appleton (not pictured). [photo courtesy of USC University Archives]

services added, increasing numbers of students began to stay on campus over the weekends. According to Appleton: "We really did, I think, integrate other aspects of campus life so that sororities and fraternities were not the only vehicles for high-quality social experiences."

Concurrently, USC's increasing diversity was another major factor that contributed to the enrichment of student life. A sign of the times was a survey designed by the American Council on Education Cooperative Institutional Research Program showing that USC's class of 1978 not only was the largest in the university's history, but also included more women and more members of ethnic minorities than ever before. USC had taken a number of proactive measures to support this trend.

Evolving out of meetings between President Hubbard and Latino student leaders on campus, Raul Sotelo Vargas was hired as the university's new director of Mexican-American programs in 1972. The following year, El Centro Chicano opened its doors, envisioned as a place that would provide culturally sensitive, student-centered programs to foster the academic and personal success of Latino students at USC. Vargas and several alumni formed the Mexican American Alumni Association

(MAAA) in 1974. The group had the goal of providing tuition assistance to Latino students, and Hubbard agreed to match every dollar raised by the MAAA with two dollars from the university's coffers.

When Thomas Kilgore—renowned civil rights activist and pastor of Los Angeles' Second Baptist Church—presented an address at USC's baccalaureate ceremonies in 1972, Hubbard was, as he recalled, "so impressed by his manner, his appearance, his eloquence and especially his message that we had it within our institutional means to become a powerful force for progress within the whole community," that he hired Kilgore as special adviser to the president the following year. Kilgore was instrumental not only in founding the USC Black Alumni Association (originally called "Ebonics") in 1976, but also in establishing USC's Office of Special Community Affairs, which opened on July 1, 1973, to help build bridges between the university and its surrounding neighborhoods.

(Some years later, in 1982, the Asian Pacific American Support Group—precursor to the USC Asian Pacific Alumni Association—was chartered to bring together, faculty, staff, students and friends to ensure high-quality services for USC's students of Asian and Pacific descent.)

Above: Together with eight Trojan alumni, Raul Sotelo Vargas founded the USC Mexican American Alumni Association (MAAA) in 1974. The group provides tuition-assistance grants to Latino students attending the university, with the goal of ensuring that financial need is never an obstacle to enrolling at USC.

Below: After speaking at USC's baccalaureate ceremony and receiving an honorary degree in 1972, Thomas Kilgore joined the university as a special adviser to the president. The Reverend Thomas Kilgore Jr. Chapel of the Cross at the University Religious Center was later named in appreciation of his contributions to USC.

[photos courtesy of USC University Archives]

THE SPIRIT OF TROY

[USC News Service photo, courtesy of USC University Archives]

The Trojan Marching Band traces its origins to the founding of the University of Southern California in 1880, but it was not until much later that the group secured its place in history as "the greatest marching band in the history of the universe." When Arthur C. Bartner took up the baton in 1969, the band numbered 80 male student musicians and didn't boast much to set itself apart from any other collegiate marching ensemble. All of that, however, was soon to change.

Under Bartner's leadership—in concert with that of associate director and arranger Tony Fox—the Trojan Marching Band admitted women to its ranks, developed its famous "drive-it" marching style and "rock chart" sound, donned its trademark sunglasses and was christened the true Spirit of Troy.

As its fame spread, the group's numerous film and television appearances—including *Two Minute Warning* (1976), *The Gong Show Movie* (1980) and *Forrest Gump* (1994)—earned it the additional moniker of "Hollywood's Band." A real break came in 1979, when the band made a guest appearance with the rock group Fleetwood Mac on the title track for the album *Tusk*; the

record went platinum and earned worldwide notoriety for the Spirit of Troy.

From Trojan contests to Super Bowls, the Olympics and beyond, the band has lifted spirits at an amazing roster of venues. Band members performed at Ronald Reagan's second U.S. presidential inauguration in 1985, and on July 4, 1986, 40 student musicians participated in the rededication ceremonies for the Statue of Liberty in New York City. There have been international appearances as well, including one to commemorate the 50th anniversary of the D-Day landing on Normandy Beach. "If current trends continue," observed *USC Trojan Family* in 1986, "the litmus test for whether an event is of major ceremonial importance in American life will be this: Is Bartner there, and is he leading the band?"

As USC life trustee and alumnus Herbert G. Klein aptly put it: "The band's a good example of what's happening at the university. Before, you had to scratch to get players. Now you have to qualify in order to join the band."

An Evolving Neighborhood

The area surrounding the University Park campus had been the focus of an ongoing urban planning and renewal effort since the Los Angeles City Council endorsed the Hoover Redevelopment Project in January 1966. But it wasn't until the 1970s that the project moved into full swing, with USC's efforts mounted under the direction of Anthony D. "Tony" Lazzaro, vice president for business affairs. Originally covering 165 acres, the plan called for the systematic rebuilding and renovation of areas to the north, east and west of the University Park campus. Later, the Hoover Redevelopment Project was expanded to encompass 574 acres, incorporating improvements to the Figueroa and Vermont commercial corridors, the historic Adams Boulevard district, and Exposition Park and Los Angeles Memorial Coliseum.

The commercial core of the project, as originally conceived, was the University Village shopping center on Jefferson Boulevard, which celebrated its grand opening in fall 1976. On what once had been the site of a meat packing plant, University Village provided space for a variety of new shops, restaurants and other businesses as well as homes for established local merchants such as Silverwoods men's clothing store, Tam's Bookstore, University Travel and the 32nd Street Market.

Through the Hoover Redevelopment Project, the neighborhood also gained a fire station on Jefferson, situated at the southern border of University Village. Along Vermont Avenue arose new apartment complexes that were available to the public as well as USC students and staff, in addition to the Dockweiler Station office of the U.S. Postal Service and the Dr. Mary McCleod

Two generations of JEP directors compared notes when founder Barbara Gardner (left) posed with Richard E. "Dick" Cone in 1985. Tammara Seabrook Anderson (not pictured) took the helm of the program in 2002.
[photo courtesy of USC University Archives]

USC'S JOINT EDUCATIONAL PROJECT

USC students have a long history of service to the local community, embracing such longstanding Trojan institutions as Troy Camp and Songfest. In 1972, building on that rich tradition, Barbara Seaver Gardner, director of what was then the USC Center for Urban Affairs, conceived a program that would forge an even stronger relationship between the university and its surrounding urban neighborhoods by fostering intellectual connections between students' formal university coursework and community service activities. She founded USC's Joint Educational Project (JEP), which began placing students as volunteer tutors and teacher's aides in local schools. The program soon expanded, offering student volunteers who could teach "mini-courses" in a broad range of subjects, including anthropology, business, dental hygiene, mathematics and Spanish.

Headquartered since 1976 in the former residence of USC's fourth president, George F. Bovard, JEP grew to become one of the oldest and largest service-learning programs in the United States. The program links academic learning with experiences outside the classroom, and as of 2005 was placing approximately 2,000 students from the USC College of Letters, Arts and Sciences into the neighborhood as mentors, tutors, translators and assistants at schools, hospitals and service agencies each year.

Bethune Regional Branch of the Los Angeles Public Library. On Figueroa Street, a hotel and restaurants took the place of a used car lot. Occupying a site near USC's Catholic Newman Center, the B'nai B'rith Hillel Foundation Center (USC Hillel) serving the Jewish student community at USC, was also a part of the plan. Another significant feature of the Hoover Redevelopment Project was a new Los Angeles campus for Hebrew Union College-Jewish Institute of Religion (HUC), which opened its doors in July 1971.

Just as it had from the beginning, the urban renewal effort of the 1970s—and USC's participation in it—alternately raised questions and rallied support among local residents. As *Los Angeles Times* columnist Art Seidenbaum characterized it in 1976, the project could be viewed either as an attempt to insert a "buffer zone" between the university and its surrounding neighborhood or as "a major effort to make a gate, to provide mutually beneficial facilities for both communities and perhaps places of common interest." The latter explanation was borne out in the changes wrought by the project, which helped create a much more vibrant off-campus environment for students by expanding opportunities for them to interact with fellow

Above: As part of the Hoover Redevelopment Project, several older buildings on Jefferson Boulevard were demolished to make way for new businesses.

Right: Opened on the site of a former meat packing plant on Jefferson Boulevard, the University Village shopping center debuted in fall 1976.

[photos courtesy of USC University Archives]

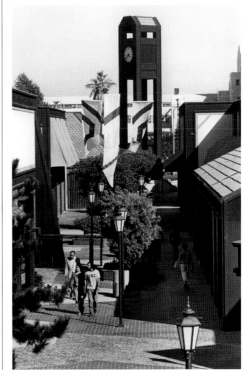

Building on programs held in previous years, USC's Office of International Students and Scholars sponsored an annual "International Week" through-out the 1970s as a way to bring the cultures and histories of other countries to the University Park campus. The festival featured food booths, fashion parades, sports competitions, lectures and exhibits of art and handicrafts. [photo courtesy of USC University Archives]

students and faculty as well as neighbors outside the classroom, while at the same time encouraging broader community participation in university life.

International Ties

Just as USC during the 1970s looked to its surrounding neighborhood as a crucial asset to a major urban univer-sity, it also reached out to a broad international constituency. "In the past half century the University of Southern California has established an enviable reputation for interna-tional activities both on and off cam-pus," Hubbard said in his 1975 annual address to USC faculty and staff. "The heritage of former chancellor Rufus von KleinSmid flourishes! It is my firm belief that this university has both a moral obligation and a lively oppor-tunity to expand and build upon its considerable international experience and expertise."

During Hubbard's tenure, USC's international connections ran the gamut from consultation on the part of individual faculty members assisting foreign organizations to full-fledged teacher-training programs in locations as far flung as Mexico, Europe and the Far East. In 1973, the university's College of Continuing Education created the Office of International Summer Session to coordinate an expanded slate of summer programs, including specialized intensive-study courses for foreign students as well as wide-ranging study-abroad opportu-nities for students based at USC. The university also operated a program of English language instruction and other activities to help spouses of international students at USC adapt to their new environment. This par-ticular program, founded in 1972 by volunteer teacher Louise Lyon and Bill Gay, then director of USC's American Language Institute, bene-fited from the enthusiastic participa-tion of USC first lady Lucy Hubbard.

By the end of the decade, USC's student body included more than 3,500 international students from some 100 countries—more than at any other U.S. university—and there were 26 Trojan alumni clubs in international locations. As Hubbard proudly proclaimed in his final faculty-breakfast address in 1979, "The campus is a truly vibrant amal-gamation of races, cultures and mores."

Yet while USC drew widespread praise for its international programs overall, its ties to the Middle East became the subject of intense public scrutiny, perhaps all the more so because of the oil crises of 1973 and 1979.

Part of the controversy related to USC's Iranian links and growing turmoil leading up to the shah's departure from Iran in January 1979. As Hubbard pointed out, USC's relationship with Iran could be traced to 1954, when the USC School of Public Administration had assisted in the establishment of a school of public and business administration at Iran's University of Tehran. By the 1970s, Iranian students at USC numbered around 500, representing the largest contingent of international scholars on campus. Several Iranian cabinet ministers, including the current minister of energy, were Trojan alumni. Stemming from this longstanding relationship, the Shah of Iran made a $1 million gift to USC in 1974, presented through the

National Iranian Oil Company, to establish an endowed professorship in petroleum engineering at the university. During a trip to Iran the following summer, Hubbard, emeritus public administration dean Henry Reining and USC Office of International Programs director K. William Leffland presented honorary degrees to the shah and to Manoutchehr Eghbal, a distinguished physician, former university chancellor and officer of the National Iranian Oil Company. Two years later, in 1977, demonstrators outside burned effigies of the shah in protest, while USC also awarded an honorary doctor of humane letters to the shah's wife, Farah Pahlavi, in a ceremony held in

USC's Norris Cinema Theatre.

Even more contentious was USC's involvement with Saudi Arabia, which, like the university's association with Iran, extended back over decades. Saudi Arabia's late King Faisal had received an honorary doctor of laws degree from USC during von KleinSmid's presidency, in 1945. Additionally, in 1976, then Saudi Arabian minister of industry and electricity Ghazi Al-Gosaibi, who had earned a master's degree in international relations from USC in 1965, presented the university with a $1 million gift, on behalf of the Kingdom of Saudi Arabia, to create the King Faisal Chair of Islamic and Arab Studies (later renamed the King

In a ceremony held in the Imperial Palace at Tehran, Mohammad Reza Pahlavi, the Shah of Iran (left), received an honorary degree from USC in 1975. Present with the shah at the ceremony were (from left) President Hubbard, Dean Emeritus Henry Reining (School of Public Administration) and K. William Leffland, head of international programs at USC. [photo courtesy of USC University Archives]

In 1973, USC's League International, a support group for international students and scholars, sponsored a campus reception for the Los Angeles consular corps. During the event, banners of many countries were displayed at the Von KleinSmid Center for International and Public Affairs, where Consul and Mrs. Mogens Edsberg of Denmark (left) joined President and Mrs. Hubbard in admiring the Danish flag. [photo courtesy of USC University Archives]

Faisal Chair in Islamic Thought and Culture). During the mid-1970s, some 200 Trojan alumni held posts in the Saudi Arabian government, and more than 150 Saudi students were enrolled at USC.

In 1978, growing out of these connections, the establishment of a Middle East studies center at USC was proposed. Although there are as many stories about the origin of the idea for the center as there are people who witnessed the unfolding events, there is agreement that a meeting took place in Santa Barbara in May 1978, involving Al-Gosaibi, USC Board of Trustees chairman J. Robert Fluor (head of the Fluor Corporation, a petrochemical engineering firm that had subsidiaries in Saudi Arabia) and the leaders of several other U.S. companies doing business with Arab countries. During this meeting, an agreement was proposed whereby the businessmen would contribute funds to a private foundation whose purpose was to support the creation and operation of a Middle East studies center at USC. Hubbard was convinced that the university could render a service to society by establishing such a center, and the USC Board of Trustees endorsed the agreement on October 4, 1978. When an announcement was made to the campus community that USC would

be home to a new Middle East studies center directed by a joint committee composed of USC trustees and the officers of the private foundation, the center—and its unconventional governance structure—became the subject of a highly publicized national debate.

Believing that the confusion derived in great part from the language of the proposed agreement, on October 26, Hubbard and Willard Beling, the USC faculty member who was to head the proposed center, issued a memorandum of understanding amending the agreement and confirming that the university would have "full control" of the center's academic, fiscal and other activities. The USC Board of Trustees and PAC convened special committees to draft recommendations about the proposed center's academic programs and operating policies, and a special *Ad Hoc* Committee on New Academic Units was assembled "to formulate procedures for the creation of new academic units associated in any way with USC." Despite these efforts to remedy uncertainties about the center's academic integrity, however, in 1979, the USC Board of Trustees voted to rescind the agreement and return the funds that already had been raised from the corporate donors.

During a gala dinner (above) held at the Century Plaza Hotel in April 1976, President Hubbard (above right) announced USC's largest fundraising effort to date, the $265,340,000 Toward Century II campaign.
[photos courtesy of USC University Archives]

Toward Century II

All the more remarkable considering the economic and public-relations challenges of the 1970s, USC carried out its largest fundraising effort to date under the aegis of "Toward Century II." Dedicated to a vision of responsible academic leadership, the program was publicly launched in April 1976, during the country's bicentennial, and culminated in the celebration of USC's 100th birthday during the 1980–81 academic year. The $265,340,000 campaign had USC trustee Leonard K. Firestone, U.S. ambassador to Belgium, as its international honorary chairman, aided by co-chairs Justin Dart, Virginia Ramo and Chancellor Norman Topping. Montgomery Ross Fisher was named chairman of the executive committee, and Thomas P. Nickell Jr., vice president for university affairs, directed the drive. At the kickoff dinner, Hubbard announced to an eager crowd at the Century Plaza Hotel:

We intend to begin our second century as a model of academic excellence without compromising our traditional dedication to sound fiscal policies. The 100th anniversary of USC is filled with historical significance not only for the university but for all of Southern California. That historical significance, however, is overshadowed by our concern for the future.

Aerol Arnold, distinguished emeritus professor of English, and his wife, USC trustee Anna Bing Arnold, are pictured here paying a visit to the newly completed Anna Bing Arnold Child Care Center in 1977. The center was created to accommodate the children of USC's faculty, staff and student parents. [photo courtesy of USC University Archives]

Looking toward that future, the campaign laid out six principal educational thrusts grounded in the work of task forces that Hubbard had established in 1972 to help chart USC's continued upward trajectory. These six objectives were: fostering a higher level of interaction between the college and USC's professional schools, ensuring a flexible and personalized educational experience for students at USC, endowing "a new generation of master professors," establishing more multidisciplinary centers of excellence, strengthening

the university's commitment to world affairs and international education, and improving the quality of urban living.

Toward Century II attained nearly half of its goal in just over a year, and topped its target two months before its official closing. The final tally was $309,273,937—nearly $44 million beyond the original goal. Thanks to Toward Century II, USC added more than 50 endowed chairs to its roster, including two funded by trustees and named in honor of faculty maestros Gregor Piatigorsky and Jascha Heifetz. All told, campaign gifts augmented the university's endowment by $72 million, for a new total of $155 million.

Under the direction of Anthony Lazzaro, 10 major academic facilities were constructed on USC's campuses during the campaign, and by campaign close, seven others were under construction or on the drawing boards. Completed buildings included the Anna Bing Arnold Child Care Center, Bing Theatre, Charlotte S. and Davre R. Davidson Continuing Education Conference Center, Corwin D. Denney Research Center, Eileen L. Norris Cinema Theatre, Grace Ford Salvatori Hall and Arnold Schoenberg Institute, as well as the $2 million Henry Salvatori Computer Science Center, which provided a focal point for access to the engineering school's newly acquired time-sharing computer. Under

Above left: USC's involvement with Santa Catalina Island can be traced to a meeting between then president Norman Topping and Philip Knight Wrigley in 1962. After Wrigley's death in 1977, his family estate provided the largest gift to the Toward Century II campaign, and his son, William (pictured), became a longtime USC benefactor and trustee.

Above right: USC awarded an honorary doctor of laws degree to Walter Hubert Annenberg, principal benefactor of the USC Annenberg School for Communication, in 1977. Posing together to mark the occasion were (from left) Justin W. Dart, Leonore "Lee" and Walter Annenberg, Leonard K. Firestone and President Hubbard.

[photos courtesy of USC University Archives]

construction was the Seeley G. Mudd Building, a $12 million classroom and laboratory facility for the USC College of Letters, Arts and Sciences funded in part by a $5 million contribution from the Seeley G. Mudd Foundation—the largest gift ever made to the university by a California foundation. Work also was under way on Mark Taper Hall of Humanities (including renovation of Founders Hall) and, at the Health Sciences campus, the Kenneth Norris Jr. Cancer Hospital and Research Institute. Structures that had been funded and were planned for construction included the Hedco Petroleum and Chemical Engineering Building as well as the Harold Lloyd Motion

Picture Scoring Stage, Marcia Lucas Post Production Building and George Lucas Instructional Building for the USC School of Cinema-Television. Under the leadership of trustee Paul Trousdale, campaign funds also were set aside for campus beautification in the form of landscaping, fountains and pedestrian malls.

The largest campaign gift came from the William Wrigley family and estate, whose contribution of $13 million, at the time the largest in USC's history, supported the USC Institute of Marine and Coastal Studies (named the USC Wrigley Institute for Environmental Studies in 1995). Walter Annenberg made major gifts benefiting his namesake

NEW MOMENTUM FOR USC'S MEDICAL SCHOOL

The period from 1970 to 1980 was one of dramatic transformation for the health sciences at USC. Under the leadership of Franz Bauer (medical dean from 1969 to 1974), USC founded the country's first department of emergency medicine in 1971. The university's Primary Care Physician Assistant Program was launched within the Department of Family Medicine in 1973. In addition, the 1970s saw the founding of two flagship components of USC's health sciences enterprise.

Roots of the USC/Norris Comprehensive Cancer Center

In 1968, the National Cancer Institute (NCI) approved a proposal developed by several USC faculty members to establish a regional cancer center as a joint project of the university and Los Angeles County (LAC). The county was to provide land and funding for construction, while USC would staff the facility and cover operating costs. G. Denman Hammond, a renowned pediatric oncologist and director of hematology and oncology at Childrens Hospital Los Angeles, was recruited as the center's founding director in 1971. That December, President Richard Nixon declared a national "war on cancer" and signed the National Cancer Act, which amounted to the country's first coordinated battle plan. Under this legislation, the USC/LAC program— still without a permanent headquarters—was designated in 1973 as one of the first eight comprehensive cancer centers in the United States. Plans were quickly developed to construct a 96-bed facility on the grounds of LAC+USC Medical Center.

Benefactor Kenneth T. Norris Jr. (left) and cancer center director G. Denman Hammond are pictured here with a detailed model of the Kenneth Norris Jr. Cancer Research Institute. [photo courtesy of USC University Archives]

Despite these initial successes, however, the road ahead proved rocky. Facing a serious budget crisis in mid-1976, the Los Angeles County Board of Supervisors placed a $40 million bond issue on the November ballot to raise the county's share of money for the facility. With precious little time to rally public support, USC launched a celebrity-studded advertising campaign spearheaded by Chancellor Topping and Justin Dart, chairman of the USC Board of Trustees—but the measure fell short of the two-thirds majority required for passage, jeopardizing the NCI grant, which was contingent on partnership with the county.

Determined to retain federal funding, Hammond went back to the drawing board and submitted a new proposal for a smaller hospital located on USC's Health Sciences campus. USC received the award.

In May 1979, thanks to lead gifts from Kenneth Norris Jr. and the Kenneth T. and Eileen L. Norris Foundation, ground was broken for the USC Kenneth Norris Jr. Cancer Hospital and Research Institute. It was the largest building project in USC's history, and an undertaking that President Hubbard described as having "survived more perils than Pauline ever knew." The $40 million, 60-bed facility was dedicated in February 1983.

The Estelle Doheny Eye Hospital

In 1971, the USC School of Medicine became formally associated with the Estelle Doheny Eye Foundation, which was established in 1947 by the late philanthropist Carrie Estelle Doheny, widow of oil magnate Edward L. Doheny and mother of USC alumnus Edward L. Doheny Jr., after her personal experience with glaucoma. The alliance was the outcome of an arduous negotiation.

The Estelle Doheny Eye Hospital opened on USC's Health Sciences campus in 1985. [photo courtesy of USC University Archives]

The foundation had had its primary facility at St. Vincent Medical Center and for more than two decades had considered affiliating with a university to expand its scope. Despite this ambition, however, Father William G. Ward, Mrs. Doheny's personal confessor, and other members of the foundation's board were concerned that the Doheny entity would become "gobbled up" in the larger university administration.

Thanks to the efforts of Hugh Edmondson, emeritus chair of pathology at USC and a member of the Doheny board, an agreement between the two entities was finally cemented, and USC recruited an internationally recognized young surgeon, Stephen J. Ryan, from Johns Hopkins to head USC's newly a established ophthalmology department. The foundation agreed to provide research funds and to construct a facility on USC's Health Sciences campus.

Ryan arrived at USC in 1974, and the 35-bed Doheny Eye Hospital opened in 1985. It was augmented with a four-story expansion in 1992.

THE SEELEY G. MUDD ESTATE

Since 1979, USC's presidential families have made their home at the Seeley G. Mudd Estate, a San Marino mansion constructed in 1934. [photo courtesy of USC University Archives]

In spring 1979, the Hubbards became the first of USC's presidential families to reside at the Seeley G. Mudd Estate, the university's new "White House." Designed by architect Reginald Johnson, this 14-room San Marino mansion was built in 1934 as a home for the family of Seeley Greenleaf Mudd, who served for some 40 years on the USC Board of Trustees and was dean of the university's medical school from 1941 to 1943. (Seeley G. Mudd was the son of Seeley Wintersmith Mudd, for whom USC's Mudd Memorial Hall of Philosophy is named.) When Mudd passed away in 1968, he stipulated that the house would be transferred to USC, after his widow no longer needed it, to serve as a residence for the university's chief executive officer. USC acquired the property in 1978.

Over the years, USC's "first families" have made several changes to the estate: Lucy Hubbard added a swimming pool, and both Marilyn Zumberge and Kathryn Sample improved the interior and exterior of the house to better accommodate the official entertainment needs of the university. But the "bones" remain the same. With its spacious interior—including a formal living room paneled in 18th-century Georgian pine—and a sweeping lawn the size of a football field, the house and grounds have provided an exemplary setting for countless university-related functions.

school as well as the Center for the Study of the American Experience. More than $3 million in campaign contributions was earmarked for the USC University Libraries, and the USC School of Urban and Regional Planning received $2 million from the James Irvine Foundation, at the time the largest single grant in the foundation's 40-year history. In addition, a gift from trustee Kenneth T. Norris Jr. made possible a major renovation of Bovard Auditorium that was completed during the winter of 1979–80.

In the end, *Trojan Family* hailed Toward Century II as the second most successful fundraising effort ever undertaken in higher education (after Yale)—even more remarkable for having been achieved during a major national recession—and as one of the first three capital programs in academic history to exceed $300 million.

Passing the Torch

At a press conference held on February 7, 1979, Hubbard made public his retirement plans. "The close of USC's first 100 years of service in 1980, culminating a decade of considerable progress," he said, "would be an appropriate time for a new president to take the university into its second century." He was to step down on August 3, 1980, 10 years

THEMATIC OPTION

USC's vaunted freshman honors program, Thematic Option, had its unlikely beginnings in a five-year, $750,000 start-up grant from the National Endowment for the Humanities. USC received the grant in 1974 to develop an undergraduate curriculum that would be relevant to a contemporary urban university. At the time of the award, the grant was among the largest ever made for curriculum development at a private university.

With an explicit emphasis on "relevance," the original intention was to create a program that would stress philosophical and ethical values in relation to career and professional pursuits—but in the eyes of the program's founders, the first courses missed the mark. Karen Segal, a former executive director of general studies at USC who was hired to develop Thematic Option, told USC's faculty/staff newsletter: "The grant was based on the idea that the demands of the late '60s had not been taken seriously enough, that there was a need to be more modern, relevant and urban. But [by 1975] there had already been a massive move in that direction and a loss of historical consciousness and declining literacy." In light of these trends and in tandem with USC's efforts to strengthen liberal arts education in the college, Segal approached the NEH program officer about a change in focus. Approval was granted, and USC overhauled the curriculum to create an honors program that didn't include "honors" in its title.

[photo courtesy of USC University Archives]

Thematic Option's centerpiece was a series of four required core courses organized around themes rather than disciplines —"Quality of Life," "Change and the Future," "Symbols and Structures" (later changed to "Symbols and Conceptual Systems") and "The Process of Change in Science"— coupled with intensive writing tutorials. By design, the course structure allowed instructors flexibility in covering material as they saw fit, so that one section on "The Process of Change in Science," for example, might examine the topic through the lens of major developments in physics, whereas another might take a sociological point of view.

Thematic Option proved enormously popular among students as well as instructors from the onset, and thanks to the advocacy of John H. "Jack"Marburger III, dean of the USC College of Letters, Arts and Sciences from 1977 to 1979, it was fully institutionalized as part of the university budget by the time the NEH grant concluded. Immortalized in the 1980s as "Traumatic Option" in a student film, the program helped lay the foundation for many subsequent improvements in the undergraduate curriculum at USC.

In February 1979, President Hubbard convened a press conference in his office and announced his plans to retire in August of the following year.
[photo courtesy of USC University Archives]

to the day after he had taken office as USC's eighth president.

Hubbard had seen the university make significant strides in terms of national standing. In 1970—and in fact as late as 1975—USC's faculty included no members of the National Academy of Sciences or the National Academy of Engineering. By 1979, it had 11, with four members newly elected that year. With respect to federal research and development funding, USC's national ranking rose from 33rd to 19th under Hubbard's watch. Many academic programs had grown in stature with the addition of modern facilities, such as John Stauffer Pharmaceutical Sciences

Center on the Health Sciences campus, which in November 1974 replaced the University Park campus headquarters in Science Hall (later renamed James H. and Marilyn E. Zumberge Hall) that had housed the USC School of Pharmacy for more than 50 years. The university's music school, too, gained a splendid new facility with the opening of Virginia Ramo Hall of Music in 1974.

The 1970s also ushered in a number of enhancements aimed at better serving the extended Trojan Family, such as an alumni travel bureau and the University Credit Union, which had enjoyed a booming business since opening its doors in 1973. Additionally, many campus facilities had been fitted with ramps and other features to provide access for people with disabilities, including a new elevator in Bovard Administration Building.

On May 15, 1980, the university hosted an open-air retirement reception for Hubbard in Alumni Memorial Park. A special *Chronicle* feature titled "Looking Back at President Jack" described the "lively speaking program," for which USC baseball coach and longtime Hubbard friend Rod Dedeaux served as emcee. Zohrab Kaprielian talked about the previous decade as having been "one of the most dynamic and productive periods in the life of the University of Southern California," while trustee Carl Hartnack praised Hubbard for his refusal to compromise on quality. On a more personal note, football coach John Robinson admitted that, "while he would miss Hubbard's familiar figure on the sidelines during Trojan football games, he thought the team might be able to fare reasonably well even without Hubbard to send in plays."

Throughout his administration, President Hubbard was a familiar figure on the sidelines during Trojan football games. [photo courtesy of USC University Archives]

University Park campus beautification took a major step forward during the Zumberge administration as the intersection of Trousdale Parkway and Childs Way was transformed into Hahn Central Plaza in preparation for the 1984 Olympics. [photo courtesy of USC University Archives]

Chapter Seven

Gaining Momentum (1980–1991)

By Annette Moore

The 15-month quest for USC's ninth chief executive was fraught with obstacles and unfolded very much in the public eye. Not only was there contention among the members of the selection committee about which candidate to choose, but the names of the first round of finalists—Richard C. Atkinson, director of the National Science Foundation (who later became president of the UC system); Thornton F. Bradshaw, president of Atlantic Richfield Company; and David P. Gardner, president of the University of Utah (who later preceded Atkinson as UC president)—also were leaked to the press. The process quickly unraveled, and both Bradshaw and Gardner ultimately withdrew. Ostensibly to plug leaks to the media, a new committee was convened in February 1980, this one headed by trustee Carl E. Hartnack (president and chairman of the board of Security Pacific Bank) and made up of only five trustees. Shrouded in secrecy, the search proceeded until May 1980, when the Board of Trustees unanimously elected James Herbert Zumberge as the ninth president of USC.

Zumberge came with impressive credentials indeed. He had been president of Southern Methodist University since 1975, and before that had served as chancellor of the University of Nebraska-Lincoln (1972–75), dean of the College of Earth Sciences at the University of Arizona (1968–72) and founding president of Grand Valley State College in Michigan (1962–68). A noted glaciologist, he was the author of a widely used geology textbook and had led two expeditions to Antarctica's Ross Ice Shelf. Throughout his tenure as president of USC, he continued to make active contributions to polar research, serving as president of the international Scientific Committee on Antarctic Research from 1982 to 1986 and as chair (on appointment by President Ronald Reagan) of the newly formed U.S. Arctic Research Commission from 1984 to 1987.

"It is the highlight of my whole career to be president of USC at the beginning of its second century," Zumberge declared in a press conference shortly following his election, adding that USC had been the

Below left: James Herbert Zumberge was formally inaugurated as USC's ninth president on May 10, 1981, in a ceremony that was the capstone of USC's 100th anniversary commemoration.

Below: President Zumberge's inauguration introduced several elements that were new to USC. A set of heraldic banners (pictured here arranged in a circle around the "Youth Triumphant" fountain) was designed for each academic unit that confers degrees. Additionally, USC adopted a cardinal robe with gold panels, a modified hood and a velvet cap for past and future recipients of USC doctoral degrees; a dark-cardinal robe with gold velvet chevrons on the sleeves for university officers; and a presidential medallion minted as a tangible symbol of the authority vested in the president.

[photos courtesy of USC University Archives]

farthest thing from his mind only six weeks before, when the selection committee first approached him.

Taking Stock of Athletics

As quickly as he had made the transition to USC, Zumberge had even less time to adjust to his new job. On the morning of his first day at the office, he was confronted by reporters asking what he intended to do about the fact that the Pacific-10 Conference had put USC—along with four other Pac-10 schools—on athletic probation. On his desk he found reports prepared by three committees that Hubbard had appointed the previous spring to look into questions about the academic performance of student athletes.

The new president wasted no time in setting to work, and in barely two months, Zumberge set a precedent of addressing issues face-on by issuing a lengthy statement about the academic conduct, advisement and counseling, and admission of student athletes at USC—making clear his expectations that USC would take a leadership role in restoring public faith in university athletic programs. The fact that USC was one of several institutions of higher learning that had come under scrutiny for rules violations in the area of intercollegiate

Mayor Tom Bradley (seated, right) chatted with President Zumberge and Carl E. Hartnack, chairman of the USC Board of Trustees, during Zumberge's inauguration ceremony. Trustee Anna Bing Arnold can be seen the background (seated, far right). [photo courtesy of USC University Archives]

athletics, he wrote, suggested that higher education may well have come to a turning point in its relationship to competitive sports. In an interview with *USC Chronicle*, he spelled out this view: "I believe USC ... has a responsibility, because it believes in the importance and validity of intercollegiate athletics within the American system of values and higher education, to assume a leadership role in the sponsorship of reform that will bring back into focus the true purposes and ideals of competitive amateur sports."

Under the new policies, all admissions decisions—including those for student athletes—were to be made strictly by the USC Office of Admissions. Additionally, academic advisement responsibility for student

Above and below: USC's ties to Los Angeles Memorial Coliseum (shown here during construction in 1922 and as it appeared in 1980) date back to the stadium's beginnings: The Trojans played in the first varsity football game ever held there on October 6, 1923, trouncing Pomona College 23–7.

[photos courtesy of Los Angeles Memorial Coliseum and the USC University Archives]

athletes was transferred from the athletics department to the academic units. The position of student athlete program director was created to created to help ensure that student athletes were making regular progress with their studies. "[W]e need to be accessible to those students who show promise and a capacity for 'making it' in this environment," Zumberge explained, "So when we make provisions for taking marginal students, we also accept the responsibility of providing them whatever special help may be needed to elevate them into our normal academic community."

Despite these decisive measures, the National Collegiate Athletic Association (NCAA) launched a follow-up inquiry in September 1981, levying further sanctions against USC related to the sale of players' tickets by an assistant football coach and excess compensation, due to clerical error, of at least two student athletes for work performed during a vacation period. Zumberge strongly denounced the penalties as excessive but was unable to prevent the NCAA from banning the Trojan football team from bowl games and live television for a period of two years. The latter was a particularly stiff penalty for the Trojans, who had enjoyed the status of being television's top-rated college team for the past decade.

USC'S CENTENNIAL

Right: Visitors flooded the University Park campus to celebrate USC's centennial in 1980.

Far right: USC's 100th anniversary party featured a 100-foot-long birthday cake.

[photos courtesy of USC University Archives]

While Zumberge was attending to pressing policy and administrative matters during his first year as USC president, plans for the university's centennial were shifting into high gear. The celebration had its official launch with a five-day "Super Weekend" in November 1980, although concerts, a guest lecture series based on a "frontiers" theme and other anniversary-related events punctuated the entire 1980–81 academic year. "Super Weekend" festivities ranged from academic programs to a homecoming parade, exhibits, guided tours and the joint effort of actor and alumnus Michael Landon and USC Homecoming chairman Barbara Galpin in cutting a 100-foot-long birthday cake—all leading up to the Trojans' victory over Arizona State.

USC's centenary also saw publication of *The Trojan Gallery*, a beautiful "coffee-table" book that was the culmination of an effort initiated in 1976 to create a comprehensive pictorial history of the university's first 10 decades.

Zumberge's inauguration on May 10, 1981—part of a three-week academic festival that included a colloquium on the university's role in the community as well as a speech by Coretta Scott King—marked the capstone of the yearlong affair.

"USC is not a 'me too' university," USC's ninth president declared in his inaugural address. "Its characteristics do not derive from trying to emulate some prestigious institution. USC has reached its present state by seeking its own destiny, by charting its own course and by blazing its own trail." In closing, he likened the university's quest for excellence to an ascent toward a mountain summit. "… [L]et us now close the celebration of our 100th anniversary," he said. "It is time to shoulder our packs and move on toward the destiny that beckons us."

Paul E. Hadley, who had joined USC in 1945, was instrumental in developing the concept of a comprehensive program in comparative literature at USC, created the university's program in Latin American studies and founded the USC College of Continuing Education. He directed USC's Emeriti Center—which was founded by President Hubbard in 1978—from 1996 to 2001, and headed the Emeriti College (a community outreach component of the Emeriti Center) from 1990 to 1998. [photo courtesy of USC University Archives]

Hardships notwithstanding, USC emerged from the crisis with an elevated standing on the national athletic scene. Thanks to his forthright communication—not to mention a subsequent trip to Washington, D.C., to take part in an American Council for Education committee that reviewed academic admission standards for athletes—Zumberge helped create a platform for reforms in college athletic programs not just at USC, but nationwide.

At the same time Zumberge was dealing with the contentious issue of Pac-10 and NCAA sanctions, another football controversy was brewing at USC. In response to the plan to move the Oakland Raiders into Los Angeles Memorial Coliseum in 1982, a heated debate broke out over proposed alterations to the historic stadium— in particular, the Raiders' desire to tear out existing seats and construct luxury suites, resulting in a considerable net loss of seating overall. At the height of the dispute, UCLA (which had played at the Coliseum since 1933) made a decision to relocate to the Rose Bowl in Pasadena. For a while USC, too, pondered a move to a new venue, but instead fought valiantly to retain its fabled home. After a three-year stalemate centered on issues spanning seating, advertising, rent and NCAA rules prohibiting

financial contacts between professional and amateur teams, the university signed an unprecedented 11-year lease with the Coliseum Commission in May 1983—an agreement that was reached in great part thanks to the negotiation skills of Zumberge-appointed athletic director Mike McGee and vice president for business affairs Anthony D. "Tony" Lazzaro.

Administrative and Financial Reforms

A second order of business demanding immediate attention during Zumberge's first months in office was a series of administrative reforms, including the reorganization of USC's upper-level management. The discord evidenced in the search process leading up to Zumberge's appointment was symptomatic of a rift in the university's top administration following a period of what one USC publication characterized as "rapid and often divisive growth." University officers were at loggerheads, divided into factions clustered primarily around executive vice president Zohrab A. Kaprielian and Thomas P. Nickell Jr., vice president for university relations, who had helped steer USC's fundraising efforts for some 30 years.

On Monday morning following the 1980 Thanksgiving recess,

Zumberge announced the creation of the USC Office of the President. The new office consisted of the president and three new senior vice presidents —for academic affairs, administration, and development and university relations. As part of this restructuring, which was endorsed by the USC Board of Trustees, the positions of executive vice president, vice president for academic affairs and vice president for university relations were eliminated. Kaprielian, while retaining his status as engineering dean, would no longer hold a universitywide position; Nickell revealed that he would be leaving the university at the conclusion of the academic year; and Paul E. Hadley, vice president for academic affairs, was planning to retire. Rather than considering internal candidates, Zumberge decided to look outside the university in selecting individuals to fill the three new senior vice presidencies because, as he told the *Los Angeles Times*, "renewal at the administrative level is just as important as renewal on the faculty."

The first of the three positions was filled when Jon C. Strauss, former vice president for budget and finance at the University of Pennsylvania, joined USC as senior vice president for administration in May 1981. The following July, Cornelius J. "Neal" Pings, who had served as vice provost

and dean of graduate studies at Caltech since 1970, was appointed senior vice president for academic affairs. The additional title of provost was added in 1982, reflecting Pings's dual role as what *USC Trojan Family* termed "both intellectual leader and administrator." Around this same time, Robert P. Biller, former dean of USC's School of Public Administration, was named to the newly created role of vice provost, responsible for planning, budgetary policy, curriculum review and personnel policy.

The third senior vice presidency was filled only after a couple of false starts. Initially, Zumberge brought in Michael Radock, whose previous performance at the University of Michigan had earned him a reputation as one of the top educational fundraisers in the United States. Stellar qualifications notwithstanding, Radock proved not a good fit for USC. Then, in an unexpected move following Radock's resignation, Zumberge appointed John Robinson, USC's beloved head football coach since 1976, to the post. In making the announcement, Zumberge told *USC Trojan Family* magazine: "John Robinson has all the attributes we were seeking in a new senior vice president. He is well known and respected by alumni, students, faculty and staff. In this

Above: Thomas P. Nickell Jr., who left USC in 1981, had joined the university's development office during the Fagg administration. He played a key role in the success of the Master Plan as well as the Toward Century II campaign, and he also was instrumental in forming the USC Associates, developing the concept of support groups and helping the schools more effectively involve their alumni in raising funds. Known as the "father of modern fundraising at USC," Nickell changed the way fundraising was done at USC, and perhaps even in higher education overall. [photo courtesy of USC University Archives]

Below: As senior vice president for administration from 1981 to 1985, Jon C. Strauss helped put in place a decentralized system of financial management at USC. [photo by Irene Fertik, courtesy of USC University Archives]

community and throughout the country, he has an unquestioned identification with USC. ... He is stepping from his role as coach into an assignment as a leader and interpreter of the broader life of the university." If the Trojan Family was surprised when Robinson took the job in November 1982, it was heartbroken when he left two and a half months later to become head coach of the Los Angeles Rams. Fortunately, however, the third time proved to be the charm when, in 1983, Zumberge announced that Roger F. Olson—a 23-year veteran of development work at USC whose fundraising experience spanned both

the Master Plan and Toward Century II—would return to the university to help guide the planning process for USC's next major capital campaign.

Another far-reaching administrative reform that Zumberge implemented during his first year as USC president was a restructuring of the academic calendar. With the goal of making more efficient use of time and facilities, all university classes now were scheduled to begin on the hour. Additionally, the semester structure was reconfigured so that the fall term would end before the winter break, and the spring term after the second week in May.

To improve services for students and provide more timely responses to student requests, Zumberge also reorganized Student Administrative Services at USC and created the position of dean of admissions and financial aid.

While all of these reforms were under way, Zumberge became all too aware that USC was facing an ever-tightening budget crunch. The title of an article published in USC's faculty/staff newsletter in March 1981 said it all: "University's Budget: The Frill is Gone." True to form, Zumberge acted decisively and transparently, issuing a comprehensive report—replete with

By 1986, President Zumberge's top administrative team was composed of (from left) senior vice president for administration Lyn Hutton, provost and senior vice president for academic affairs Cornelius J. "Neal" Pings, James Zumberge, senior vice president for university relations Roger F. Olson and senior vice president for business affairs Anthony D. "Tony" Lazzaro.
[photo by Lois Gervais, courtesy of USC University Archives]

charts and graphs—laying out the fiscal state of the university. "The problem is that our resources and our expenditures are diverging at an increasing rate," he wrote. Just as in the preceding decade, recession, inflation, federal deficits, soaring oil prices, dwindling government support of university-based research and student aid, rising costs and a shrinking pool of college-age students all contributed to a bleak financial forecast for the 1980s. USC had just undergone its third midyear budget cut in three years, and Zumberge solicited the "wit and wile" of the entire university community in judiciously planning where future reductions would be made. Additionally, supplementing the work of groups such as the Committee on the Use of Classroom Space and the Energy Task Force, he created the Task Force on Budget Incentives to develop "a system in which there are positive benefits to accomplishing budget reductions."

Based on the work of this latter task force—and in acknowledgment of the complexity of the university as an organization—Zumberge and senior vice president for administration Jon Strauss oversaw the implementation of a new, decentralized system for financial administration. Known as revenue center management, the system was in operation by July 1982,

placing financial authority in the hands of deans and directors by allocating revenues and expenditures to individual academic and auxiliary units (the revenue centers). "The schools, which have always been vested with academic authority, would now be vested with fiscal responsibility as well," wrote John Curry, then executive director of the university budget, in the task force report.

Equally significant for USC's long-term fiscal management, under Zumberge's leadership USC merged its

John Robinson (right) coached USC's football team from 1976 to 1982, when President Zumberge appointed him senior vice president for development and university relations—a position he held for only two and one-half months before leaving to coach the Los Angeles Rams. Robinson returned to USC for a second stint as head football coach from 1993 to 1997. He is pictured here in fall 1980 with tailback Marcus Allen, who went on to become USC's fourth Heisman Trophy winner in 1981.
[photo courtesy of USC University Archives]

USC AND THE OLYMPICS

Dating from 1904, USC's Olympic history includes a star-studded roster of athletes who have attended USC before, during or after their Olympic appearance, but Troy's Olympic legacy encompasses much more than competition alone. When the Xth Olympiad came to Los Angeles in 1932, USC first lady Elisabeth von KleinSmid was appointed to the executive board of the international hostess committee, and Trojan athletic director (then called graduate manager) Gwynn Wilson served as associate manager of the Olympic games.

USC's participation in the 1984 Olympics—which included hosting the swimming and diving competitions as well as serving as the city's largest Olympic Village—was literally years in the works. During the late 1970s, the university passed a resolution to cooperate in attracting the games to Los Angeles, and USC's own John Argue (LL.B. 1956) was widely regarded as the person responsible for making that happen. In 1979, newly apponted Olympics general manager Peter Ueberroth named Gwynn Wilson to his "kitchen cabinet," and from then on, Olympic fervor gradually heated up to fever pitch. The McDonald's

Corporation announced in 1980 that it would build a pool facility on the University Park campus, and campus beautification efforts began in earnest around that same time. Also in anticipation of the games, USC's 1983 Homecoming festivities drew more than 120 of the university's 180 living Olympians to Los Angeles Memorial Coliseum for "A Salute to USC Olympians" under a dazzling display of fireworks and stars.

As a member of the Board of Directors for the Los Angeles Olympic Organizing Committee (LAOOC), President Zumberge played an instrumental role in planning for the games. Additionally, based in part on the tremendous mutual admiration that existed between Zumberge and UCLA chancellor Charles E. "Chuck" Young, USC worked closely with its cross-town rival, which served as Los Angeles' other Olympic Village, building a strong relationship off the field that would endure for years to come.

Zumberge appointed Anthony Lazzaro as USC's chief liaison officer with the LAOOC, charging him with the thorny task of ensuring that USC would still be able to function as a university even while handing over all of its dormitories and many other facilities to the committee. "They [the LAOOC] wanted a fence around the entire campus, and I told them we couldn't do that," Lazzaro recalled. "They wanted Doheny Memorial Library to go out of circulation. Under no circumstances could the Olympic Organizing Committee fail, but under no circumstances could we, either."

Thanks in great part to Lazzaro's efforts, USC continued to fulfill its academic mission throughout the Olympics. What's more, Lazzaro personally negotiated agreements with the LAOOC totaling some $19 million in reimbursement for direct expenses incurred in connection with hosting the Olympic Village. "More than any other," president Zumberge observed, "Anthony Lazzaro deserves the credit for the success of USC's involvement with the Olympics."

And that success was unqualified. U.S. President Ronald Reagan took up residence in Lazzaro's office before officiating at the opening ceremonies, and USC welcomed record-breaking crowds to a campus that had undergone a stunning transformation as the asphalt and curbs of residual city streets gave way to pedestrian malls, fountains, benches, trees and flowerbeds.

Equally remarkable, the 31 Trojan alumni and students who participated in the 1984 Olympics brought home 24 medals, bringing the total number of USC Olympians since 1904 to 240, and the total number of medals claimed by USC Olympic athletes to 161. As of the Athens Olympics in summer 2004, those tallies had risen to 361 athletes and 234 medals.

Opposite left: Looking ahead to the summer Olympics in 1984, USC's 1983 Homecoming celebration included "A Salute to USC Olympians."

Opposite right: USC's Olympic-themed 1983 Homecoming lit up the Coliseum with a fireworks display.

Above left: Alumnus John C. Argue led the successful bid that eventually brought the 1984 Olympics to Los Angeles. He was elected to the USC Board of Trustees in 1984 and served as its chairman from 2000 until his death in 2002.

[above photos courtesy of USC University Archives]

Above center: On opening day of the 1984 Olympics, U.S. President Ronald Reagan turned down an offer of temporary space in Bovard Administration Building, opting instead to take up office in Anthony Lazzaro's suite in Owens Hall. Reagan (second from left) is shown here shaking hands with Lazzaro, while first lady Nancy Reagan and USC President Zumberge look on. [official White House photo, courtesy of Anthony Lazzaro]

Above right: When the Olympics arrived in summer 1984, the University Park campus had been transformed into Los Angeles' largest Olympic Village. [photo courtesy of USC University Archives]

Above: As assiduously as President Zumberge strived to elevate USC's academic stature, he and his wife, Marilyn—pictured here in the living room of the Seeley G. Mudd Estate in 1986—saw to it that the extended Trojan Family enjoyed a warm welcome at the university's presidential residence. In great part thanks to Mrs. Zumberge's gracious style of entertaining, the Mudd Estate became a hugely popular venue for university events throughout the Zumberge administration.

Right: Albert S. Raubenheimer, affectionately known as "Raubie," came to USC in 1923 as a teacher and later played a key role in the development of Doheny Memorial Library as well as USC's music school. He served as dean of the College of Liberal Arts (renamed the College of Letters, Arts and Sciences during his tenure) from 1937 to 1947, and as vice president for academic affairs from 1948 until his retirement in 1960. The Raubenheimer Music Faculty Memorial Building was named in his honor in 1980, and that same year USC established the Albert S. Raubenheimer Distinguished Faculty Award to salute college faculty members who "make a difference in the lives of USC students" through outstanding teaching, scholarship and service.

[photos courtesy of USC University Archives]

various endowed funds into a central endowment pool and diversified its investments, generating much greater opportunity for endowment growth.

Despite all of these cautionary measures, Provost Pings announced the need for staff reductions in spring 1982 to achieve a balanced budget. Several administrative offices were closed or reorganized, and schools and other revenue centers were called upon to increase tuition, boost enrollment and step up development efforts to help close the budget gap.

Strategic Excellence: An Academic Plan

Parallel to the management initiatives, at the core of USC's advancement during the Zumberge administration was an academic plan developed by deans and faculty members in the early 1980s. The planning process, intended to generate an academic blueprint for the decade ahead, identified four major priorities. At the top of the list was strengthening undergraduate education, followed by the enhancement of key doctoral programs and related research, expansion of the professional schools and health sciences initiatives, and improvement of relations between USC and its neighbors.

In the realm of undergraduate

education, the university implemented a full-need financial aid policy for all undergraduates in 1982–83, and funds were raised to support 300 endowed scholarships and fellowships. "We intend this policy to be a sign of USC's continuing commitment to provide an educational opportunity for high-quality students regardless of their financial means," Zumberge said.

Budget allocations were adjusted to give precedence to academic units with large undergraduate enrollments, and professional schools received incentives for developing relevant and challenging general education courses. USC also launched a pilot program of credit/no credit courses called the Freshman Seminars in fall 1986. "We want to ... [offer] freshmen the opportunity to study

something really exciting to the person teaching it, something at the research boundary, to study it in close connection with the teacher and with other students, and to study it because it interests them, as opposed to grade-grubbing," said Sylvia Manning, a former executive vice provost at USC who was instrumental in

establishing the Freshman Seminars. The program proved so successful that it was still a prominent feature of USC's undergraduate curriculum as the university observed its 125th anniversary in 2005.

Extending the learning environment outside the classroom, the McDonald's Olympic Swim Stadium, a legacy from the 1984 Olympics, and the General William Lyon University Center provided USC students with much-needed recreational facilities; and the new University Bookstore, opened in July 1989, offered one of the largest collections of trade journals and texts in Los Angeles. In addition, a faculty fellows program brought professors and students together in USC's residence halls.

USC initiated a number of measures to support faculty in their teaching efforts as well. Launched in

1985, the Fund for Innovative Teaching (later known as the Fund for Innovative Undergraduate Teaching) awarded special grants to help instructors improve their undergraduate courses. Likewise, the Center for Scholarly Technology was created in 1988 to assist faculty members and other academic staff in enhancing teaching and learning through the use of digital and communications technology in USC's classrooms and libraries.

"We often say that it is the quality of undergraduate education at an independent institution which distinguishes it from that available at public universities," Zumberge said in his 1985 state-of-the-university address. "If that is true, how do we ensure that that distinction is a real one? How do we do a better job of educating and of helping young

Above left: USC's new bookstore debuted in 1989, offering a substantial increase in reference, reading and technical book selections as well as an expanded gift and clothing store. The facility was named Pertusati University Bookstore in 1993, in appreciation of a gift from Joseph Pertusati (class of 1930).

Above right: The Trojan warrior, Ronald McDonald and Sam the Eagle (official mascot of the 1984 Olympics in Los Angeles) joined USC swimmers to celebrate the addition of McDonald's Olympic Swim Stadium to the University Park campus in 1983. After serving as the site of the swimming and diving competitions during the 1984 Olympic games, the stadium became the home facility for USC's swimming, diving and water polo teams.

[photos courtesy of USC University Archives]

people become thoughtful, thinking and productive adults?"

To answer this question, Zumberge raised the bar on the academic plan's mandate to improve undergraduate education by establishing a special President's Commission on Undergraduate Education (CUE) composed of faculty, administrators, students and alumni. "A solid undergraduate program is … fundamental to USC's ascent to the top echelon of schools," confirmed Lawrence A. Singer, commission chair. In 1990, after two years of work, the commission issued a voluminous report—touching on topics ranging from walkway lighting to on-campus residential colleges and required courses in cultural diversity—that would inform USC's undergraduate programming well into the 1990s. Among the CUE recommendations acted on during Zumberge's tenure was the creation of the USC Center for Excellence in Teaching, which was founded to provide awards for out-standing teaching by faculty members and teaching assistants.

In implementing these measures to improve undergraduate programs, the university also moved increasingly toward putting the College of Letters, Arts and Sciences at the conceptual center of the institution. As many historians and longtime administrators agree, USC had come into prominence as a group of fine professional schools clustered around a college—a liberal arts core—that traditionally didn't receive a lot of attention. With mounting intensity as the decade of the 1980s progressed, there was a growing consensus among the university's deans and other academic leaders that first-rate universities needed to have first-rate colleges, and that USC, therefore, needed to make a significant investment in its college.

With respect to the second priority identified in the academic

Chemistry professor Lawrence A. Singer, chair of the President's Commission on Undergraduate Education, was also responsible for organizing USC's Chemistry Club and chemistry honors pro-gram. He later became director of the USC Postbaccalaureate Premedical Program, which was founded in the late 1990s to help post-baccalaureate students complete the core science and mathematics requirements for admission to medical school.
[photo courtesy of USC University Archives]

plan, USC's doctoral education and research programs grew in stature in the 1980s thanks to the advancement of several path-breaking interdisciplinary initiatives. In fall 1982, the Neurological, Informational and Behavioral Sciences program (later known as NIBS, and eventually reorganized as the Neuroscience Research Institute in 2005) began training graduate students in neurobiology, offering a unique melding of biology and neurology with computer science, engineering, gerontology, linguistics, mathematics, psychology and other disciplines to explore the frontiers of the brain and central nervous system.

The USC Center for Photonic Technology, established in 1985, helped steer the university's engineering programs into a new, non-defense-related direction. By the end of the decade, USC had emerged as one of the country's premier centers for photonics research, which uses photons—or light—just as electronics uses electrons as the medium for transmitting and processing information.

Another innovation that gave USC's graduate and research programs a considerable boost during Zumberge's tenure was the designation of funds contributed by the W. M. Keck Foundation to endow several

chairs and fellowships that were administered by the USC Office of the Provost—adding flexibility and muscle to the university's efforts to recruit and retain distinguished scholars and promising graduate students in a range of scientific fields. Additionally, the Faculty Research and Innovation Fund, inaugurated in 1983–84, provided a formal mechanism for fostering investigations by junior faculty members. The fund also supported new directions in research by established faculty and provided seed money for ground-breaking initiatives that might have difficulty attracting funds from external sources. Zumberge said in announcing

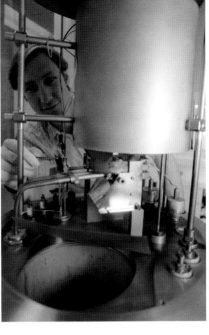

Above left: A pioneer in processing seismic data, inferring Earth's inner structure and measuring earthquake sizes, geophysicist Keiiti "Kei" Aki joined USC's faculty in 1984 and became founding director of the Southern California Earthquake Center in 1991.

Above right: Headed by P. Daniel Dapkus, USC's Center for Photonic Technology was designated by the Defense Advanced Research Projects Agency (DARPA) as a national center during the Zumberge administration, bringing together researchers from USC, Columbia, MIT, Princeton and UCLA.

[photos courtesy of USC University Archives]

Far left: In June 1987, National Medical Enterprises chairman Richard Eamer (left, class of 1955, LL.B. 1959) and President Zumberge took a ride on a bulldozer at the groundbreaking ceremony for USC University Hospital. [photo by Richard Miller, courtesy of USC Health Sciences Campus Public Relations and Marketing]

Left: The two central structures of USC's Cinema-Television Complex, dedicated in 1984, were the George Lucas Instructional Building (encompassing the Johnny Carson Television Stage and Harold Lloyd Motion Picture Scoring Stage) and the Marcia Lucas Post Production Building (including the Steven Spielberg Music Scoring Stage). [photo courtesy of USC University Archives]

the creation of the fund: "This is the first time in the history of USC that the university has established a fund in support of scholarly activities of the faculty. It is my intent that this fund become a permanent part of the university scene." In fact the fund was institutionalized at USC, and it was later renamed in Zumberge's honor.

Significant progress in advancing the third strategic priority—expansion of USC's professional schools and health sciences programs—was made with the 1984 dedication of USC's Cinema-Television Complex, funded by gifts from celebrities such as George Lucas, Steven Spielberg and

Johnny Carson. Likewise, the USC School of Urban and Regional Planning, which celebrated its tenth anniversary in 1984, entered a period of significant growth with the formation of the USC Lusk Center for Real Estate and the receipt of a major gift from Ralph and Goldy Lewis that would provide the school with a permanent, high-tech home in 1999.

On the health sciences front, USC launched a new Department of Nursing, in partnership with California Hospital Medical Center, that welcomed its first students in September 1982. (Primarily due to financial concerns, the school was closed in

2004.) Spearheaded by Joseph Van Der Meulen, vice president for health affairs, a medical faculty practice plan was approved by the USC Board of Trustees on June 1, 1983, enabling the university's faculty physicians to generate income over and above their salaries by seeing private patients. The practice plan also paved the way for a university-operated hospital, and soon the USC Health Sciences campus nearly doubled in size with the acquisition of land and existing buildings from Los Angeles County. Ground was broken for the Richard K. Eamer Medical Plaza, a cooperative project of USC and National Medical Enterprises, in 1987. With the creation of the Institute for Molecular Medicine (later called the Institute for Genetic Medicine) in 1988, and the recruitment of acclaimed researcher Laurence H. Kedes to direct the new program, USC began to position itself as a leader in the burgeoning field of biotechnology. In 1989, USC became the first university in the world to offer a doctorate in occupational science. By time Zumberge left office, the university also was in the final stages of fundraising for a major building addition to the USC Kenneth Norris Jr. Cancer Hospital and Research Institute (part of the USC/Norris Comprehensive Cancer Center and

USC'S NEIGHBOR TO THE NORTH: HEBREW UNION COLLEGE

Taking part in Hebrew Union College-Jewish Institute of Religion's 1987 commencement ceremonies were (from left) HUC-JIR executive vice president Uri Herscher, USC president James Zumberge and HUC-JIR president Alfred Gottschalk. [photo courtesy of USC University Archives]

The United States' first Jewish institution of higher learning, Hebrew Union College (HUC) was established in Cincinnati in 1875—five years before USC's founding—by Rabbi Isaac Mayer Wise. In 1954, it affiliated with the Jewish Institute of Religion in New York, which had been established in 1922 by Rabbi Stephen S. Wise, and in 1954, a Los Angeles branch was founded in the Hollywood Hills to serve Southern California's growing Jewish community. The college opened a fourth campus in Jerusalem in 1963.

Growing out of a friendship among USC president Norman Topping, HUC president Nelson Glueck and HUC Los Angeles branch dean Alfred Gottschalk in the 1960s, a decision was made to relocate HUC's Los Angeles branch to a site near the USC campus as part of the Hoover Redevelopment Project. The new facility opened in 1971.

Over the years, based on a shared understanding that was only later formalized in writing, the two institutions introduced a variety of cooperative academic ventures, including a joint doctoral degree in religion and social ethics with a concentration in Judaic ethics, arrangements whereby USC undergraduates could take HUC courses to fulfill general education requirements or lead toward a specialization in Judaic studies, and dual-degree programs between HUC's School of Jewish Communal Service and USC's schools of social work, public administration and gerontology.

Even with all of these cooperative efforts under way, it wasn't until 1989 that a formal memorandum of understanding was forged between the two institutions. By that time, Uri Herscher, HUC executive vice president and dean of faculty, estimated that HUC was attracting some 500 USC students each year. As of 2005, more than 600 USC undergraduates—including a substantial number who were not Jews—were taking courses through HUC and the USC School of Religion.

Above: In 1976, Robert P. Biller left a post at UC Berkeley to return to USC, his alma mater, as head of public administration. He was appointed vice provost in 1982 and went on to serve in a broad array of administrative capacities at the university, including vice president for external affairs. In the early 1980s, he played a key role in conceptualizing USC's highest honor, the Presidential Medallion—an award he was to win in 1998.

Above right: USC's annual Academic Honors Convocation had its origins in a special centennial faculty convocation held in October 1980. "This ceremony is a symbol of the debt we owe to those who have contributed to the first 100 years of academic achievement at USC," said President Zumberge at the event. Among the honorees were (from left) Anton Burg, J. Paul Guilford, Harold von Hofe, Morris M. Mautner, Robert Vivian, Hugh Edmondson, Halsey Stevens and Arlien Johnson.

[photos courtesy of USC University Archives]

Hospital), which had opened in 1983.

Providing a forum for celebrating the university's burgeoning research and educational prowess, the Academic Honors Convocation was instituted in 1982 to recognize faculty, staff and students for outstanding service and scholarly achievements. As Pings told a university reporter, "It is a wonderful opportunity to honor the excellence that is in our midst and remind ourselves about the noble mission of our institution of higher learning."

In a similar vein, Zumberge established a new university award, the Presidential Medallion, to recognize "achievement of the highest distinction on the part of a member of the campus community, or an outside friend of the university." Zohrab Kaprielian and internationally known cancer researcher Charles Heidelberger were named as the first recipients of the award—both posthumously—at the Academic Honors Convocation in 1983.

Over the years, USC reaped tangible rewards from Zumberge's firm adherence to the academic plan. By the end of the decade, USC ranked 19th among all colleges and universities in terms of federal research and development funding, and had enjoyed a doubling of sponsored research activity in the 1980s alone.

Forging Stronger Community Connections

The fourth priority identified in the academic plan of the 1980s was community relations, reflecting Zumberge's oft-stated contention that the quality of the academic experience on campus was in direct proportion to the quality of life surrounding that experience. Accordingly, the university invested considerable energy and resources into building bridges between itself and its neighbors.

In October 1982, the Community Consortium, composed of representatives from local neighborhood organizations as well as university offices involved in community relations, approved its constitution and its mission of fostering teamwork and communication to more fully control the destiny of the Hoover-Exposition area. "It will make for better understanding and cooperation," Thomas Kilgore, then director of USC's Office of Special Community Affairs, said about the new group. "We're no longer talking about 'we' and 'they.' It's 'us.'"

The following year, in 1983, Zumberge appointed a Task Force on the University Community, with the immediate charge of helping frame a university response to the current phase of urban renewal in the USC-

Exposition Park area and the longer-range goal of analyzing ongoing issues affecting the university and the community. Chaired by university chaplain Alvin Rudisill, the task force submitted its report in January 1984, urging the appointment of a highly placed administrator whose primary responsibility would be the coordination of community relations and services. Based on this recommendation, the USC Office of Civic and Community Relations was created, with Rudisill serving as its director. By this time, Kilgore had announced plans to retire at the end of the academic year, and the functions of the USC Office of Special Community

Alvin S. Rudisill, a recognized authority on the role of churches in urban society, served as USC's university chaplain from 1969 to 1994. In 1983, he headed President Zumberge's Task Force on the University Community, whose report provided the basis for the creation of the USC Office of Civic and Community Relations. [photo courtesy of USC University Archives]

Affairs, which he directed, were incorporated into this new office.

"The university has had a very fragmented connection with the community," Zumberge said in announcing the creation of the new unit. "We are now consolidating everything into one office to bring consistency and continuity to our relationship with the neighborhood, and I think that's an important step. The new office at last will give the university the opportunity to speak with one voice to all of the diverse interests that comprise our surrounding community."

Based on another recommendation of the Task Force on the University Community, Zumberge created the USC Community Advisory Council in 1985. Bringing to the table diverse leaders and other representatives from USC's neighborhoods, the council had the original mission of advising the USC Office of the President and the Office of Civic and Community Relations regarding how best to promote neighborhood revitalization and improvement. This group—still in operation in 2005—was instrumental in obtaining a landmark planning grant from the Ford Foundation to foster the economic development of USC's surrounding community.

Additional strategies for cultivating stronger university-community relations during the Zumberge era included a for-profit Real Estate Development Corporation that had the goal of developing property around the university's two campuses for faculty housing and commercial use. It was this corporation that was responsible for acquiring, relocating and renovating the Forthmann House (the sixth-oldest house in Los Angeles, later dubbed USC Community House), which provided a home for a number of USC's community-oriented programs. In 1987, in a move that Zumberge called "yet another indication of USC's 107-year commitment to the development of Los Angeles," the university purchased the historic Embassy Hotel in downtown

EMBASSY RESIDENTIAL COLLEGE

University of Southern California

Above right: In 1987, USC purchased the storied Embassy Hotel in downtown Los Angeles and converted it into the Embassy Residential College. USC's first residential college, the facility provided opportunities for students to benefit from a "live-work-study" setting with faculty members.

Left: In November 1988, the Forthmann House—the sixth-oldest house in Los Angeles—was moved to the intersection of Hoover and 28th streets. Later named USC Community House, it served as a home for various USC departments until 1999, when the Office of Civic and Community Relations took up residence in the historic structure.

[photos courtesy of USC University Archives]

THE "USC SEVEN"

Outraged by stories of Russian Jews who, upon application to emigrate, had been stripped of their earned academic degrees, dismissed from their appointments, denied access to libraries and forced to remain in the USSR under conditions of social and economic ostracism, a group of USC faculty members joined forces in 1982 to investigate the plight of Jewish scientists in the Soviet Union. In an effort spearheaded by USC professors Michael Melnick and Cedric Minkin —in consultation with Rabbi Laura Geller, then director of Hillel at USC; electrical engineering professor Solomon Golomb; and mathematics professor Mark Kac, co-chairman of the New York-based Committee of Concerned Scientists and himself a Polish émigré—the group identified seven distinguished *refusenik* scholars whose human rights and academic freedoms had been blatantly denied. Enlisting the support of Irwin C. "Chet" Lieb, who was vice president and dean of the USC College of Letters, Arts and Sciences at the time, Melnick and Minkin then began consulting with university departments to determine whether, in the event of openings, these scientists' qualifications met the normal criteria for faculty appointments. Based on these meetings, in February 1983, USC was prepared to offer one- or two-year visiting professorships for all seven, and Melnick and Lieb flew to Moscow to deliver the invitations.

Although other American institutions, notably the University of Wisconsin and Rutgers University, had taken action in support of Jewish *refusenik* scientists, USC was the first to offer

Of the seven Soviet *refusenik* scientists offered positions at USC, two—Semion Katz (left) and Victor Kipnis—eventually joined the university faculty.
[photo courtesy of USC University Archives]

them faculty positions. Even if the scholars were not permitted to leave the Soviet Union to accept their USC appointments, the hope was that this public acknowledgment of their situations would help shield them from imprisonment and other severe forms of harassment.

In fact, two of the *refuseniks* eventually did accept their offers from USC. The first to arrive was Victor Kipnis, an expert in applied mathematical statistics and econometrics who joined the USC faculty in 1986 as a visiting professor of economics. Kipnis described the beginning of his odyssey in an interview for *USC Transcript*:

I was very much surprised [when] Michael Melnick called me [in 1983]. "It's a friend," he said. "May we see you?" They speak English to you, so you trust them—sometimes. You never may be sure if that's not some trick of the KGB. But as soon as I saw Michael Melnick, I knew he could not be a trick—and Doctor Lieb as well. I remember him wearing this very, very thin coat, and [this] unproper hat for Russian winter, and these business shoes with very thin soles. I was sure they [were] not KGB men.

The following year, renowned Soviet geophysicist Semion Katz began a two-year appointment as a visiting professor of geological sciences at the university.

By 1988, partly as a result of USC's efforts, six of the so-called "USC seven" had been granted exit permits. After serving time in jail for "anti-Soviet agitation," the seventh *refusenik* eventually was allowed to leave the Soviet Union as well.

Sherry P. May served as dean of the USC College of Continuing Education from 1983 to 1986.
[photo courtesy of USC University Archives]

Los Angeles, creating USC's first residential college. (After being closed for reinforcement of masonry following the 1994 Northridge earthquake, Embassy Residential College was never reopened, and the university sold the building in 1998.)

Yet another benchmark project in USC's community outreach effort had its origin in 1989, when USC vice provosts Sylvia Manning and Barbara Solomon drafted a proposal to create the USC Neighborhood Academic Initiative (NAI). With the goal of increasing USC's enrollment of low-income, underrepresented youths from families residing in neighborhoods contiguous to campus, the NAI used public, private and corporate resources to provide educational enrichment programs and social services aimed at helping seventh- and eighth-grade students acquire the skills they need to achieve academic success. The program, which expanded considerably in subsequent years, accepted its first students in 1991 and saw its first scholars take diplomas in spring 1997.

Streamlining

In concert with its execution of the academic plan, the Zumberge administration introduced the notion of strategic excellence as a guiding principle for the development of academic initiatives as well as for the reorganization and elimination of others. "In adhering to this concept," Zumberge wrote in his *Review of the Decade, 1980–1990*, "… the university concedes that it cannot do all things well, admits that it should not do some things at all, and acknowledges the necessity of choosing to do those things which enhance the university's competitive advantage in the academic marketplace."

Among the academic units targeted in this streamlining effort was the USC College of Continuing Education. Beginning as early as 1982, selected for-credit courses that previously had been overseen by the College of Continuing Education were moved into the USC College of Letters, Arts and Sciences. Eventually the entire program was disbanded, and responsibility for extended education was transferred to the individual professional schools.

In 1985, an *ad hoc* university review committee was convened to examine the status of USC's Institute for Safety and Systems Management

In fall 1986, President Zumberge announced a new fundraising effort—the Campaign for the University of Southern California. [photo and image courtesy of USC University Archives]

(ISSM), which had been founded in the 1950s when the U.S. Air Force approached USC with a request to provide courses in aircraft safety and systems management at military bases. From these humble beginnings, the institute had grown into one of the world's largest, most distin- guished distributed programs of graduate education, offering classes at locations ranging from Belgium, Holland and West Germany to Japan, Korea and the Philippines. Based on the committee's recommendations, ISSM's off-campus programs were transferred to the University of Denver, which managed them until financial difficulties forced their closure between 1990 and 1992. The entire institute was dissolved during the 1996–97 academic year.

Another program that was phased out as USC tightened its priorities during the mid-1980s was the USC School of Library and Information Management. The decision to close the school, according to Pings, was financial in nature, based on declin- ing enrollments and low levels of research funding.

Financial woes were also at the heart of USC's decision to sever ties with its Idyllwild campus in 1983. Nestled among the San Jacinto Mountains about 150 miles from University Park, the 200-acre fine arts

campus was founded in 1950 by USC music faculty members Max and Bee Krone. Under an agreement reached in 1964, the financially troubled campus had been deeded to USC, and the university had been operat- ing the Idyllwild School of Music and the Arts (ISOMATA)—at considerable cost—ever since. In the end, John Gordon, then dean of fine arts at USC, announced that a decision had been made to discontinue the relationship and invest available resources in the University Park campus.

Additional academic initiatives that were canceled under Zumberge's watch included the Master of Liberal Arts Program, the History Media Institute and the Speech Science and Technology Program in the USC College of Letters, Arts and Sciences.

Further streamlining was accom- plished through reorganization rather than elimination of programs. In a move that gave more autonomy to the university's programs in cinema- television, music and drama, for example, the USC School of Per- forming Arts was phased out as an organizational unit in 1983.

The Campaign for USC

Beyond the successes engendered by strategic program-building and fiscal belt-tightening, one of

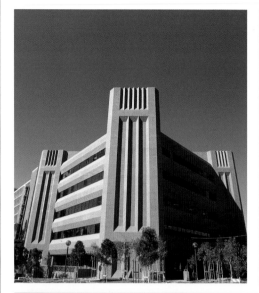

Above left: Opened in 1989, the Hedco Neurosciences Building was designed to foster interaction among faculty in USC's Neural, Informational and Behavioral Sciences (NIBS) program.

Above right: Plans for the Hughes Aircraft Electrical Engineering Center were developed in close consultation with high-technology industries.

Above: By the time the Campaign for the University of Southern California concluded in June 1990, the drive had gone on record as USC's most successful to date, bringing in $641,574,718.

[photos courtesy of USC University Archives]

Zumberge's crowning achievements was the Campaign for the University of Southern California, which was implemented under the banner of "Leadership for the 21st Century." Publicly announced in September 1986 (two years after it was quietly begun), the campaign was the largest in USC's history—$557 million. That goal was surpassed in December 1989 (six months ahead of schedule), and when the campaign ended on June 30, 1990, it had brought in a total of $641,574,718, exceeding its original target by more than $84 million. Carl E. Hartnack, chairman of the USC Board of Trustees from 1980 to 1985, served as national campaign chair.

During the Campaign for USC, the market value of USC's endowment pool grew from under $145 million in 1984 to well over $400 million in 1990. The drive yielded 41 new chairs and professorships, 18 endowed research funds and nearly 300 scholarships and fellowships—including 32 designated specifically for student athletes. The campaign spurred the creation of an important new source of continued support as well: The Presidential Associates group, bringing together donors investing $100,000 or more in USC, was created as a new gift level for the USC Associates in April 1988.

An array of new facilities

GAINING MOMENTUM 163

constructed with campaign funds provided a vital impetus for many of the objectives identified in USC's academic plan. Thanks to lead gifts of $8.2 million from the Hedco Foundation and $4 million from the Irvine Foundation, the NIBS program gained a permanent home in the Hedco Neurosciences Building, which was configured specifically to promote cross-disciplinary collaboration in teaching and research. Gifts of $2.9 million from the W. M. Keck Foundation and $1.25 million from the Charles Lee Powell Foundation paved the way for the W. M. Keck Photonics Research Laboratory, which contained the largest and best-equipped cleanroom in all of academia when it opened in 1992. The $15.9 million Hughes Aircraft Electrical Engineering Center offered crucial laboratories, office space and advanced computer systems support for electrical engineering, one of the flagship departments of the university's engineering school, and Kaprielian Hall, opened in 1989, was equipped with state-of-the-art shake tables for laboratory-based research in earthquake-related engineering. Dedicated in May 1990, the Elvon and Mabel Musick Law Center Addition, a project that encompassed extensive remodeling of the original facility, added 64,000 square feet to the

THE ALL-UNIVERSITY CATALOGUE

In 1984, Sylvia Manning was promoted to the newly created position of vice provost for undergraduate studies at USC. "It was a role that could be invented," Manning recalled some 22 years later, "and out of that role, we got the first unified catalogue in 20 years."

Since the mid-1960s, information about the university's academic programs had been decentralized, with each degree-granting unit publishing its own bulletin. As Robert Biller, then executive vice provost, explained when announcing plans for the new publication in 1985: "Every year around graduation time, thousands of students have to clear petitions because they aren't exactly straight on the graduation requirements. The catalogue will make the requirements clear, and students can steer with them. This enables [students] to have the university at their fingertips."

The finished catalogue, containing 648 pages and about the size of a local telephone directory, was published for the 1986-87 academic year. Besides serving as a single, central reference for university policies, curricula and requirements, it was also a valuable tool for making students aware of the tremendous range of programs offered at

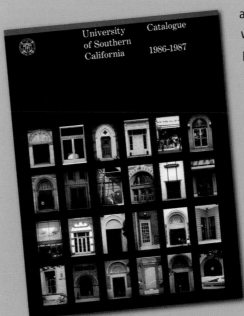

USC. According to Kristine Dillon, assistant vice president of student affairs when the catalogue was in the planning phase, "We say to students now who register in a major, 'You've made your decision; here's your bulletin, your slice of the pie.'" With the new catalogue, students—many of whom change their majors—gained access to information about course offerings across the university.

Said Manning, "It was one of the small, symbolic ways in which the campus was being pulled together into a more coherent whole."

[photo courtesy of USC University Archives]

THE FREEMAN HOUSE

The USC School of Architecture formally assumed stewardship of an extraordinary historic structure in March 1986, after Harriet Freeman deeded her family home to the university. Erected in 1924, the Freeman House is one of just a few textile-block buildings designed by Frank Lloyd Wright for the Hollywood Hills. Intended as experimental prototypes of low-cost, mass-produced housing, the homes were constructed with thousands of individually cast concrete blocks patterned with designs abstracted from nature. Wright himself created the molds.

As the residence of Harriet and Samuel Freeman, the house served as a center of avant-garde artistic and political activity in Los Angeles for more than 50 years. Beginning in the 1920s, visitors and resident guests included such well-known figures as Xavier Cugat, Clark Gable, Martha Graham and Edward Weston. The house also contains one of the best collections of custom-designed Rudolph Schindler furniture.

Because many of the techniques used in its construction were so experimental, the building suffered structural problems from the beginning. Under the supervision of USC architects, however, it underwent a major seismic upgrade and as of fall 2005 was in the process of being fully restored. Once restoration work is complete, the USC School of Architecture plans to use the home as a residence for advanced students and distinguished visitors, a setting for conferences and seminars, and a resource for its programs in historic preservation.

Faculty member Jeffrey Chusid took advantage of his role as director of the Freeman House to introduce USC students to the field of historic preservation. He went on to initiate the School of Architecture's Summer Preservation Program in 1993. [photo courtesy of USC University Archives]

existing building for USC's Gould School of Law.

Ambassador Walter H. Annenberg was the campaign's largest contributor, providing $28.2 million in gifts to support the USC Annenberg School for Communication as well as university endowment and operating funds. Additional major gifts came from Thomas Lord, who gave $10 million for research and graduate teaching; from Katherine Bogdanovich Loker, who provided $7 million for the Loker Hydrocarbon Research Institute and a new Katherine B. Loker Wing; and from Harold E. Moulton, who designated $6.5 million for programs in organic chemistry.

Students' recreational needs were served by the Kennedy Family Aquatics Building, a gift from the Jack Kennedy III family, as well as the General William Lyon University Center, completed in September 1989 following a lead gift of $6.5 million from General William Lyon and his wife, Willa Dean. In addition, in a move that marked the largest corporate gift to the campaign, the May Department Stores Company combined a sale and a charitable donation to transfer property located on the east side of the Harbor Freeway to USC. A six-story warehouse on the site was converted into the USC Parking Center, providing some 1,760 much-needed parking spaces for USC students, faculty and staff.

By the time the campaign closed on June 30, 1990, eight new buildings had been completed or were under construction, 14 had been renovated and an additional 11 capital projects were in the planning stages—all under the direction of then vice president and special adviser to the president Anthony Lazzaro.

USC's libraries—a high personal priority for Zumberge—also benefited from the campaign. Not only did Doheny Memorial Library undergo a major renovation, but 27 endowed book funds also were created, and library holdings were augmented with donations such as a 60,000-volume collection of Latin American materials that created the Boeckmann Center for Iberian and Latin American Studies in 1985. Named for USC's seventh first lady, the $1.2 million Helen Topping Architecture and Fine Arts Library, outfitted with a skylit reading room and an exterior patio, opened in fall 1990. At campaign's end, plans also were well under way to build a revolutionary new undergraduate teaching library (the Thomas and Dorothy Leavey Library, opened in 1994) that would provide sophisticated technological resources to enhance instruction, learning and scholarship at USC.

Above: Although confined to a wheelchair due to illness, Helen Topping gave a brief speech at the groundbreaking for her namesake library—the Helen Topping Architecture and Fine Arts Library—in 1986. With her were (from left) President Zumberge, Chancellor Emeritus Norman Topping, fine arts dean John S. Gordon and architecture dean Robert S. Harris. [photo by Wendy Rosin Malecki, courtesy of USC University Archives]

Right: Enriching student life outside the classroom at USC, the General William Lyon University Center, opened in 1989, provides facilities to meet students' recreational needs. [photo courtesy of USC University Archives]

In announcing his retirement, President Zumberge expressed his desire to spend more time at his family cabin in Jackson Hole, Wyoming, and to work on a ninth edition of his textbook, *The Elements of Geology*. [photo courtesy of USC University Archives]

"To the Mountains"

On February 7, 1990, James Zumberge, aged 66, asked the USC Board of Trustees to begin a search for the university's next president. "I will remain at my post and continue to serve as president with vigor and enthusiasm until my successor reports for duty," he said in his statement to the board.

Zumberge called his association with USC "one of the most rewarding experiences I have had in 25 years as a university president." He had inherited a university that was, as he declared in one of his first major addresses after taking office, "still on the rising curve of its expectations." Now, having stewarded USC's ascent to ever-greater heights by steering an enormously successful fundraising campaign, beefing up academic programs and spearheading a significant era of campus expansion, he was ready for a change. In announcing his decision to the broader university community, Zumberge—whose name in German means "to the mountains" —expressed his desire to work on a ninth edition of his well-known geology textbook, *The Elements of Geology*, and possibly to teach at USC. Closer to his heart, he wanted to spend time

A PACIFIC UNIVERSITY

Anticipating a trend that would extend well beyond his tenure at USC, one of the major themes of Zumberge's presidency was the opportunity presented by USC's participation in the development of the Pacific Rim.

"[T]he last 100 years have seen the Pacific coastline of the United States change from a frontier to a gateway, from a natural geographic boundary to an open door to the lands and peoples of the Pacific Rim," Zumberge said in his remarks at the annual faculty breakfast in October 1983. He pointed to the growing potential for cultural and economic exchange between the United States and other countries bordering the Pacific basin, and to the inexorable shift of the world's population from the north Atlantic region to the Pacific Rim.

USC had already begun to cultivate strong ties to the area through initiatives such as the USC College of Letters, Arts and Sciences' East Asian Studies Center and the business school's International Business Education and Research (IBEAR) program, both of which were founded in the 1970s. Furthermore, the very composition of USC's student body bore witness to Southern California's emergence as a Pacific gateway: Whereas students from the Middle East had formed the largest foreign contingent in USC's student body during the 1970s, by 1990, students from areas along the Pacific Rim—including Indonesia, Hong Kong, Taipei, Korea and Japan—represented USC's largest undergraduate student delegation. Zumberge encouraged units universitywide to take an active role in expanding USC's horizons and sphere of influence by launching research projects, providing educational services and offering consultation to governments, corporations and other institutions.

"Since our beginnings, USC has always been identified with Southern California in general and Los Angeles in particular," Zumberge affirmed. "We are a Pacific people. Los Angeles is a Pacific city. To continue to serve Los Angeles, USC must increasingly be a Pacific university."

with his wife, Marilyn, and their children and grandchildren at the family cabin in Jackson Hole, Wyoming.

"There is a time to come and a time to go, and I think the time to go is now," he told an interviewer for the *Los Angeles Times.* "I'd rather make the decision myself than have my doctor make it or the Board of Trustees make it or the good Lord make it."

In retrospect, his statement was tragically prescient: In August 1991, just months after stepping down from the USC presidency, Zumberge was diagnosed with a brain tumor. He died at the age of 68, in April 1992.

Although Zumberge's passing was a tremendous loss for the Trojan Family, he left a vibrant, indelible legacy at USC. George T. Scharffenberger, chairman of the USC Board of Trustees during the final years of Zumberge's presidency, described the Zumberge decade as "an era of extraordinary academic accomplishment for USC" and expressed deep gratitude for Zumberge's leadership. "He set high standards and created a climate of shared responsibility," Scharffenberger said. "And the academic planning mechanism he initiated has enabled the university to seize opportunities that will have an impact on this institution for generations."

"PROFESSOR OF THE CENTURY"

USC mourned the end of an era with the passing of emerita professor of biology Irene A. McCulloch in 1987. McCulloch had joined the USC faculty in 1924, when the university's marine research apparatus consisted of one 14-foot skiff. The lack of facilities, however, didn't deter her from using hand-held dredges and plankton nets to conduct extensive research on marine invertebrates (foraminifera), which provide valuable clues about ocean currents and pollution. Eventually, McCulloch piqued the interest of Capt. G. Allan Hancock in her work, which ultimately led to the formation of the Hancock Foundation and a blossoming of marine research at USC. McCulloch also is credited with persuading Hancock to construct his namesake building on the University Park campus—for which she designed many of the research and library spaces—and to

purchase most of the library of the Boston Society of Natural History in 1944, forming the core of the Hancock Collections and Archives at USC.

Although she retired in 1952, McCulloch continued to walk the few blocks from her home to campus every weekday to continue her research—a schedule she maintained well into her 99th year. In 1969, a group of her former students and colleagues established a foundation in her honor, dedicated to education and research in marine biology. Additionally, after being hailed by generations of USC students as "professor of the century," McCulloch was formally recognized in 1971 by the Los Angeles City Council, which passed a resolution lauding her for "a lifetime of teaching and scientific research."

McCulloch's name is memorialized at USC in the Irene McCulloch Foundation monograph series as well as in the USC College of Letters, Arts and Sciences' McCulloch-Crosby Chair in Marine Biology, which was created in 1991. Additionally, the McCulloch Townhomes, a 27-unit housing complex built for USC faculty and staff on the site of McCulloch's former residence at 30th and Hoover streets— which she bequeathed to the university— were opened in 1990.

[photo courtesy of USC University Archives]

At the time of USC's 125th anniversary in 2005, the 226-acre University Park campus had become the crown jewel of the L.A. Arts & Education Corridor, which extends from downtown Los Angeles to University Park and Exposition Park.

[photo © John Livzey]

Chapter Eight

A World-Class University (1991–2005)

By Annette Moore

The University of Southern California's tenth president, Steven Browning Sample, took office on March 31, 1991, after nearly a decade at the helm of the State University of New York (SUNY) at Buffalo. His election marked the end of an arduous quest that had begun in spring 1990 with the appointment of a 20-member presidential search committee, headed by University Professor Warren Bennis, which sifted through hundreds of potential candidates before forwarding a slate of finalists to the USC Board of Trustees.

"He [Sample] has all the tickets academically, but he also has a very broad experience running a major university," said Forrest N. Shumway, chairman of the USC Board of Trustees, when he made the announcement to the *Los Angeles Times* on December 5, 1990. "Look at his track record in Buffalo. It's absolutely spectacular."

of Nebraska in 1974. He joined SUNY-Buffalo (UB) in 1982, where he was credited with helping turn a foundering campus in an economically depressed region into the flagship of the SUNY system. Under Sample's leadership, UB in 1989 became the first public university in New York or New England ever elected to membership in the Association of American Universities (AAU).

It was an impressive record of achievement, but looking back some 15 years later, the clincher, according to USC life trustee Malcolm R. Currie, was the fact that a consortium of California institutions, of which USC was a part, had lost out to SUNY-Buffalo in nabbing a National Science Foundation grant to establish a major earthquake research center back in the mid-1980s. "We figured it was a shoo-in for the California team, because we have all the earthquakes out here," Currie recalled. "But we lost the competition to the State University of New York at Buffalo, and we thought, 'Gee, how the heck did they do that?' Well, there was an outstanding leader there at Buffalo, Steve Sample, and he took it away from California. So we all decided that if the guy could do that, then, boy, he had a lot on the ball."

Shumway cited yet another important factor in Sample's selection:

USC Board of Trustees chairman Forrest N. Shumway (left) showed the Samples around campus in December 1990. [photo by Irene Fertik, courtesy of USC University Archives]

A musician, outdoorsman and electrical engineer, Sample had completed three degrees from the University of Illinois by the age of 24 and was awarded tenure as an associate professor of engineering at Purdue University by age 29. He invented a digital electronic control system that has been installed behind the touch panels in more than 500 million microwave ovens and other home appliances around the world. After leaving Purdue, he served as deputy director for academic affairs at the Illinois Board of Higher Education before moving on to accept an appointment as executive vice president for academic affairs and dean of the Graduate College at the University

"We were also impressed with Kathryn Sample, who clearly understood the responsibilities associated with being a president's wife."

Kathryn Brunkow Sample, a certified surgical technologist who has worked professionally in Nebraska, New York and California, had been actively involved in the lives of several universities, including the University of Nebraska and the State University of New York at Buffalo. Her husband described her as "an indispensable ally and my most trusted adviser."

The prospects appeared auspicious from the new president's perspective as well. Sample told the *Los Angeles Times* that he had been attracted to Los Angeles because "in some ways it is the center of our culture." Likewise, he welcomed the shift from public to private higher education. "I think that while private universities have to work much harder than public institutions to get their money, they have much more flexibility in how that money is spent," he said to *USC Trojan Family*. "Private universities can move much more quickly, much more aggressively, and that is appealing to me." Even more important, from the beginning Sample called out a certain defining characteristic of the Trojan Family. He described it in this way:

USC officially welcomed Steven and Kathryn Sample into the Trojan Family in spring 1991. [photo by Irene Fertik, courtesy of *USC Trojan Family Magazine*]

I got the sense from the search committee and the trustees that they all were clear about wanting USC to emerge as one of the very best private universities in the country. It's a very good institution now, it's clearly a very strong research university, but I think there is a desire, a real desire, on the part of the people I spoke with to make it better. That's not true at most universities in the United States. Most universities are relatively happy with where they are. They may talk vaguely in terms of getting better, but they're not really committed to it, they're not hungry for it to the point where they are willing to make really tough comparisons between themselves and their peers.

Above left: USC's four living presidents—(from left) Norman H. Topping, James H. Zumberge, Steven B. Sample and John R. Hubbard—got together for a formal portrait in 1991. [photo by John Livzey, courtesy of USC Public Relations Projects]

Above right: At Steven Sample's inauguration on September 20, 1991, Faculty Senate president Martin L. Levine (right) presented the ceremonial silver mace to the university's newly installed tenth president. [photo courtesy of USC Public Relations Projects]

That quality—the sense of never being fully satisfied, of always striving to be better—resonated with Sample's own sensibilities.

A Tumultuous "Freshman Year"

In one of two front-page stories that the *Los Angeles Times* published following the public announcement of Sample's appointment in December 1990, Robert J. Wagner, UB's vice president for university services, was quoted as suggesting that USC staff members ought to take their vacations before Sample arrived. " ... [O]nce he

gets there, it's going to be non-stop," Wagner said. "It's a high commitment, but Steve doesn't ask you to do something he doesn't do himself."

The warning was well advised. Clearing his desk of anything not specifically conducive to university business, Sample set to work.

By the time of his formal inauguration—which was held on September 20, 1991, and included a ceremonial "March of Commitment" by 10,000 people representing all dimensions of the Trojan Family—Sample already had formulated carefully thought-out priorities for the period immediately ahead.

These were: strengthening undergraduate programs; developing the USC Health Sciences campus; aggressively recruiting the very best doctoral and postdoctoral students; continuing and expanding USC's tradition of public service, with a particular emphasis on the neighborhoods in the immediate vicinity of the University Park and Health Sciences campuses; and pruning, consolidating and refocusing programs and services in order to raise quality and conserve resources. In his inaugural address, he also articulated a principle that would become a leitmotif of his administration:

I do not believe it would be appropriate for USC to rest on its laurels and survey with satisfaction the thousands of colleges and universities it has already surpassed. Rather we should focus our attention on those very few universities which are in some sense academically superior to us, especially the 10 or so best AAU private universities. When we judge USC from this perspective we find ourselves challenged in a most exciting and formidable way.

Before the end of Sample's first year in office, the university found itself formidably challenged indeed—but in an entirely unexpected way. With the country's slow economic recovery following the 1990–91 recession, USC was confronting a serious budget shortfall resulting in great part from lower-than-expected tuition income, greater-than-expected financial aid expenses, skyrocketing health insurance costs and decreased return on investments due to low interest rates. The offices of the three senior vice presidents (for academic affairs, administration and university relations) instituted hiring freezes in all administrative areas under their jurisdictions effective November 1, 1991, and academic and administrative staff salaries were frozen through the 1992–93 fiscal year.

USC'S FIRST NOBEL LAUREATE

In 1994, USC's George Olah received the highest honor in science, the Nobel Prize, for his creation of "superacids" —substances billions of times more acidic than conventional acids— and his pioneering use of them in the field of hydrocarbon chemistry.

Olah, who left his native Hungary after the Soviet invasion of 1956, came to USC from Cleveland's Case Western Reserve University in 1977. His arrival, coinciding with the decade's second major energy crisis, spurred USC to establish a research institute dedicated to the study of hydrocarbons. As founding director of the new institute, Olah set to work at once, conducting experiments in temporary basement quarters until, thanks to benefactors Katherine B. and Donald P. Loker, a new facility was opened in 1979.

Hydrocarbons form the basic building blocks of life. They occur naturally in substances such as petroleum, natural gas and coal, and they also are key components of industrial products ranging from fuels to

Back on campus after attending the Nobel Prize ceremony in Sweden, 1994 Nobel laureate George Olah and benefactor Katherine Loker (class of 1940) got together for a photo-op.
[photo © Patricia Tryforos, courtesy of *USC Trojan Family* magazine]

plastics and even pharmaceuticals. Many important hydrocarbon processes have been difficult to study, however, because they entail a succession of exceedingly short-lived chemical compounds. Using his superacids, Olah discovered a means of "freezing" these reactions, making possible numerous advances in the field—including methods for producing high-octane, lead-free gasoline in an environmentally friendly way.

The Nobel Prize was one in an impressive series of national and international honors that Distinguished Professor Olah has received, including Japan's Grand Cordon of the Order of the Rising Sun and membership in the U.S. National Academy of Sciences, the United Kingdom's Royal Society and the American Academy of Arts and Sciences. In 1995, Olah made special note of an honorary doctorate that was added to his credentials at USC's 112th commencement, telling the crowd that he was proud to take a place alongside his two sons in having a USC degree.

The riots of April 1992 constituted Los Angeles' worst episode of violence since the Watts riots of 1965. Among the structures that fell victim to widespread looting and fires was a strip mall adjacent to the University Park campus on Vermont Avenue. USC, however, remained unscathed. [photo courtesy of USC University Archives]

Regrettably, even these measures were not enough to keep USC's budget in the black. In January 1992, then senior vice president for administration Dennis F. Dougherty announced that the university needed to tighten its belt further. Consequently, in what Sample later called "the first major downsizing in our university's history," selected positions left vacant by the hiring freeze were eliminated altogether, and certain administrative units began laying off staff. Altogether, some 800 jobs were eliminated, and nearly 500 people were laid off. "This is a painful and difficult process for all of us," Dougherty said. "If we could find a way to avoid it and still balance our budget, we would."

Calling to mind this stressful period of cutbacks some 15 years

later, trustee Malcolm Currie reflected: "It was a very courageous thing he [Sample] did, just being the new guy there. But he had to do it, financially, and I think in doing that he established himself as a leader."

In concert with this belt-tightening, just before Thanksgiving break in 1991, Sample appointed an 11-member Strategic Planning Steering Group, with Provost Cornelius J. "Neal" Pings as chair, to develop a strategic framework for charting USC's academic progress in the decade ahead. By commencing the self-assessment and planning process with this small leadership group—as opposed to starting with the individual academic units, as had been the case with USC's 1982–84 academic plan—Sample laid the groundwork for a program that would take into account the institution's overall resources as well as universitywide issues such as undergraduate and doctoral education, libraries, interdisciplinary programs and facilities. The planning effort was intended to ensure USC's ability to build momentum while navigating the financial crisis facing all of higher education in the 1990s, but Sample acknowledged that many imponderables lay ahead. "If we were planning two or three years ago, nobody in their right mind would have thought the Soviet Union would dissolve," he noted. "That event has had enormous implications. It's going to change how the government spends its money. It's going to change the country's research policies, which is going to affect USC to a great extent."

Little did Sample know how closely such an unforeseeable contingency loomed on the horizon. On Wednesday, April 29, 1992, a controversial "not guilty" verdict in the case of police assault against Rodney King unleashed mayhem throughout many parts of Los Angeles. In the city's worst eruption of violence since the Watts riots of 1965, an estimated 55 people were killed. Looting and fires inflicted approximately $1 billion in property damage.

Yet while Los Angeles was in upheaval, USC emerged remarkably unscathed. "There has been no reported damage to property on campus save for one broken window in a parking kiosk, and no reported damage whatsoever to off-campus housing and fraternity and sorority houses," Sample wrote in a letter to parents, alumni and supporters. "Our Health Sciences campus … was not affected at all…." He continued:

It was my privilege to spend all of Thursday and Friday night on campus, including sleeping on the floor of my office Thursday night. As I walked around the campus at about 11 p.m. Thursday evening, chatting with students, security officers, maintenance staff and food service people, I developed an almost overwhelming sense of pride in the Trojan Family. Where one might have found fear and despair, I instead found strength and quiet confidence. Never in my life have I felt so fortunate or so well rewarded.

It was no miracle that USC was spared. Thanks to the university's longstanding commitment to serving Los Angeles and Southern California, community residents had come to view USC as an anchor institution and a neighbor rather than as an adversary. Reflecting on the incident for a *Daily Trojan* article some 13 years later, USC history professor William Deverell confirmed that USC had emerged unharmed largely because it "weaved itself into the neighborhood in a way that bigger businesses didn't."

Immediately following the riots, in cooperation with the Rebuild L.A. task force headed by USC trustee Peter Ueberroth, members of the Trojan Family reached out to the ravaged city in its hour of need. Pitching in with neighbors dressed alike in USC caps and T-shirts, students, faculty and staff came in with street sweepers, brooms and buckets to help with clean-up. Members of the Trojan Family also provided counseling services, distributed food and clothing and collected donations to help local businesses get back on their feet.

When Eduard A. Shevardnadze, head of the State Committee of the Republic of Georgia and former foreign minister of the Soviet Union, was unable to keep his appointment to speak at USC's 109th annual commencement on May 8, 1992, Sample stepped up to the podium and addressed a sea of some 8,000 graduates wearing caps and gowns, saying:

My message today is simple and hopeful. We have an opportunity to build our city anew—not as it was, but as it should be. We have a chance to create a new kind of city, with justice for all, with broad access to quality education and with real economic opportunities for everyone; a place in which every child has a chance for a decent and productive life. Thus we must begin to look through the crisis of the moment toward a larger goal.

He also reminded his audience of USC's institutional obligation to the city in which it was born. "The city and the university grew up together," he said. "USC needs this community just as much as this community needs USC."

As USC's provost and vice president for academic affairs from 1993 to 2005, Lloyd Armstrong Jr. oversaw some of the most significant advances in the university's history, helping transform USC into one of the most selective universities in the country. In appreciation for his extraordinary service to USC, Armstrong was honored with the Presidential Medallion in March 2006. Lauding Armstrong for his "extraordinary foresight and skill," President Sample said: "Provost Armstrong's 12-year tenure will be forever inscribed in USC's history as pivotal and far-reaching." [photo courtesy of USC University Archives]

In the wake of the riots, USC took a number of proactive steps to meet this obligation during troubled times. In January 1993, Sample established the Administrative Outreach Group (AOG), an action committee of faculty and staff members chaired by Jane G. Pisano, then dean of the USC School of Public Administration (appointed senior vice president for external relations effective January 1, 1994). The AOG promoted the economic revitalization of USC's neighborhoods through activities ranging from technical assistance for entrepreneurs wanting to start or enlarge businesses in the neighborhood, to preferential hiring at USC for longtime neighborhood residents. "The president established the AOG to help ensure that the university's walk would match its talk," Pisano said.

Then the university hit yet another unanticipated bump in the road when, in fall 1992, Cornelius Pings, USC's provost and senior vice president for academic affairs since 1981, announced that he would be leaving USC as of February 1993 to accept the presidency of the Association of American Universities in Washington, D.C. Until a permanent replacement could be found, William G. Spitzer, professor emeritus of physics, materials science and electrical engineering, was appointed to fill the office on an interim basis.

In his annual address to USC's faculty on October 9, 1992, Sample reflected: "What a freshman year for a new president: earthquakes,* riots, budget reductions, layoffs, my provost ups and quits, and our football team goes 3 and 8."

True to form, however, Sample proved unstoppable even in the face of these setbacks, immediately turning his attention to a matter of more "transcendent importance." During the course of the university's strategic planning process, Sample said, the trustees had raised a number of "embarrassing" questions about USC's mission and role in Southern California and beyond— and they requested a response that would fit on a single page. Sample invested close to 100 hours in drafting a role and mission statement for USC and trying it out on trustees, alumni, faculty, staff and students. The document began:

---

* Sierra Madre, Joshua Tree and Landers

The central mission of the University of Southern California is the development of human beings and society as a whole through the cultivation and enrichment of the human mind and spirit.

The Strategic Plan of the University of Southern California

The strategic planning process of the 1990s fired up in January 1992, when six focus groups composed of faculty, staff, students and alumni met to tackle a novel assignment. Their charge: "Imagine the university as the cover story for an issue of *Time* magazine in 2002. What would the article say? What would USC offer that would warrant its being put on the cover of a national magazine?" According to Sylvia Manning, then executive vice provost, the *Time* magazine approach was used because "it kept us focused on what will make us not just excellent, but excellent and different."

When Lloyd Armstrong Jr., formerly a professor of physics and dean of the School of Arts and Sciences at Johns Hopkins University, came on board as USC's new provost and senior vice president for academic affairs in August 1993, he quickly mobilized the broader university community to get involved in the strategic planning process. Armstrong posted drafts of the plan online and solicited comments and suggestions through a newly created newsgroup called "usc.plan." He also met with faculty to get their input.

After more than two years of work involving hundreds of members of the university community, the USC Board of Trustees endorsed and adopted the Strategic Plan of the University of Southern California in 1994. The plan set forth four overarching priorities—undergraduate education, interdisciplinary research and education, programs building on the resources of Southern California and Los Angeles, and internationalization—for building on USC's strengths and capitalizing on external trends. The goal was to move the university over the next decade "to a position of academic leadership among America's foremost private universities."

In 1998, USC conducted a systematic review of the plan and issued a four-year report, adopted by the trustees in 1998, that took stock of USC's achievements with respect to the four strategic priorities. The report also refined the plan with the addition of four critical pathways of opportunity—communications, life sciences, the arts and the urban

Above: In 1994, Noburo Nakagaki (left), director of the international center at Japan's Chukyo University, joined Lloyd Armstrong Jr., USC provost, in establishing a five-year agreement to foster cooperative research projects and student exchanges between the two universities.
[photo courtesy of USC University Archives]

Below: In keeping with the internationalization component of USC's strategic plan, a group of senior administrators and trustees spent two weeks visiting three Asian capitals in 1997. As part of that visit, Lily Chiang (left, class of 1982) welcomed President Sample, board chairman Malcolm R. Currie and trustee Ronnie C. Chan (M.B.A. 1976) to the inaugural dinner of USC's newly formed Hong Kong Alumni Club.
[photo courtesy of *USC Trojan Family Magazine*]

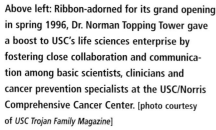

Above left: Ribbon-adorned for its grand opening in spring 1996, Dr. Norman Topping Tower gave a boost to USC's life sciences enterprise by fostering close collaboration and communication among basic scientists, clinicians and cancer prevention specialists at the USC/Norris Comprehensive Cancer Center. [photo courtesy of *USC Trojan Family Magazine*]

Above center: Ambassador Walter Annenberg's 1993 gift of $120 million to USC not only was by far the largest gift in USC's history, but also provided the impetus for a fundraising drive that would conclude as the most successful in American higher education. [Image courtesy of USC Public Relations]

Above right: In appreciation for his extraordinary support of USC, Ambassador Walter H. Annenberg (second from right) became the first recipient of the University Medallion during a special ceremony held at the Seeley G. Mudd Estate in 1994. Helping make the presentation were (from left) USC Board of Trustees chairman Forrest N. Shumway, Leonore "Lee" Annenberg and President Sample. [photo © BerlinerStudio/ BEImages, courtesy of the USC Office of the President]

paradigm—that defined major areas, interwoven with the strategic priorities, in which USC had "a special opportunity to build strength and reputation."

Besides providing a blueprint for USC's investment in its academic programs during the 1990s, the strategic plan set the stage for a truly historic fundraising campaign.

"Building on Excellence" and Beyond

In June 1993, Ambassador Walter H. Annenberg, chairman of the Annenberg Foundation, announced the largest single private donation ever made to support education in the United States. The gift, $365 million, was divided into four grants for four educational institutions: USC, the University of Pennsylvania, Harvard University and the Peddie School of

Hightstown, New Jersey (Annenberg's former prep school). USC's share was $120 million—by far the largest gift in the university's history—provided to launch the USC Annenberg Center for Communication, an interdisciplinary entity drawing faculty and resources from USC's various programs in communication, cinema-television, engineering and journalism.

At a time when institutions of higher education across the country were facing severe budget problems, this landmark gift—in combination with the university's evolving strategic plan—gave USC the impetus it needed to launch an audacious fundraising campaign. Under the banner of "Building on Excellence," USC set out to raise the unheard-of sum of $1 billion in seven years, from 1993 through 2000. After just four and a half years, the university exceeded

A MORAL COMPASS

One of President Sample's enduring legacies at USC has been the explicit interweaving of moral values into the very fabric of academic life. Although it wasn't until the early 2000s that grave ethical lapses in corporate and political America provided an external impetus for Sample actually to sit down and draft an official Code of Ethics—which was approved by the USC Board of Trustees on March 28, 2004 —adherence to the highest principles of moral conduct has represented a dominant theme throughout his administration.

In May 1991, barely a month on the job, Sample responded to negative media attention about fraternities and sororities by establishing a task force to evaluate USC's criteria for officially recognizing Greek organizations. Out of this task force the USC Minimum Standards policy was developed, imposing strict academic and behavioral guidelines for fraternities and sororities associated with the university. "A few parents complained, 'You can't do this to my child,'" recalled life trustee Forrest Shumway. "But inside of six months, the whole thing was cleaned up." Even more noteworthy, despite apprehensions about the ongoing difficulty of enforcing the standards and their potential negative impact on membership, fraternity and sorority grade-point averages had climbed above USC's all-men's and all-women's averages by the end of the decade, and the university also had seen a significant increase in the number of students wishing to join Greek-letter societies.

USC faced a thorny ethical challenge again in 2005, this time related to a noticeable rise in incidents involving alcohol during

To promote a clean, safe and family-friendly environment, USC banned alcohol during home football games at Los Angeles Memorial Colisuem, effective fall 2005. [photo courtesy of USC Public Relations]

sports events at the Coliseum. Under Sample's leadership and in cooperation with the Coliseum Commission, USC joined the ranks of its Pac-10 partners and banned alcohol sales and consumption during home football games, starting with the season opener on September 17. While many Trojans hailed the move as a positive measure that would promote a family-friendly environment at the stadium, the ban was not without dissent. Nonetheless, Sample urged the Trojan Family to support the new rules and to join him "in modeling civility and good sportsmanship" at the stadium. "It was the right thing to do," said life trustee Kenneth Leventhal. "You can trust Sample to do the right thing. And he does it well."

Grounded in this unwavering commitment to "doing the right thing," and in accord with the university's longstanding tradition of community service, USC's Code of Ethics begins by reminding the members of the Trojan Family about their connection to other people: "At the University of Southern California, ethical behavior is predicated on two main pillars: a commitment to discharging our obligations to others in a fair and honest manner, and a commitment to respecting the rights and dignity of all persons." Ultimately, the code provides a powerful reminder that the core values of honesty, fairness and mutual respect are essential elements of USC's overall academic mission.

Above left: In recognition of his tireless work as national chair of the Building on Excellence campaign, USC presented Kenneth Leventhal (pictured with his wife, Elaine) with a "tin cup" trophy for being the "biggest hero" of the fundraising drive. That award, however, was not the only honor USC was to bestow upon the Leventhals. Philanthropist Elaine Otter Leventhal and entrepreneur Kenneth Leventhal both received honorary doctorates at the university's 117th commencement in 2000, and Kenneth Leventhal won USC's top honor, the Presidential Medallion, at the 23rd annual Academic Honors Convocation in 2004. [photo by Avra Photography, courtesy of the USC Office of the President]

Above right: USC's $19 million Jane Hoffman Popovich and J. Kristoffer Popovich Hall, dedicated October 10, 1999, was credited with making the USC Marshall School of Business the most technologically advanced business school in the country. [photo courtesy of USC Public Relations]

that goal, and the trustees decided to raise the bar to $1.5 billion. As of December 1999, that target, too, had been surpassed. In what Sample characterized as a "Grand Canyon moment"—that is, "a point where you see how far you've come (and get to indulge in a little self-congratulation), and then you look at where you want to be and, far from being daunted or depleted, you become energized"—the trustees elected to increase the goal yet again, to $2 billion, and extended the timeline to December 31, 2002.

USC passed the $2 billion mark quickly and pressed ahead; when the books closed, the campaign had brought in a total of $2,850,143,933 in cash and pledges. All the more extraordinary for having been achieved even after the dot-com

boom of the mid-1990s collapsed, Building on Excellence was at the time the most successful fundraising drive in the history of American higher education.

The campaign broke other records as well. During the course of Building on Excellence, USC became the first university ever to receive four nine-figure gifts—$120 million from Walter Annenberg in 1993; $113 million from Alfred E. Mann, given in 1998 to establish the Alfred E. Mann Institute for Biomedical Engineering (later increased to $163 million); $110 million from the W. M. Keck Foundation, given in 1999 to support the university's medical school (which was renamed the Keck School of Medicine of the University of Southern California); and $100 million from the Annenberg

Foundation, given in 2002 to support the USC Annenberg School for Communication. Five schools received naming gifts, each of which was, at the time of its announcement, the largest ever made to a program of its kind. Besides the Keck grant, these naming gifts were: $15 million in 1995—later increased to $25 million—from longtime trustee Kenneth Leventhal (who also served as campaign chair) and his wife, Elaine, for the USC Leventhal School of Accounting; $35 million in 1996 from alumnus and trustee Gordon S. Marshall for the USC Marshall School of Business; $20 million in 1998 from alumna and trustee Barbara Rossier and her husband, Roger, for the USC Rossier School of Education; and $25 million in 1999 from Flora Laney Thornton for the USC Thornton School of Music.

In addition, two departmental naming gifts were received. The engineering school's Daniel J. Epstein Department of Industrial and Systems Engineering was named in appreciation for an $11 million gift from trustee Daniel J. Epstein, and the medical school's Aresty Department of Urology was named in recognition of $11 million in cumulative campaign gifts from Catherine and Joseph Aresty.

Campaign contributions also made possible a dramatic physical

Above left: The Zilkha Neurogenetic Institute building—designed with the vision of attracting top researchers to study the genetic basis of neurological diseases and behavioral disorders—opened its doors in March 2003. Pictured in front of the new structure is benefactor Selim K. Zilkha. [photo © Steven A. Heller, courtesy of USC Health Sciences Campus Public Relations and Marketing]

Above, upper right: Doing some symbolic heavy lifting at the groundbreaking for the Harlyne J. Norris Cancer Research Tower in June 2003 were (from left) Norris Foundation board member William Corey, USC/Norris Comprehensive Cancer Center director Peter Jones, USC trustee and foundation chair Harlyne Norris, President Sample and USC medical dean Stephen Ryan. Dedicated to making cancer a disease of the past, the facility was designed to nearly double the laboratory space at USC/Norris. [photo by Jon Nalick, courtesy of USC University Archives]

Above, lower right: Ronald Tutor Hall, a $50 million research and instructional complex designed to support work in biomedical technology, information technology and nanotechnology, officially opened its doors in February 2005. Officiating at the grand opening were (from left) School of Engineering dean C. L. Max Nikias, former dean Leonard M. Silverman, President Sample and USC trustee Ronald N. Tutor. [photo by Irene Fertik, courtesy of the USC Viterbi School of Engineering]

transformation of USC's two campuses. On the Health Sciences campus, the 125,000-square-foot Zilkha Neuro-genetic Institute was dedicated in March 2003 and named in honor of Los Angeles businessman Selim K. Zilkha, who contributed $20 million to the project. With a lead gift of $15 million from the Kenneth T. and Eileen L. Norris Foundation, construc-tion began on the Harlyne J. Norris Research Tower, a major addition to the USC/Norris Cancer Center and Hospital that was named for trustee Harlyne Norris, in June 2003. On the University Park campus, Jane Hoffman Popovich and J. Kristoffer Popovich Hall, housing the graduate programs

of the USC Marshall School of Business, opened in 1999. Ronald Tutor Hall, a state-of-the-art, $50 million engineer-ing research and instructional complex that officially opened its doors in February 2005, was named in honor of USC trustee Ronald Tutor. Additionally, McCarthy Quad, a landscaped green space between Leavey Library and Doheny Memorial Library on the University Park campus, was completed in 2001 and named in honor of the family of USC alumna and trustee Kathleen Leavey McCarthy.

Campus athletic facilities got a boost from the campaign as well. New additions included the Loker Track and Field Stadium, named for alumna and

honorary trustee Katherine B. Loker, whose $17 million campaign gift included $2 million for the stadium; the Louis J. and Helene Galen Athletic Center, an athletics-themed restaurant facility adjacent to Heritage Hall; and a major renovation of USC's historic Dedeaux Field.

Just as they enhanced USC's physical landscape, campaign funds infused academic programs across the university with new vitality and direction. Among 25 institutes and centers expanded or initiated during the campaign were the Casden Institute for the Study of the Jewish Role in American Life, the Donald P. and Katherine B. Loker Hydrocarbon

In October 2001, USC's historic Edward L. Doheny Jr. Memorial Library reopened after 18 months of earthquake upgrades, repairs and renovation. "As the first academic library of its size in Southern California, it has served generations of students, faculty and scholars to produce important and original research in humanities and social sciences," said Los Angeles mayor James K. Hahn after ceremonially unlocking the doors. "I foresee a great relationship between this library and USC in general and the City of Los Angeles." [photo courtesy of USC Public Relations]

Research Institute, the Lloyd Greif Center for Entrepreneurial Studies, the Harold E. and Henrietta C. Lee Breast Center, the Wrigley Institute for Environmental Studies and the Robert Zemeckis Center for Digital Arts. USC also received $27 million from an anonymous donor to support the Women in Science and Engineering (WiSE) program—including the creation of the Gabilan Chair for a female faculty scientist or engineer—and to fund capital improvements for the USC School of Social Work.

In all, more than 350,000 individuals, foundations and corporations made gifts to USC during the campaign. Approximately half of the funds raised went into endowment, helping create 125 new endowed faculty chairs and professorships and generating a more than fourfold increase in USC's endowment, which grew from $490 million at the end of the 1989–90 fiscal year to $2.1 billion by the end of 2001–02. Another significant campaign accomplishment was the impressive increase in alumni giving—a key measure used in rating American colleges and universities—from 13 percent at the start of the campaign to 34 percent in 2001–02. "Donations from USC alumni alone exceeded our original $1 billion goal," Sample said in his 2003 state-of-the-university address.

"However," he added, "the fact that more than half of our campaign money came from other universities' alumni stunned our competitors nationwide." This circumstance was something that Alan Kreditor, senior vice president for university advancement since 1992, attributed to USC's "compelling excellence." "The dramatic rise in USC's quality helps explain why donors are reaching deeper into their pockets to help the institution," he told the *Los Angeles Times* on February 26, 2003.

The momentum generated by Building on Excellence continued to fuel USC's fundraising efforts, not to mention its ascent into the top echelon

In March 2001, Hollywood turned out big-time as the USC School of Cinema-Television's Robert Zemeckis Center for Digital Arts marked a new era in the making of motion pictures. At the head table were (from left) Avid Technology CEO David Krall, filmmakers George Lucas (class of 1966), Robert Zemeckis (class of 1973) and Steven Spielberg, and Dean Elizabeth Monk Daley. [photo © Lee Salem Photography, courtesy of USC Public Relations]

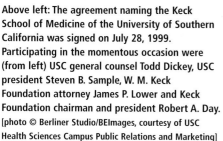

Above left: The agreement naming the Keck School of Medicine of the University of Southern California was signed on July 28, 1999. Participating in the momentous occasion were (from left) USC general counsel Todd Dickey, USC president Steven B. Sample, W. M. Keck Foundation attorney James P. Lower and Keck Foundation chairman and president Robert A. Day. [photo © Berliner Studio/BEImages, courtesy of USC Health Sciences Campus Public Relations and Marketing]

Above right: In March 2004, members of the Trojan Family came in droves to applaud the $52 million gift from alumnus Andrew Viterbi and his wife, Erna, that resulted in the naming of the USC Viterbi School of Engineering. [photo © Jason Dziegielewski, courtesy of the USC Viterbi School of Engineering]

of American research universities, well beyond the campaign's end.

With the receipt of the $110 million Keck naming gift in 1999, the Keck School of Medicine of USC implemented its own fundraising drive, setting its sights on hiring 135 new faculty members and raising $1 billion within a 10-year time-frame—all toward the end of elevating the school into the ranks of the top 10 medical schools in the United States. The financial goal was doubled to $2 billion in October 2004, encompassing the campaigns of Keck School partners Childrens Hospital Los Angeles, Doheny Eye Institute and Health Research Associates—and the original target of $1 billion was in hand by November 2005.

In September 2002, the USC College of Letters, Arts and Sciences

and its dean, Joseph Aoun, captured national attention with the announcement of the $100 million Senior Faculty Hiring Initiative, an effort to increase the ranks of the college's faculty by 25 percent with the addition of 100 world-class scholars whose work cuts across traditional disciplinary boundaries. Around the same time, the college made public its ambition to become one of the very best colleges in an American research university by the end of the decade, with the 2013 National Research Council survey to be a measure of its success. Energizing this quest, a $400 million fundraising initiative was launched in fall 2005.

The university's highly ranked engineering school, too, stepped up to the plate. Led by its charismatic dean, C. L. Max Nikias, the school embarked on its own seven-year, $300 million initiative. An early high point was reached in spring 2004, when Trojan alumnus and celebrated engineer Andrew Viterbi and his wife, Erna, made the largest-ever naming gift to a U.S. engineering school— $52 million—to endow and name the USC Andrew and Erna Viterbi School of Engineering. And the momentum kept going. A $22 million gift from alumnus and trustee Mark A. Stevens and his wife, Mary, in late 2004 created the USC Mark and Mary

"THE ART AND ADVENTURE OF LEADERSHIP"

Every spring since 1996, President Steven B. Sample and University Professor Warren Bennis—whom *Forbes* magazine dubbed the "dean of leadership gurus"— have co-taught a course called "The Art and Adventure of Leadership" at USC. The hugely popular class, open to juniors and seniors by application only, exposes undergraduates to the study and practice of leadership in many settings, examining the lives of leaders ranging from King David and Socrates to Elizabeth I and Eleanor Roosevelt.

"One of the things that makes this course so exciting is that it brings together the best and brightest students from every discipline," Sample said. "So while we admit only 40 students to the class, we make sure that we have humanists, business majors, social scientists, physical scientists, engineers, filmmakers, public administration majors and so forth. And this course has been a great laboratory and testing ground for some of my own ideas about leadership."

In fact, largely growing out of his experience in teaching the course, Sample wrote a book, *The Contrarian's Guide to Leadership* (published by Wiley's Jossey-Bass division in 2002, with author's royalties used to fund undergraduate scholarships at USC), that takes the university's explosive growth since 1991 as a case study. The book spells out Sample's unconventional approach to "doing"—as opposed to just "being"— a leader, offering such contrarian counsel as, "Never make a decision today that can reasonably be put off until tomorrow." It also points out the many ways in which USC has profited from this unorthodox point of view. In the early 1990s, for example, USC opted to inaugurate an extensive merit-based aid program, reduce the target size of the freshman class and have core undergraduate courses taught by senior faculty in small classes. All of these decisions were counter-intuitive in light of the university's budget problems at the time, but they ultimately helped bring about a dramatic improvement in the quality of undergraduate education at USC.

President Sample (left) and leadership guru Warren Bennis began co-teaching their popular undergraduate course in spring 1996. [photo by John Livzey, courtesy of USC Public Relations Projects]

On the evening of June 3, 2003, McCarthy Quad was transformed for a gala soirée celebrating the conclusion of the $2,850,143,933 Building on Excellence campaign. [photo © Lee Salem Photography, courtesy of the USC Office of Protocol and University Events]

Stevens Institute for Technology Commercialization, which later was designated as the university's central resource for technology transfer and development. In fall 2005, the newly merged Mork Family Department of Chemical Engineering and Materials Science was named in recognition of a $15 million gift from alumnus John Mork and his family.

A Distinctive Undergraduate Education

From the time he took office, Sample spelled out his intention to improve undergraduate education at USC,

building on a thrust that had been gaining momentum since the Hubbard administration. In his inaugural address, he spoke to the need for research universities overall to improve their undergraduate offerings, and pointed to the Freshman Seminars, Thematic Option program, smaller classes and the recent report of former president Zumberge's Commission on Undergraduate Education (CUE) as indicators of USC's frontrunner status in this area. Then Sample quickly set in motion a process aimed at creating an exemplary program stressing critical thinking and writing skills. A major goal was to ensure that undergraduates would benefit from the university's special distinctions by taking advantage of educational offerings in USC's unusually broad array of first-rate professional schools, participating in leading-edge research, making use of Los Angeles as a living laboratory and enjoying a small-college atmosphere even while studying at a large university.

As early as October 1991, the Office of the Provost issued a report tracking implementation of the 124 CUE recommendations. Among the 64 that already had taken effect were teaching incentives and the formation of a faculty programming committee for the new teaching library.

Still under discussion at the time were the establishment of an on-campus residential college and a requirement that students pass at least one course dealing with issues related to gender, race, ethnicity, sexual orientation, language, religion and social class in order to graduate. In a memo, Provost Pings underscored the fact that "USC, like the nation, state and city in which it stands, is a community of men and women with enormous differences." He went on to note that these differences constituted a basis for social conflict just as they represented a value to society, and confirmed his perception that "the preparation of our students for citizenship in this complex and hetero-geneous society should include education in these matters." USC officially implemented the new graduation requirement in fall 1993, with an initial roster of courses that spanned the fields of anthropology, occupational therapy, English and ethnic studies, to name a few.

With an eye to improving student selectivity, USC began to revamp its student recruitment, admissions and financial aid, and undergraduate advising programs as well. The university inaugurated an extensive merit-based aid program, beefed up need-based grants for highly qualified applicants and reduced the target size

of the freshman class. Additionally, the Student Academic Record System (STARS) was implemented to provide progress-toward-degree reports every semester for advisers and students beginning in the sophomore year.

Jump-starting the drive to improve the educational experience for undergraduates was the opening of USC's Thomas and Dorothy Leavey Library—the realization of a 10-year dream—in fall 1994. This new facility, dubbed the "gateway to ideas," rep-resented a sea change for the USC Libraries, shifting the focus from collecting books and journals to pro-viding students with electronic access

Above: With the start of the fall term in 1994, USC's long-awaited Thomas and Dorothy Leavey Library opened its doors. The high-tech teaching library was designed to bring students and faculty together in an atmosphere of collegial learning. [photo © John Livzey]

to texts, journals and visual materials from around the world.

The centerpiece of the strategic initiative in undergraduate education, the highest priority identified in USC's 1994 strategic plan, was a far-reaching overhaul of USC's general education requirements. The goal was to develop a program that would help increase USC's undergraduate retention rate, link students to each other through a solid body of basic knowledge and provide a distinctive academic "signature" to set USC students apart from undergraduates at other universities. "We're establishing an identifiable core," said Michael A. Diamond, then executive vice provost, in announcing plans for the new curriculum in September 1996. "We can say, 'This is what you'll get only if you come to USC,' as opposed to offering a smorgasbord of courses."

Two and a half years in preparation, the new curriculum was approved in summer 1996 and fully operational in fall 1997. It encompassed six core courses spanning the humanities, natural sciences and social sciences—all taught exclusively by tenured and tenure-track professors and centrally overseen by the USC College of Letters, Arts and Sciences— that applied to bachelor's-level students in all of the university's schools, from business to fine arts. By significantly cutting back the number of required general-education credits, the curriculum freed up electives so that students could complete a second major, a minor or another secondary emphasis, and it also enabled them to change majors more easily. As Provost Armstrong told *USC Chronicle* in September 1996,

"We want our students to be able to sample, in some depth, a broader spectrum of subjects than has been possible in the past."

This approach was grounded in Sample's realization that, at elite universities such as USC, the undergraduate program in many ways was becoming preparatory—in the way high school used to be—for further specialization at the graduate or professional-school level. USC was among the first universities in the country to understand this emerging change in the nature and purpose of the baccalaureate degree. Because the bachelor's degree was not likely to be the terminal degree for its students, USC needed to create an educational foundation that would be both strong and diverse in order to serve its graduates well into the 21st century.

Accordingly, hand-in-hand with the new core curriculum, USC

Speaking to a capacity crowd in Bovard Auditorium, former Israeli prime minister Shimon Peres opened the 1996–97 season of the USC President's Distinguished Lecture Series. His talk was covered by ABC, NBC, CNN, United Press International, Voice of America, Reuters and a number of local television and radio stations. [photo by Irene Fertik, courtesy of USC University Archives]

A STRONGER TROJAN FAMILY

[photo courtesy of USC Public Relations]

The years since 1991 have witnessed an inspiring expansion and revivification of the Trojan Family. The university's 1993 Role and Mission Statement drew attention to the "extraordinary closeness and willingness to help one another" that are evident among USC students, alumni, faculty and staff—but the compass of this supportive community has extended far beyond those four constituencies. As President Sample put it in his 2000 state-of-the-university address:

> Who is a part of the Trojan Family? Who is actually under the Trojan tent? Well, it's a very, very big tent. It includes alumni, students, parents of students, faculty, staff and emeriti. It includes members of our Board of Trustees and our boards of councilors, along with donors, athletic fans and neighborhood partners. All of these people are heavily invested in USC, both emotionally and economically.

"Sample is a person who values inclusiveness and not exclusiveness," confirmed Stanley P. Gold, chairman of the USC Board of Trustees since 2002, "... and I think the university is better for it."

By the same token, when the General Alumni Association changed its name to the USC Alumni Association in 1998–99, William C. (Bill) Allen, association president, coined a new watchword for the group: "lifelong and worldwide." Both the name and the slogan signaled a redoubled commitment to outreach and diversity, and a conviction that all alumni—wherever they might find themselves—ought to have a connection to their university for the rest of their lives.

Even in the face of this growing inclusiveness within the university community, USC's skyrocketing stature since 1991 and the subsequent stiffening of academic standards caused some to fear that fewer legacies (that is, children and grandchildren of Trojan alumni) would be admitted. Yet in fact the opposite occurred. Whereas in 1991 about 10 percent of freshmen in USC's entering class were legacies, that percentage had risen to about 20 percent by 2005.

With increasing momentum as the Trojan Family has expanded, its collective vision, spirit and determination have become a powerful force in USC's upward movement. Reflecting on USC's progress in recent decades, longtime USC administrator Robert Biller described it in this way: "The single most important thing that's happened is that the community—faculty, staff, students and alumni—gradually came to believe that the place didn't need to be a third-rate regional school, that it could be first rate, and applied itself to it."

Kicking off the second year of the President's Distinguished Artist Series, jazz great Wayne Shorter—accompanied by the USC Thornton Symphony—performed before a packed house in Bovard Auditorium on September 8, 2000. [photo © Lee Salem Photography, courtesy of the USC Office of the President]

developed an array of new academic and professional minors, offering students the opportunity to study subjects across widely separated fields. Under this arrangement, a student majoring in the arts and sciences now was able to take a minor in business, cinema-television, engineering, public administration or another professional field—an opportunity that, according to Sample, simply wasn't available at most private research universities. As of fall 2005, USC offered approximately 120 different minors—the broadest selection of any university in the United States—and the notion of "breadth with depth" had become a hallmark of undergraduate education at USC.

To recognize outstanding students who have taken advantage of the educational opportunities unique to USC by studying subjects widely separated across the academic landscape, the university announced its distinctive Renaissance Scholars program in 1999. Fully implemented with the naming of USC's first 14 Renaissance Scholars the following spring, this program—believed to be the first award of its kind in American higher education—offers $10,000 prizes to as many as 20 graduating seniors each year who have distinguished themselves in two or more broadly divergent fields of study. Sample articulated the philosophy underlying the scholarships when he addressed the newly minted graduates at USC's 2000 commencement exercises: "Due to extraordinary anticipated advances in medical science, I would expect that most of you will live beyond the age of 100 and work past the age of 80. You will probably have three or four different careers during your lifetimes…. USC has tried to prepare you for this new reality."

Further enhancements to USC's undergraduate program included the establishment of several new residential colleges, expanded opportunities for undergraduates to participate in research, and the creation of the position of dean of religious life to support campus ministers and help students address moral and spiritual concerns. Additionally, in 1993, USC launched an innovative eight-year B.A./M.D. program—a joint effort of the medical school and the College of Letters, Arts and Sciences—to encourage high-achieving students to balance their pre-med studies with a liberal arts education by assuring them admission to the medical school, contingent upon the successful

completion of their baccalaureate degree, maintenance of their GPAs and requisite MCAT scores. USC Spectrum (part of the Division of Student Affairs) was created to augment arts and cultural programming. Sample also inaugurated the President's Distinguished Lecture Series in 1996, bringing men and women who have distinguished themselves in contemporary life—people such as Madeleine Albright, Shimon Peres, Gen. Colin Powell, Gen. H. Norman Schwarzkopf (M.S. 1964) Margaret Thatcher and Lech Walesa—to campus to discuss significant issues of the day. This program was followed by the President's Distinguished Artist Series, through which artists such as violin legend Isaac Stern, Chicana novelist and poet Sandra Cisneros and jazz great Wayne Shorter have come to USC.

Within a remarkably brief period of time, it became patently clear that an improvement in undergraduate education would be one of the triumphs of Sample's administration. In the 1997–98 academic year, USC for the first time in its history accepted fewer than half of the students who applied as new freshmen—thereby acquiring the status of a "highly selective institution" according to the standards of numerous college rating services. By 1999–2000, USC ranked within the top 1 percent of all U.S. colleges and universities in terms of selectivity. The 2001 edition of the *Newsweek/Kaplan How To Get Into College* guide named USC one of America's nine "hottest schools" based on its ethnic diversity, abundant scholarships, small classroom sizes and sterling academic reputation. Likewise, in 2001, the

Since 1995, USC's annual Friends and Neighbors Service Day, sponsored by the USC Volunteer Center, has teamed students with community residents to paint, sweep, shovel, weed and provide general clean-up at schools, shelters and nonprofit organizations in the vicinity of the University Park campus. The one-day "volunteer blitz"—which expanded to include the Health Sciences campus in 2000—was conceived to integrate faculty, staff and students, especially freshmen, into the community, and to serve as a portal to other volunteer opportunities. [photo courtesy of the USC Office of Civic and Community Relations]

Left: USC had been sending student volunteers and researchers to work at Norwood Street Elementary School for some 20 years before the Family of Five Schools formalized the relationship in 1994. In 1995, Norwood fourth- and fifth-graders gathered around a duct tape-wrapped Tommy Trojan together with (back row, from left) USC Office of Civic and Community Relations executive director Kay Kyung-Sook Song, vice president for external relations Jane Pisano and Norwood teacher Cora Anderson. [photo courtesy of the USC Office of Civic and Community Relations]

Below: Serving children from kindergarten through sixth grade in the Family of Schools, the USC ReadersPlus program places Trojan students, such as Kimberly Bonner (pictured, right), in local schools to provide one-on-one tutoring in reading and math. [photo by Claudio Cambon, courtesy of the USC Office of Civic and Community Relations]

Association of American Colleges and Universities singled USC out as one of 16 "leadership institutions" in recognition of its innovations in undergraduate education both within and outside of the classroom.

At the time of its 125th anniversary in 2005–06, USC had become regarded nationally as a pacesetter in undergraduate education. With students clamoring for admission, the university was attracting 11 applications for every freshman opening— more than double the number in 1991—and the average SAT score for USC's entering freshmen had risen from 1070 in fall 1991 to 1364 in fall 2005. No other university had increased its SAT scores as quickly or as spectacularly as this. Also during that same period, the number of National Merit Scholars enrolled at USC rose from 33 to 194.

A Strong Culture of Public Service

USC's time-honored tradition of service to community vigorously took root and blossomed during Sample's administration—and in so doing, it became a pivotal factor in the enhancement of the university's undergraduate programs as well as in the burgeoning strength, prestige and outward reach of the institution overall.

While the Trojan Family was galvanized to help rebuild the ravaged City of Angels in the aftermath of the civil unrest of spring 1992, Sample returned to a "priority point" he had raised in his inaugural address. To fulfill its civic responsibility while ensuring that time and money would not be spread too thin, he called upon the university to "pull in its horns" and concentrate on making visible improvements in the neighborhoods immediately surrounding USC's two campuses. "Regardless of where we live," he said, "every person who works at USC has a tremendous stake in the surrounding community—financially and morally."

Extensive consultation with campus neighbors revealed that the two most important priorities for the community were good public schools and safe streets. If those two priorities constituted the paramount programs of USC's community outreach efforts, university administrators believed, other improvements would naturally follow. The value of this approach was borne out in the next few years.

As a formal mechanism for coordinating USC's community-service efforts, Sample announced the formation of a nonprofit corporation, USC Neighborhood Outreach, Inc., that would receive funds through the United Way to launch new,

"signature" university assistance programs. Charged with developing these various projects was the Administrative Outreach Group headed by Jane Pisano. "We want to touch our neighbors in multiple ways," Pisano said, "by pulling together resources from across the university."

In its first comprehensive, universitywide community-service effort, USC initiated an ambitious United Way appeal in fall 1993, encouraging staff and faculty to contribute to university outreach through the United Way of Greater Los Angeles. A significant outcome of this first appeal was the Neighborhood Resource Center, administered by the USC School of Social Work, which was established to provide counseling, information and assistance to local families in need of health and social services.

The following year, in fall 1994, USC launched an independent giving campaign that invited staff and faculty to invest directly in efforts to "visibly improve" the neighborhoods surrounding USC's two campuses. This new drive, dubbed the Good Neighbors Campaign, offered a mechanism for giving that was administered by the university rather than United Way. While United Way remained an option, giving directly to USC Neighborhood Outreach meant

Jane G. Pisano joined USC in 1991 as dean of the School of Public Administration. Going on to hold the posts of vice president and senior vice president for external relations, she conceptualized and implemented USC's Good Neighbors Campaign, spearheaded the Family of Five Schools partnership and helped organize the Kid Watch program. [photo by Irene Fertik, courtesy of *USC Trojan Family* magazine]

Above left: Among the programs sponsored by the university's Business Expansion Network (BEN) was FastTrac, an entrepreneurial training program for aspiring business owners developed with support from UNOCAL and the City of Los Angeles during the 1980s. In this picture, USC BEN director Debra Esparza (far right) applauded FastTrac participants as part of BEN's fourth anniversary celebration in 1997. [photo by Irene Fertik, courtesy of the Office of Civic and Community Relations]

Above right: University Park residents Carmen Perez (left) and Guadalupe Andrade, pictured here in 2002, formed part of a broad network of community members dedicated to creating a small-town atmosphere by watching out for each others' children through USC's Kid Watch program. [photo by Katharine Díaz, courtesy of the Office of Civic and Community Relations]

that 100 percent of donations were used to fund joint-venture projects involving groups at USC and community-based organizations in an effort to improve the neighborhoods surrounding the University Park and Health Sciences campuses.

The flagship program of USC Neighborhood Outreach was founded in 1994, when USC partnered with five schools near the University Park campus to provide educational, cultural and development opportunities for pre-kindergarten to 12th-grade neighborhood youths. Among the most successful projects implemented through this partnership—originally called the "USC Family of Five Schools" —was Kid Watch, launched in 1996, which mobilized volunteers to ensure safe passage for schoolchildren as they walked to and from school, local parks, museums, libraries and other

neighborhood institutions near the University Park campus. Kid Watch won a community policing award from the International Association of Chiefs of Police in 1999, inspired a similar citywide effort sponsored by the Los Angeles Unified School District in 2000 and as of fall 2005 involved nearly 1,000 volunteers and some 9,000 children. Likewise, the USC Family of Five Schools—later renamed the USC Family of Schools—expanded from five school partners to eight. A similar program, the Health Sciences Campus Partner Schools, was launched in 1999 with four schools in the neighborhood surrounding USC's Health Sciences campus.

All told, as of fall 2005, USC's Good Neighbors Campaign had raised over $7 million in voluntary contributions from faculty and staff.

USC also stepped up its efforts

to provide educational support to children in its local neighborhoods through the Neighborhood Academic Initiative (NAI), rewarding students who completed the six-year college-preparation program and met USC's competitive admission requirements with a full 4.5-year financial package. Of the more than 370 scholars who had graduated from the NAI as of fall 2005, 125 were attending or had graduated from USC, and 164 were attending or had graduated from another four-year college.

Under the direction of Carolyn Webb de Macias, appointed vice president for external relations in 2002, the Community Education Academy was created to help focus USC's wide-ranging efforts—including oversight of national programs such as Head Start and Upward Bound—to enhance educational opportunities for neighborhood children.

Adding yet another dimension to its community-building efforts, the university implemented the Neighborhood Homeownership Program in 1995. This program provided financial incentives to help faculty and staff purchase and occupy homes in communities surrounding USC's two campuses. Additionally, USC's Local Vendor Program, Small Business Development Office and Business Expansion Network (later anchored in the Los Angeles Metropolitan Minority Business Development Center, which it has operated since 1996) were created to promote the success of small businesses and entrepreneurs in local neighborhoods.

This far-reaching investment in community became a national mark of distinction when the editors of the *Time/Princeton Review College Guide*—a co-publication of *Time* magazine and *The Princeton Review* —declared USC "College of the Year 2000," calling the university out for organizing "the most ambitious social-outreach program of any private university in the nation." "More institutions might do well to emulate USC's enlightened self-interest," the editors pronounced, "for not only has the 'hood dramatically improved, but so has the university."

Sample beamed in his 2000

Above: Since 2004, the USC School of Cinema-Television's Electronic Arts Game Innovation Lab has provided a think tank-type environment in which students can expand the frontiers of game design by developing, prototyping and testing new concepts. [photo courtesy of the USC School of Cinema-Television]

Below left: The editors of the *Time/Princeton Review College Guide* named USC "College of the Year 2000" in recognition of the bonds the university had forged with local schools, neighborhood residents, police, businesses and community organizations. [photo courtesy of USC Public Relations]

annual address to the faculty: "USC has developed something for which other universities and colleges would give their right arm—a strong culture of public service among our undergraduates."

An Academic Powerhouse

USC already had strong academic programs in a variety of fields by the time Sample came on board in 1991, but he was determined to elevate the university to ever-greater heights. He delivered on this promise by pushing USC to concentrate on programs that leveraged its unique institutional strengths in tandem with its unparalleled competitive edge in what he consistently underscored as the three prime criteria for real estate—"location, location and location." It was precisely this emphasis on USC's role as an anchor institution in Southern California that led to the identification of the four critical pathways to excellence (life sciences, communications, the arts and the urban paradigm) that were outlined in the four-year update on USC's 1994 strategic plan. By focusing its energies in this way, USC—the oldest private university in the West—emerged as one of the leading private research universities in the United States.

One of the most tangible measures of this dramatic gain in academic prowess under Sample's watch has been the increasing eminence of USC's faculty. Sponsored research by USC faculty investigators nearly doubled in the 1990s, and by fall 2005, USC ranked among the top 10 private universities in terms of extramurally funded research— bringing in some $430 million a year in contract and grant funds. The faculty included 44 scholars elected to membership in the three national academies recognized by the AAU (National Academy of Engineering, National Academy of Sciences and

Below left: Opened in fall 2000 with a $45 million grant and a challenge from the U.S. Army to develop virtual-reality and simulation technologies to help prepare troops to make critical on-the-ground decisions, the Institute for Creative Technologies (ICT) draws researchers from the USC Viterbi School of Engineering, School of Cinema-Television and Annenberg School for Communication. In fall 2004, the Army awarded ICT a new five-year, $100 million contract—the largest ever received by USC. [photo courtesy of USC Public Relations]

Below center: Priya Vashishta joined USC as part of a trio of researchers who were recruited in 2002. Together with colleagues Rajiv Kalia and Aiichiro Nakano, Vashishta received a joint appointment in engineering and the college. The team became part of USC's High Performance Computing and Communications program, whose supercomputer was ranked the second most powerful computer system in an academic setting as of November 2005. [photo © John Livzey, courtesy of USC Public Relations]

Below right: More than 400 alumni, trustees, faculty, administrators and guest speakers attended the 2004 USC Asia Conference in Seoul, Korea, which focused on national security, healthcare, technology, urban development and economic issues facing the Pacific Rim. Thanks to the hard work of the USC Korean Alumni Association, the program also featured cultural events, including a performance of traditional Korean dance. [photo courtesy of the USC Asia Conference]

DISTANCE LEARNING

USC's earliest forays into distance education can be traced to the "University of the Air," an educational radio program that debuted in 1934, and English professor Frank Baxter's wildly popular "Shakespeare on TV" venture in 1953. But it wasn't until the 1970s that the notion of distance education gained a truly firm foothold at USC.

In 1968, USC electrical engineering professor Jack Munushian hit on a way of expanding the engineering school's successful industrial outreach program by using television as a medium for instruction. He persuaded the Olin Foundation to make an unprecedented third gift to the university, this time to support the school in establishing the Norman Topping Instructional Television Center and the Instructional Television Network (ITV) in 1972. Decades ahead of its time, the ITV used closed-circuit television to beam lectures directly from USC to the corporate offices of Hughes Aircraft and Aerospace Corporation (Munushian's former employers) as well as other aerospace companies throughout Southern California. Expanding from a regional to a national and international focus, the program migrated to cable and satellite delivery in the 1980s, and ultimately to a high-speed Internet-based delivery system. It was renamed the Distance Education Network (DEN) in 2002, and as of 2005 had become the largest graduate engineering e-learning program in the United States.

Jack Munushian
[photo courtesy of the USC Viterbi School of Engineering]

Other units as well have pushed the frontiers of distance education at USC. Beginning in 1972, the university's business school operated the Flexible Education Program, which was built around instructional texts used in conjunction with audio- and videotapes. With the advent of Internet technology, the USC Davis School of Gerontology in 1998 launched "AgeWorks," an online master's degree program, soon branching out to offer undergraduate as well as graduate degrees. In 1999, President Sample appointed a special Presidential Commission on Distance and Distributed Learning, which recommended that the university develop new initiatives in this area, structured around the needs of individual colleges and schools.

Jump-starting this effort, in January 2006, Provost C. L. Max Nikias announced that USC would put in place an infrastructure to enable faculty and students across the university to experiment with new teaching and learning paradigms involving instructional technology, multimedia and the Internet. The plan, directed primarily at master's-level graduate students and students in the university's continuing education programs, called for the establishment of 12 studio classrooms outfitted expressly for technology-enhanced and distance learning on USC's various campuses. It also encompassed training for faculty members, seed funding for large-scale development projects and advisement for deans and their leadership teams.

In January 2002, students moved into the International Residential College at Parkside (pictured above), USC's first new on-campus residence hall since Pardee Tower opened in 1982. Faculty master and University Professor Kevin Starr (pictured below left, with student Sara Corbett), then also California state librarian, established Monday night faculty master dinners at the new facility, which had the mission of fostering cross-cultural understanding and learning among students from the United States and abroad. [photos by Irene Fertik, courtesy of USC Public Relations]

Institute of Medicine). Distinguished Professor George A. Olah's receipt of the Nobel Prize in chemistry marked yet another outward sign of USC's rising academic stature. At a campus reception honoring him following the announcement of the award in 1994, Olah said: "I hope that this recognition will put USC on the map as a center for science. I think this prize is another indication of the way that USC is maturing."

An International University

Continuing to raise USC's global profile has been yet another major thrust of the Sample administration, and in 1994, to give the university what Sample called a coherent

"foreign policy," the position of vice provost for international affairs was created. Moreover, in recognition of the significance of its location in Los Angeles, USC began to concentrate its international efforts even more intently on the Pacific Rim. Sample was the first leader in Los Angeles to articulate the city's position definitively as *the* capital of the Pacific Rim. He focused on this theme in his 1999 annual address to the faculty: "The capital city of the Pacific Rim is not Tokyo or Hong Kong or Singapore or San Francisco or Seattle. Rather, the capital city— the 'Rome of the Rim,' if you will—is Los Angeles, and USC is located right in the heart of this new capital."

Reinforcing this connection, USC partnered with UCLA, UC Berkeley and Caltech to establish the Association of Pacific Rim Universities (APRU), with Sample serving as the group's founding chairman during the 1997–98 academic year. From those modest beginnings, the APRU has grown into a consortium of 36 leading universities from 16 economies around the Pacific Rim, all working together to contribute to economic, scientific and cultural advancement in the Pacific Rim.

Additionally, USC sponsored its first international conference, a three-day gathering held in Hong Kong, in fall 2001. The event show-

GLORY DAYS FOR TROJAN ATHLETICS

In January 1993, USC's own Mike Garrett returned to Troy as USC's athletic director. He replaced Mike McGee, who resigned in November 1992 to take a position at the University of South Carolina. Upon assuming his new post, Garrett stressed that his first priority was to make sure USC's student-athletes received the best education; his second priority was to win.

There can be no doubt that winning—both on and off the playing field— was the only thing Garrett knew how to do. As a USC student, he had been a star football tailback—a two-time All-American and the university's first Heisman Trophy winner (1965). After earning a degree in sociology from USC in 1967, he went on to an illustrious NFL career, playing in two Super Bowls and becoming the first player to rush for 1,000 yards for two teams. In 1986, he earned a law degree from Western State University College of Law in Fullerton, California, later serving as director of business development for the Great Western Forum, working in the San Diego district attorney's office and holding management positions in the retail, construction and real estate industries.

Mike Garrett
[photo courtesy of USC
University Archives]

Not surprisingly, Garrett proved to be a phenomenal athletic director—and one of his crowning achievements was building a coaching staff that returned the Trojan football team to its glory days.

The feat was not without a few false starts. In December 1997, Garrett fired John Robinson, five seasons into his second head-coaching tenure at USC, and brought in Paul Hackett, who had been an assistant coach in the late 1970s. Hackett's hard work failed to translate into wins after three years, however, and Garrett relieved him of his duties. Replacing Hackett was Pete Carroll, who came to USC in 2000 with 26 years of NFL and college coaching experience. "I offered the job to Pete Carroll three years ago, but he couldn't take it," Garrett said in making the announcement. "I'm excited that he's finally here. We've recruited very well in the last few years and, at the same time, our football team has had great academic success. Now, it's time to have success on the field. With Pete Carroll, I believe we will do that."

Garrett couldn't have been more right.

In 2002, Carroll's second season at USC, the Trojans beat Iowa in the Orange Bowl and posted an 11–2 overall record, USC's first 11-win season

since 1979 and its highest ranking since 1988. The team went on to rack up four consecutive Pac-10 titles from 2002 to 2005, and back-to-back national championships in 2003 and 2004. Between 2002 and 2005, USC set a record by having three Heisman Trophy winners—Carson Palmer, Matt Leinart and Reggie Bush. What is more, USC's 37 wins from 2003 to 2005 represented the winningest three-year period in Trojan football history.

And with Garrett at the helm, USC's athletic achievements haven't been limited to the gridiron. The Trojan water polo teams also moved into the limelight, with the men's team capturing national crowns in 1998, 2003 and 2005, and the women's team in 1999 and 2004. In fact, the 2004 women's team was the first in NCAA championship history to go undefeated during the regular season. Coaching both teams was Jovan Vavic, who was named coach of the year for the men's team in 2003 and 2005, and for the women's team in 2004.

On January 21, 2004, the Los Angeles City Council honored three national champions from Troy—the football, women's volleyball and men's water polo teams—by declaring the day "USC Trojans Day in L.A." The following month, in yet another tribute to USC's triumvirate of championship teams, Congress passed HR 511, a resolution extolling the extraordinary talent, efforts and achievements of the university's student-athletes and coaches.

As of USC's 125th anniversary, Trojan athletics programs had accumulated a total of 16 national titles under Garrett's watch. Garrett also had bolstered women's sports and scholarships, boosted fundraising for USC's athletic programs and overseen the greatest expansion of facilities in the history of Trojan athletics. When a long-awaited campus events center began taking shape at the southeast corner of Jefferson Boulevard and Figueroa Street in December 2004, President Sample gave the credit to Garrett: "For more than 50 years Trojans have dreamed of having an arena like this, but it took a leader like Mike Garrett to make it happen." Officially named the Galen Center in honor of longtime fans Helene and Louis Galen, who gave $50 million to support it, this splendid new facility—opened in fall 2006—encompasses a 255,000-square-foot arena with 10,258 seats to benefit USC's basketball and volleyball teams as well as arts and cultural events.

AN UNPRECEDENTED BUILDING BOOM

Much more than a home base for USC's basketball and volleyball teams, the Galen Center was built with the entire community in mind. The new facility plays host to concerts, lectures, dance performances, commencement ceremonies and more. [photo by Philip Channing, courtesy of USC Public Relations]

By the time of its 125th anniversary year, USC was in the midst of the largest building boom in its history, adding more than a million square feet of new research, classroom, student-activity, residential and parking space. Besides the Galen Center, Troy's much-anticipated campus sports and cultural events venue, a high priority of the program was the enrichment of student life. By nearly doubling housing opportunities for students, the new construction would ensure USC's transformation from a commuter school to a residential university.

Most of the construction, however, was intended to open up new opportunities for USC's life sciences and medical enterprises. Accordingly, major facilities already completed by the 2005–06 academic year included the Dornsife Cognitive Neuroscience Imaging Center (opened in 2004) and the Molecular and Computational Biology Building (dedicated in spring 2005) on the University Park campus. Additionally, a new medical office building, Healthcare Consultation Center II, opened on the Health Sciences campus in spring 2004. In parallel with these USC projects, the County of Los Angeles had moved ahead with construction of a 600-bed, $1 billion replacement for the aging LAC+USC Medical Center, which suffered damage in the 1994 Northridge earthquake.

Yet another project on the medical horizon was a planned biomedical research park adjacent to USC's Health Sciences campus. Making the most of USC's institutional strengths and crystallizing Southern California's status as what Sample has repeatedly referred to as "the world capital of the biotechnology industry," this new enterprise was conceived to catalyze the work of entrepreneurs not only from USC, but also from UCLA, Caltech and other local medical institutions. With the goal of providing both a hub for integrative biomedical research on USC's Health Sciences campus and an anchor for the new research park, the Eli and Edythe Broad Foundation made a gift of $25 million in February 2006 to create the Broad Institute for Integrative Biology and Stem Cell Research at the Keck School of Medicine of USC.

A guiding philosophy underlying all of the new construction was the notion of an integrated campus. "With these new buildings and projects, USC maintains the architectural grace, elegance and integrity of a distinguished past while meeting the needs of the 21st century," Sample said.

cased the university's global reach while promoting networking among some 250 attendees with business, commercial and educational interests in Asia. Subsequent conferences were held in Shanghai in 2002, and in Seoul in 2004.

With Sample at the helm, USC opened international offices in Hong Kong, Jakarta, Mexico City, Tokyo and Taipei. Furthermore, as of the time of the university's 125th anniversary, four members of the USC Board of Trustees were from overseas (Hong Kong, Japan, Korea and India).

The effects of this broad international focus extended to USC's student population as well. The university had attracted students from foreign lands almost since its founding, and by fall 2005, USC was enrolling a student body representing more than 100 different countries. A survey conducted by the Institute of International Education showed that USC, for the fourth consecutive year, had the highest number of international students of any university in the United States, with the majority of foreign students hailing from areas on the Pacific Rim. In a world of increasingly intermingling cultures, the opportunity to develop a network of friends and acquaintances from around the world offered an undisputed advantage for USC's domestic and international students alike.

Inventing the Future: USC's Plan for Increasing Academic Excellence

In his 2003 state-of-the-university speech, Sample commended the USC community for having completed a record-breaking fund-raising drive, undergirded by the university's "resoundingly successful" strategic plan. But then he quickly revisited a theme he had introduced in his inaugural address:

> This is decidedly not the time for us to slow up or take a breather. Rather, we must keep pressing upward toward increasingly lofty goals. We must fire up the furnaces of ambition to a white heat, and take advantage of the extraordinary and exciting opportunities before us. Thus our celebration of the completion of our Building on Excellence campaign does not mark the close of our efforts to make USC a better university; rather, it signals a new beginning.

In short order, Sample clarified his vision of precisely what this "new beginning" should entail. In his 2004 address to the faculty, he explained:

> In order to elevate USC to a higher position in the academic

USC's Bovard Auditorium was the site of a live-broadcast Democratic presidential primary debate on February 26, 2004, sponsored by CNN and the *Los Angeles Times*. Standing before more than 700 students and special guests attending the forum were (above, from left) *Times* editor John Carroll, President Sample, candidates John Edwards, John F. Kerry, Dennis J. Kucinich and the Rev. Al Sharpton, and moderator Larry King. [photos © Lee Salem Photography, courtesy of USC Public Relations]

The Molecular and Computational Biology Building, opened in April 2005, for the first time united the USC College of Letters, Arts and Sciences' molecular and computational biology faculty in a shared physical space—paving the way for pathbreaking research on the frontiers of genomics as well as molecular biology, genetics, bioinformatics and molecular evolution. The building was slated to be rededicated as Ray R. Irani Hall in February 2007. [photo by Brian Morri/211 Photography, courtesy of USC Public Relations]

firmament, we have aggressively and successfully pursued excellence as measured by conventional yardsticks. Now, because of our achievements and our upward momentum, we have an opportunity to help develop new yardsticks by which we and our competitors will be measured. In other words, USC has the opportunity to help define new metrics and set new standards for research universities throughout the world.

To guide the university in seizing this opportunity, a new strategic plan was approved by the Board of Trustees on October 6, 2004. Titled "USC's Plan for Increasing Academic Excellence: Building Strategic Capabilities for the University of the 21st Century," the document—developed over the course of two years by a committee of senior faculty and deans headed by Provost

Armstrong—enjoined the university not to lose sight of the strategies set forth in the 1994 and 1998 plans, nor to abandon its traditional core values and shared ethical principles of ensuring freedom of academic inquiry, upholding the standards of the Trojan Family, pursuing an entrepreneurial approach to challenges and committing itself to ethical conduct. At the same time, the plan acknowledged the need for more flexible strategies that would enable USC to accelerate its progress in the face of rapidly evolving external circumstances.

With the goal of making USC "one of the most influential and productive research universities in the world," the new plan set forth three key approaches: meeting societal needs, expanding USC's global presence and promoting learner-centered education. The first two approaches addressed the growing demand to blend strong theoretical research with practical applications, and to ensure USC's continued effectiveness and influence on an international scale; both also built on USC's traditional strengths and entrepreneurial heritage. The third approach, on the other hand, would require the university to sharpen its focus on the educational needs of students rather than developing programs based on the structure and needs of the institution.

INTERNATIONAL ALUMNA OF THE 20TH CENTURY

Far left: President Sample presented alumna Lei Jieqiong—101 years of age —with USC's International Alumna of the Century Award in May 2006. [photo by Stanley P. Gold]

Left: Formal portrait of the young Lei Jieqiong [photo courtesy of Valerie Naso]

In May 2006, members of the USC Board of Trustees took a historic trip to the Chinese capitals of Beijing, Shanghai and Hong Kong, marking the trustees' third official visit to China. The first occurred in 1978, when USC became the first U.S. university to visit Beijing during the reestablishment of diplomatic relations between the two countries. Nearly two decades later, in 1997, President Sample led a delegation to China to establish the Association of Pacific Rim Universities.

While in Beijing on this most recent trip, President Sample announced the creation of the USC U.S.-China Institute, an interdisciplinary institute dedicated to research on contemporary relations between China and the United States. He also took the occasion to honor one of the university's most inspiring alumnae for her accomplishments on the world stage. USC's International Alumna of the 20th Century Award was bestowed upon Lei Jieqiong (M.A. 1931), an eminent educator and sociologist who played a key role in the development of the social sciences in China.

Lei was born in 1905 near Canton, China, and traveled to the United States in 1924 to study chemistry at Stanford University. Distressed by events at home, however, she developed an interest in sociology. After learning about the work of USC's Emory S. Bogardus in diagnosing social problems, she moved to Los Angeles in 1926 and enrolled as a graduate student in the sociology department at USC.

While at USC, Lei gave lessons in Cantonese to earn money. Most of her students were children of Chinese immigrants, and Lei was struck by the way in which they were alienated from both their heritage and American society. With the encouragement of her professors, Lei conducted wide-ranging interviews with members of Los Angeles' Chinese community and completed a master's thesis, titled "A Study of American-Born and American-Reared Chinese in Los Angeles." Her work documented the human effects of discrimination as well as her hope that American-educated Chinese would benefit from the "ability to interpret the oriental and occidental cultures which are now meeting across the Pacific Basin."

After receiving her degree in 1931, Lei returned to China and began teaching at Yenching University in Beijing. During the war, she became an organizer. Her career as an educator and administrator continued after the communist victory with her service on a special commission on education, and on various bodies dealing with women and children.

On the political front, Lei was a founding member of the Central Committee of the China Association for Promoting Democracy, formed in Shanghai in 1945. In 1956, she was elected as a delegate to the National Peoples' Congress, a China-wide legislative body of which she later became vice chair. She also held posts as vice chair of the Standing Committee of the National People's Congress, vice chair of the National Committee of the Chinese People's Political Consultative Conference, and vice mayor of Beijing.

President Sample (right) officiated as former engineering dean C. L. Max Nikias was formally installed as USC's new provost and senior vice president for academic affairs on September 22, 2005. [photo © Lee Salem, courtesy of USC Public Relations]

To meet these ambitious goals, the plan enumerated four strategic capabilities—expanding interdisciplinary research and teaching, linking basic and applied research, continuing to build networks and partnerships, and increasing the university's responsiveness to the needs of learners—for positioning USC to meet challenges that are unknowable today. "It's not a roadmap with detailed directions and a final destination," said Sample in describing the plan. "Rather, it's a treasure map of possibilities for pushing out our current frontiers in order to encourage interdisciplinary research, lifelong learning, the strengthening of our Pacific Rim connections, the proliferation of technology transfer, and collaborations with industry and other universities."

Looking Ahead

In fall 2004, Lloyd Armstrong, who had served as USC's provost and senior vice president for academic affairs for 12 years, announced that he would retire the following June and return to teaching. Armstrong stepped down having led some of the most dramatic academic advances in the history of the university.

Taking Armstrong's place at the dawn of the university's 125th year was C. L. Max Nikias, USC's engineering dean, outstripping more than 160 candidates who applied or were nominated for the position. As dean, Nikias had established strong connections with a wide range of federal and private funding agencies. He also had been instrumental in bringing two NSF-funded Engineering Research Centers to USC—the Integrated Media Systems Center, of which he was founding director; and the Biomimetic MicroElectronic Systems Center, directed by the Keck School of Medicine's Mark Humayun, developer of the first retinal implant—along with the country's first Homeland Security Center of Excellence, developed in conjunction with the School of Policy, Planning, and Development.

Nikias assumed his new duties on June 1, 2005. In his installation speech the following September, he praised the university for having created "what others only pay lip service to: a bridge-building, cross-disciplinary culture that serves society's real needs." He also voiced his intention to heed Sample's caveat that USC must not pause, but rather accelerate its upward momentum.

True to form, USC took yet another step forward in September 2005, when Sample announced that the Shoah Foundation would become part of the USC College of Letters, Arts and Sciences with the launch of the USC Shoah Foundation Institute for Visual History and Education. Academy Award-winning filmmaker and USC trustee Steven Spielberg created the Shoah Foundation (named for the Hebrew word for catastrophe or devastation) in 1994 when, after making the film *Schindler's List*, he decided to collect and preserve historical testimony about the Holocaust. Over time, the collection grew to become the world's largest visual history archive, offering a digital library of nearly 52,000 testimonies of survivors and other witnesses to the Holocaust collected in 56 countries and in 32 languages. "We are pleased to welcome the Shoah Foundation as part of USC," Sample said. "It is a significant addition to our strengths in the humanities and social sciences...." Eventually, the intention is to expand the focus of the archive chronologically, geographically and topically. "Imagine educational products built around testimonials of Rwandan survivors, Darfurian survivors, even survivors of the Hurricane Katrina," said Douglas Greenberg, president and CEO of the Shoah Foundation, in an interview with the *Los Angeles Times*. "Our larger mission is documenting the experience of the people in the 21st century so that people in subsequent centuries will understand what the world was like."

Similarly, while USC observed its 125th anniversary with an ardent focus on what lies ahead, Sample paused to take a lesson from the past in his 2005 state-of-the-university address:

From our vantage point in the doorway of USC's 125th year, we have two views: one is the sepia-toned image of 53 students studying in a small, two-story frame building, situated in a mustard field and bearing the pretentious name "The University of Southern California" over its front door. The other is a sweeping view of the comprehensive research university which is USC today—comprising two campuses on 305 acres, a liberal arts college and 17 professional schools, some 32,000 students, a $2.5 billion endowment, over 3,000 full-time faculty and an international reputation for excellence. We have truly grown into the pretentious name with which we were christened 125 years ago.

As USC looks forward to redefining the research university of the 21st century, it takes on an audacious task indeed. But if past achievements are any indication of future prospects, there is every reason to believe that USC will fulfill its charge. Its trajectory is on the rise. "Change and success in universities are measured in terms of generations and sometimes even centuries," said Dennis F. Dougherty, USC's senior vice president for finance and chief financial officer. "But the change that [Sample] has brought about has taken place in the span of just over a decade. This is extraordinary."

Chairing the Board of Trustees at the time of USC's 125th anniversary was alumnus, attorney and corporate governance expert Stanley P. Gold, pictured here with his wife, Ilene. While ever-conscious of the continuing need for USC to "keep the pedal to the metal" as it moves into the future, Gold expressed optimism about USC's ability to maintain its upward momentum. "The thing I like best [about USC] is the huge diversity within the university, the fact that it is complex, multifaceted and multidisciplined," he said. "And when it all begins to work together, it's like a fine engine that is purring." [photo courtesy of USC University Archives]

Trojan victory signs held high, members of the Trojan Family filled Hahn Central Plaza during Festival 125. [photo © Lee Salem Photography, courtesy of the USC Office of Protocol and University Events]

USC's 125th Anniversary:

Inventing the Future, Honoring the Past

By Annette Moore

In 2003, USC embarked on a multi-year tribute to 125 years of Trojan history. The USC 125th Anniversary Project was conceived to showcase the ways in which USC set out to redefine the research university of the 21st century, while honoring its proud heritage as one of the oldest continuing academic and cultural institutions in the West. Activities ranged from special exhibits, lectures and performances to the publication of a book about the evolution of the University Park campus and its surrounding neighborhoods as well as this history—all organized under the theme of "Inventing the Future, Honoring the Past."

Taking advantage of the anniversary as a milestone in USC's focus on the road ahead, the university rolled out a new strategic plan in 2004, envisioning USC as one of the most influential and productive research universities in the world, and as a model for American higher education in the 21st century. A variety of academic conferences and a special scientific symposium co-sponsored with the journal *Science* in April 2006 reinforced this theme.

Left: USC commissioned a detailed pewter replica of Bovard Administration Building, painstakingly reproduced from original blueprints, as a memento of the university's 125th anniversary.

Right: A commemorative 18-month wall calendar featured historical entries as well as never-before-seen photographs of the modern campus.

In an effort spearheaded by first lady Kathryn Sample, USC also launched a project to discover and preserve the stories of its presidential spouses. The book *USC's First Ladies: A Trojan Family Album* was published to document the contributions of the wives of USC's presidents to the university's progress. Additionally, USC's "Gallery of First Ladies" debuted in May 2005. Established by the USC Board of Trustees and located on the second floor of Bovard Administration Building's north wing, the gallery displays portraits of the wives of USC's 10 presidents.

The showpiece of USC's anniversary celebration was "Festival 125," a four-day all-university open house that kicked off on October 6, 2005— 125 years to the day after USC welcomed its first students. Following an academic convocation featuring speeches, presentations by star faculty and a musical salute to the Trojan Family, the Spirit of Troy filled Hahn

USC's "Gallery of First Ladies," displaying portraits of the university's 10 presidents' wives, was conceived by Kathryn Sample and established by the Board of Trustees as part of the observation of USC's 125th anniversary. Attending the dedication ceremony in May 2005 were USC's three living first ladies (from left): Marilyn Edwards Zumberge (USC's ninth first lady), Kathryn Brunkow Sample (USC's tenth first lady) and Lucy Hubbard Haugh (USC's eighth first lady).

USC's First Ladies: A Trojan Family Album was published in 2005, giving readers a view of the development of the university through the lives and works of its presidential families. Posing with a copy of the newly minted book was USC's current first family (from left): Michelle Sample Smith, President Steven B. Sample, Kathryn Brunkow Sample and Elizabeth Sample.

[photos courtesy of the USC Office of the President]

Bovard Auditorium was packed to the gills for the academic convocation that kicked off USC's Festival 125. [photo © Lee Salem Photography, courtesy of the USC Office of Protocol and University Events]

Below left: Colorful banners proclaimed USC's 125th anniversary along the streets surrounding the University Park and Health Sciences campuses as well as up and down the Figueroa Corridor. [photo courtesy of USC Public Relations]

Below right: "You don't have to be a Trojan," said Los Angeles mayor Antonio Villaraigosa at Festival 125, "to respect USC's uncompromising commitment to Los Angeles." [photo © Lee Salem Photography, courtesy of the USC Office of Protocol and University Events]

Central Plaza with the strains of USC's best-loved songs as the Trojan Warrior burst out of a giant birthday cake.

The birthday party continued with a picnic lunch in Alumni Memorial Park. That evening, accompanied by the USC Thornton Symphony, virtuoso violinist Itzhak Perlman regaled a packed Bovard Auditorium as part of a gala concert that also marked the world premiere of *Capriccio for Piano and Orchestra*, a piece composed by USC faculty member Donald Crockett and specially commissioned for USC's 125th anniversary.

Giving the keynote address at Festival 125, Los Angeles mayor Antonio Villaraigosa praised USC for its commitment to community. "I want to say how lucky we all are to live in a city with a research university like USC," he said (Villaraigosa is an alumnus of UCLA). "There is no university that has played such an important role in the lives of its residents. You can take my word on that, because I graduated from the school down the street." The festival —which coincided with Trojan Parents Weekend and the Class of 1955 Reunion—saw the University Park campus thronged as some 100,000 students, parents, alumni, faculty, staff and neighbors enjoyed a full slate of performances, picnics, lectures and demonstrations. USC also

took the occasion to unveil its new 125th anniversary fountain. Located off of Exposition Boulevard, the fountain was a finishing touch to USC's new grand entry, completing a view northward to the university's first building, Widney Alumni House, at the end of Pardee Way.

USC Alumni Association-sponsored activities included a two-year slate of "USC on the Road" events that brought some of the university's most stimulating faculty, deans, administrators and graduates to speak to Trojan alumni groups in cities such as Chicago, Dallas, Honolulu, Mexico City, Sacramento and Seattle. Plans also were laid to equip the University Park and Health Sciences campuses with additional history stations, enameled plaques that present snapshots of Troy's history and traditions.

The observation of USC's 125th anniversary culminated in May 2006 with the 73rd annual Alumni Awards Dinner, the university's premier celebration of the Trojan Family.

Above: Festival 125's academic convocation included a rousing musical salute to the Trojan Family featuring the USC Thornton Jazz Orchestra (right) and the Fresh Start Community Gospel Choir (left).

Below: Members of the Half Century Trojans joined current students on the Bovard stage for Festival 125.

[photos © Lee Salem Photography, courtesy of the USC Office of Protocol and University Events]

Above, far left: At Festival 125, band director Arthur C. Bartner led the Spirit of Troy as it regaled the crowd with an assortment of USC's favorite songs.*

Left: Inside the Festival Pavilion, historical photos and artifacts displayed alongside exhibits of technological advances pioneered at USC gave visitors the opportunity to experience the dual themes of USC's 125th anniversary: Inventing the Future, Honoring the Past.*

Below left: Performances, lectures, demonstrations and exhibits on a series of stages and in buildings across campus gave Festival 125 participants a broad sampling of research, educational, cultural, athletic and community-service programs at USC. [photo by Michael Kloss, courtesy of the USC Office of Protocol and University Events]

Below center: Balloons and streamers wafted skyward as the Trojan Warrior burst from a giant birthday cake.*

Below right: Fourth- and fifth-graders from neighborhood schools enjoyed an art workshop sponsored by the USC Office of Civic and Community Relations and conducted under the watchful eye of Trojan Vision, the university's student-operated television station. [photo by Katharine A. Díaz, courtesy of the USC Office of Civic and Community Relations]

* [photos © Lee Salem Photography, courtesy of the USC Office of Protocol and University Events]

Clockwise from above left: Accompanied by the USC Thornton Symphony with conductor Larry Livingston, Itzhak Perlman—widely heralded as one of the greatest violinists of our time—gave a moving performance in Bovard Auditorium as part of the special USC Festival 125 concert. [photo © Lee Salem Photography, courtesy of the USC Office of Protocol and University Events]

Making a majestic statement for the University Park campus's main entrance at Pardee Way and Exposition Boulevard, USC's 125th anniversary fountain was unveiled on Saturday, October 8, 2005. [photo © Lee Salem Photography, courtesy of USC Public Relations]

At the fountain dedication, celebrants looked to the sky as 125 white doves were released. [photos © Lee Salem Photography, courtesy of USC Public Relations]

On Saturday, October 8, a traditional tailgate party brought together parents, students and Trojan football fans of all stripes for pregame festivities prior to cheering the team on for Troy's 27th straight win—a 42-to-21 victory against Arizona. [photo by Michael Kloss, courtesy of the USC Office of Protocol and University Events]

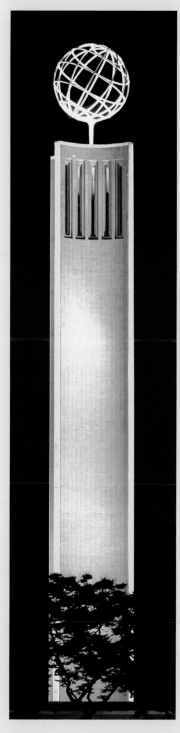

Clockwise from left: To celebrate USC's 125th anniversary as well as the university's proud connection to the city of Los Angeles, the Von KleinSmid Center tower was fitted with powerful lights, creating a stunning effect that was visible for miles. It was the first time the tower had been illuminated since the 1984 Olympics. [photo by Michael Kloss, courtesy of the USC Office of Protocol and University Events]

As part of the USC Alumni Association's "USC on the Road" program, President Sample delivered an inspiring talk—titled "USC: 125 Years of Reinvention and Renewal"—to update members of the Trojan Family in San Diego about the history, current trends and future of their university. [photo courtesy of the USC Alumni Association]

USC's 125th anniversary celebration concluded in May 2006 with the 73rd annual Alumni Awards Dinner, held in Town and Gown on the University Park campus. Pictured at the event are (from left): dinner committee chair William C. Allen (class of 1979); Alumni Service Award winner Carol Campbell Fox (class of 1962); Alumni Merit Award winner Jack Dyer "J. D." Crouch II (class of 1980, M.A. 1981, Ph.D. 1987); President Steven B. Sample; Asa V. Call Achievement Award winner Andrew Viterbi (Ph.D. 1962); Alumni Merit Award winner Thom Mayne (class of 1969); Alumni Service Award winner Reginald Lathan (class

of 1976); and Judith F. Blumenthal (M.B.A. 1984, Ph.D. 1988), associate vice president, alumni relations. [photo © Lee Salem Photography, courtesy of the USC Alumni Association]

In commemoration of their shared 125th anniversaries, USC joined forces with the journal *Science* to present a one-day symposium titled "Global Horizons: America's Challenge in Science and Innovation" in April 2006. The event brought together some of the world's foremost luminaries in science policy, including USC alumnus and trustee Andrew Viterbi, cofounder of QUALCOMM Incorporated, to examine topics ranging from stem cell research to the United States' standing with respect to China and India. Moderating the day's final session was Chris Matthews (left), host of MSNBC's "Hardball with Chris Matthews," with panelists John Seely Brown (former chief scientist at Xerox Corporation), Gururaj "Desh" Deshpande (cofounder and chairman of Sycamore Networks, Inc.), Judith Jackson Fossett (director of the USC African American Studies Program), Raymond Kurzweil (acclaimed futurist, inventor and entrepreneur), USC Nobel laureate George Olah and Alan Leshner (executive publisher of *Science* and chief executive officer of the American Association for the Advancement of Science). [photo © Steve Cohn, courtesy of the USC Office of Protocol and University Events]

Appendix I

Senior Administration

(as of December 2006)

Steven B. Sample
President

C. L. Max Nikias
Provost and Senior Vice President, Academic Affairs

Todd R. Dickey
Senior Vice President, Administration
General Counsel and Secretary of the University

Dennis F. Dougherty
Senior Vice President, Finance
Chief Financial Officer

Martha Harris
Senior Vice President, University Relations

Alan Kreditor
Senior Vice President, University Advancement

Carol Mauch Amir
Secretary of the University

Ruth Wernig
Treasurer

Elizabeth Garrett
Vice President, Academic Planning and Budget

Michael L. Jackson
Vice President, Student Affairs

Carolyn Webb de Macias
Vice President, External Relations

Curtis D. Williams
Vice President, Capital Construction

Michael Garrett
Athletic Director

USC's senior administrative team in 2005 (standing, from left): Michael Garrett, Michael L. Jackson, Curtis D. Williams, Carolyn Webb de Macias and Ruth Wernig; (seated, from left): Martha Harris, Dennis F. Dougherty, Steven B. Sample, C. L. Max Nikias, Alan Kreditor and Todd R. Dickey. (Carol Mauch Amir and Elizabeth Garrett joined the group in 2006.) [photo © Lee Salem Photography, courtesy of USC Public Relations Projects]

Appendix II

USC Board of Trustees

(as of February 2007)

As a private corporation, USC is governed by a board of trustees that has approximately 50 voting members. The board is a self-perpetuating body, electing one-fifth of its members each year for a five-year term of office.

Appendix III

Academic Deans

(as of February 2007)

Randolph P. Beatty
USC Leventhal School of Accounting

Geoffrey Cowan
USC Annenberg School for Communication

Robert A. Cutietta
USC Thornton School of Music

Elizabeth M. Daley
USC School of Cinematic Arts

Gerald C. Davison
USC Davis School of Gerontology

Marilyn Flynn
USC School of Social Work

Karen Symms Gallagher
USC Rossier School of Education

Thomas Gilligan
USC Marshall School of Business

Brian E. Henderson
Keck School of Medicine of USC

Jack H. Knott
*USC School of Policy, Planning,
and Development*

Qingyun Ma
USC School of Architecture

Edward J. McCaffery
USC Gould School of Law

Madeline Puzo
USC School of Theatre

Harold C. Slavkin
USC School of Dentistry

Peter Starr
USC College of Letters, Arts and Sciences

Randall L. "Pete" Vanderveen
USC School of Pharmacy

Ruth E. Weisberg
USC Roski School of Fine Arts

Yannis C. Yortsos
USC Viterbi School of Engineering

Appendix IV

Distinguished Professors

(as of December 2006)

The title of Distinguished Professor is bestowed very selectively upon those faculty members whose accomplishments have brought special renown to the University of Southern California

Leonard M. Adleman
Henry Salvatori Distinguished Chair in Computer Science

Norman Arnheim
Distinguished Professor of Biological Sciences, Molecular Biology and Biochemistry, and Ester Dornsife Chair in Biological Sciences

Warren Bennis
University Professor and Distinguished Professor of Business Administration

T. Coraghessan Boyle
Distinguished Professor of English

Stephen Hartke
Distinguished Professor of Theory and Composition

Brian E. Henderson
Distinguished Professor of Preventive Medicine, May S. and John Hooval Dean's Chair in Medicine, and Kenneth T. Norris, Jr. Chair in Epidemiology

Peter A. Jones
Distinguished Professor of Biochemistry and Molecular Biology, and H. Leslie Hoffman and Elaine S. Hoffman Chair in Cancer Research

Francine R. Kaufman
Distinguished Professor of Pediatrics

Michael M. C. Lai
Distinguished Professor of Molecular Microbiology and Immunology, and Neurology

Edward E. Lawler III
Distinguished Research Professor of Business

Alexandra M. Levine
Distinguished Professor of Medicine and Ronald H. Bloom Family Chair in Lymphoma Research

George A. Olah
Distinguished Professor of Chemistry and Donald P. and Katherine B. Loker Chair in Organic Chemistry

Shahbudin H. Rahimtoola
Distinguished Professor of Medicine and George C. Griffith Chair in Cardiology

Vaughn A. Starnes
Hastings Distinguished Professor of Cardiothoracic Surgery

Walter Wolf
Distinguished Professor of Pharmaceutical Sciences

Appendix V

University Professors

(as of December 2006)

The title of University Professor is bestowed upon outstanding faculty at the University of Southern California based on multidisciplinary interests and significant accomplishments in several disciplines.

Michael A. Arbib
University Professor, Fletcher Jones Chair in Computer Science, and Professor of Biological Sciences and Biomedical Engineering

Lloyd Armstrong, Jr.
University Professor, Professor of Physics and Professor of Education

George A. Bekey
University Professor Emeritus and Professor Emeritus of Computer Science

Warren Bennis
University Professor and Distinguished Professor of Business Administration

Leo B. Braudy
University Professor and Leo S. Bing Chair in English and American Literature

Alexander M. Capron
University Professor, Scott H. Bice Chair in Healthcare Law, Policy and Ethics, and Professor of Law and Medicine

Marshall Cohen
University Professor Emeritus and Professor Emeritus of Philosophy and Law

Richard A. Easterlin
University Professor and Professor of Economics

Caleb Finch
University Professor, ARCO/William F. Kieschnick Chair in the Neurobiology of Aging, and Professor of Gerontology and Biological Sciences

Solomon W. Golomb
University Professor, Andrew and Erna Viterbi Chair in Communications, and Professor of Electrical Engineering and Mathematics

Robert W. Hellwarth
University Professor, George T. Pfleger Chair in Electrical Engineering, and Professor of Physics

Thomas Jordan
University Professor, W. M. Keck Foundation Professor of Geophysics, and Professor of Earth Sciences

Marsha Kinder
University Professor and Professor of Critical Studies, Spanish and Portuguese, and Comparative Literature

Malcolm Cecil Pike
University Professor and Professor of Preventive Medicine

Jean C. Shih
University Professor, Boyd P. and Elsie D. Welin Professor of Molecular Pharmacology and Toxicology, and Professor of Cell and Neurobiology

Kevin O. Starr
University Professor and Professor of History and Policy, Planning, and Development

William G. Tierney
University Professor and Leslie Wilbur and Norma Lash Wilbur–Evelyn Kieffer Professor of Higher Education

Stephen E. Toulmin
University Professor and Adjunct Professor of Anthropology, International Relations and Religion

Michael S. Waterman
University Professor, USC Associates Chair in Natural Sciences, and Professor of Biological Sciences and Mathematics

Appendix VI

National Academy Members

(as of December 2006)

National Academy of Sciences

Leonard M. Adleman
Sidney W. Benson
Richard A. Easterlin
Alfred G. Fischer
Solomon W. Golomb
Robert W. Hellwarth
Thomas H. Jordan
George A. Olah
Richard F. Thompson
Michael S. Waterman

Institute of Medicine

Alexander M. Capron
Antonio Damasio
Clifton O. Dummett
Brian E. Henderson
Francine R. Kaufman
Barbara M. Korsch
Malcolm C. Pike
Stephen J. Ryan
William B. Schwartz
Harold C. Slavkin
Robert E. Tranquada

National Academy of Engineering

Leonard M. Adleman
Mihran S. Agbabian
George A. Bekey
Barry W. Boehm
H. K. Cheng
Malcolm Currie
P. Daniel Dapkus
Solomon W. Golomb
Robert W. Hellwarth
Ralph L. Keeney
William C. Lindsey
Alfred Mann
Tony Maxworthy
Sanjit K. Mitra
Philip E. Muntz
Gerald Nadler
Allen E. Puckett
Irving S. Reed
Steven B. Sample
Stan F. Settles
Leonard M. Silverman
John B. Slaughter
Richard J. Stegemeier
Ronald D. Sugar
Lloyd R. Welch

Appendix VII

The Role and Mission of the University of Southern California

The central mission of the University of Southern California is the development of human beings and society as a whole through the cultivation and enrichment of the human mind and spirit. The principal means by which our mission is accomplished are teaching, research, artistic creation, professional practice and selected forms of public service.

Our first priority as faculty and staff is the education of our students, from freshmen to postdoctorals, through a broad array of academic, professional, extracurricular and athletic programs of the first rank. The integration of liberal and professional learning is one of USC's special strengths. We strive constantly for excellence in teaching knowledge and skills to our students, while at the same time helping them to acquire wisdom and insight, love of truth and beauty, moral discernment, understanding of self, and respect and appreciation for others.

Research of the highest quality by our faculty and students is fundamental to our mission. USC is one of a very small number of premier academic institutions in which research and teaching are inextricably intertwined, and on which the nation depends for a steady stream of new knowledge, art, and technology. Our faculty are not simply teachers of the works of others, but active contributors to what is taught, thought and practiced throughout the world.

USC is pluralistic, welcoming outstanding men and women of every race, creed and background. We are a global institution in a global center, attracting more international students over the years than any other American university. And we are private, unfettered by political control, strongly committed to academic freedom, and proud of our entrepreneurial heritage.

An extraordinary closeness and willingness to help one another are evident among USC students, alumni, faculty, and staff; indeed, for those within its compass the Trojan Family is a genuinely supportive community. Alumni, trustees, volunteers and friends of USC are essential to this family tradition, providing generous financial support, participating in university governance, and assisting students at every turn.

In our surrounding neighborhoods and around the globe, USC provides public leadership and public service in such diverse fields as health care, economic development, social welfare, scientific research, public policy and the arts. We also serve the public interest by being the largest private employer in the city of Los Angeles, as well as the city's largest export industry in the private sector.

USC has played a major role in the development of Southern California for more than a century, and plays an increasingly important role in the development of the nation and the world. We expect to continue to play these roles for many centuries to come. Thus our planning, commitments and fiscal policies are directed toward building quality and excellence in the long term.

Adopted by the USC Board of Trustees, February 1993

Appendix VIII

University of Southern California Code of Ethics

At the University of Southern California, ethical behavior is predicated on two main pillars: a commitment to discharging our obligations to others in a fair and honest manner, and a commitment to respecting the rights and dignity of all persons. As faculty, staff, students, and trustees, we each bear responsibility not only for the ethics of our own behavior, but also for building USC's stature as an ethical institution.

We recognize that the fundamental relationships upon which our university is based are those between individual students and individual professors; thus, such relationships are especially sacred and deserve special care that they not be prostituted or exploited for base motives or personal gain.

When we make promises as an institution, or as individuals who are authorized to speak on behalf of USC, we keep those promises, including especially the promises expressed and implied in our Role and Mission Statement. We try to do what is right even if no one is watching us or compelling us to do the right thing.

We promptly and openly identify and disclose conflicts of interest on the part of faculty, staff, students, trustees, and the institution as a whole, and we take appropriate steps to either eliminate such conflicts or insure that they do not compromise the integrity of the individuals involved or that of the university.

We nurture an environment of mutual respect and tolerance. As members of the USC community, we treat everyone with respect and dignity, even when the values, beliefs, behavior, or background of a person or group is repugnant to us. This last is one of the bedrocks of ethical behavior at USC and the basis of civil discourse within our academic community. Because we are responsible not only for ourselves but also for others, we speak out against hatred and bigotry whenever and wherever we find them.

We do not harass, mistreat, belittle, harm, or take unfair advantage of anyone. We do not tolerate plagiarism, lying, deliberate misrepresenttation, theft, scientific fraud, cheating, invidious discrimination, or ill use of our fellow human beings — whether such persons be volunteer subjects of scientific research, peers, patients, superiors, subordinates, students, professors, trustees, parents, alumni, donors, or members of the public.

We do not misappropriate the university's resources, or resources belonging to others which are entrusted to our care, nor do we permit any such misappropriation to go unchallenged.

We are careful to distinguish between legal behavior on the one hand and ethical behavior on the other, knowing that, while the two overlap in many areas, they are at bottom quite distinct from each other. While we follow legal requirements, we must never lose sight of ethical considerations.

Because of the special bonds that bind us together as members of the Trojan Family, we have a familial duty as well as a fiduciary duty to one another. Our faculty and staff are attentive to the well-being of students and others who are entrusted to our care or who are especially vulnerable, including patients, volunteer subjects of research, and the children in our daycare and community outreach programs.

By respecting the rights and dignity of others, and by striving for fairness and honesty in our dealings with others, we create an ethical university of which we can all be proud, and which will serve as a bright beacon for all peoples in our day and in the centuries to come.

Adopted by the USC Board of Trustees, March 28, 2004

Appendix IX

Presidents of the University of Southern California

(1880–2006)

1880–1891
Marion McKinley Bovard

1892–1895
Joseph Pomeroy Widney

1895–1899
George Washington White

1903–1921
George Finley Bovard

1921–1947
Rufus Bernhard von KleinSmid

1947–1957
Frederick Dow "Fred" Fagg II

1958–1970
Norman Hawkins Topping

1970–1980
John Randolph "Jack" Hubbard

1980–1991
James Herbert Zumberge

1991–present
Steven Browning Sample

Appendix X

Presidents and Chairmen of the USC Board of Trustees

(1880–2006)

1880–1882
Robert M. Widney *(president)*

1882
Charles Shelling *(president)*

1883–1886
Edward F. Spence *(president)*

1886–1889
Asahel M. Hough *(president)*

1889–1891
Edward F. Spence *(president)*

1891–1895
Joseph P. Widney *(president)*

1895
Edward S. Chase *(president)*

1895–1899
George W. White *(president)*

1899–1903
George F. Bovard *(president)*

1903–1916
Ezra A. Healy *(president)*

1916–1924
Adna W. Leonard *(president)*

1924–1927
Albert J. Wallace *(president)*

1927–1939
George I. Cochran *(president)*

1939–1950
G. Allan Hancock *(president)*

1950–1954
Asa V. Call *(president)*
G. Allan Hancock *(chairman)*

1954–1958
Asa V. Call *(president)*
Harry J. Bauer *(chairman)*

1958–1960
Asa V. Call *(chairman)*
Harry J. Bauer *(honorary chairman [to 1961])*

1960–1964
Leonard K. Firestone *(chairman)*

1964–1967
Frank L. King *(chairman)*

1967–1971
Justin W. Dart *(chairman)*

1971–1972
Kenneth T. Norris *(chairman)*

1972–1980
J. Robert Fluor *(chairman)*

1980–1985
Carl E. Hartnack *(chairman)*

1985–1990
George T. Scharffenberger *(chairman)*

1990–1995
Forrest N. Shumway *(chairman)*

1995–2000
Malcolm R. Currie *(chairman)*

2000–2002
John C. Argue *(chairman)*

2002–present
Stanley P. Gold *(chairman)*

Appendix XI

Presidents and Executive Directors
of the USC Alumni Association

(1923–2007)

Year	President	Executive Director	Year	President	Executive Director
1923–24	E. L. Doheny Jr. (LAS '16)	Harold J. Stonier (LAS '13)	1948–49	Ron Stever (Com '26)	
1924–25			1949–50	Gwynn M. Wilson (Com '21)	
1925–26			1950–51	Francis J. Conley (Dent '31)	
1926–27			1951–52	J. Kneeland Nunan (Engr '36)	
1927–28	Allen T. Archer (Law '10)	Frank L. Hadlock (Com '22)	1952–53	Bernard C. Brennan (Law '25)	
1928–29	James D. McCoy (Dent '06)		1953–54	Lewis K. Gough (Com '31)	
1929–30	Herbert A. Freston (Law '15)		1954–55	Kennedy Ellsworth (Com '22)	
1930–31	Merritt H. Adamson (LAS '13)		1955–56	Mulvey White (LAS '31)	
1931–32	Asa V. Call (Law '14)		1956–57	Boyd P. Welin (Pharm '27)	
1932–33	Frank W. Ott (Med '15)	Lewis K. Gough (Com '31)	1957–58	J. Howard Payne (LAS 38; Med '42)	
1933–34	Carl Wirsching (LAS '10)		1958–59	Eber E. Jaques (Com '30)	
1934–35	Clifford E. Hughes (Law '21)		1959–60	Ralph E. Smith (Law '28)	
1935–36	Fred B. Olds (Dent '24)		1960–61	E. Russell Werdin (Com '32)	Moreland Thomas ('49)
1936–37	Byron C. Hanna (Law '10)		1961–62	Bruce W. McNeil (Engr '39)	
1937–38	Carl R. Howson (Med '13)		1962–63	Michael F. B. MacBan (LAS '40)	
1938–39	Frank F. Barham (Med '06)		1963–64	G. Everett Miller (LAS '28; Law '30)	Francis V. McGinley (Bus '35)
1939–40	Elmer P. Bromley (Law '13)		1964–65	John R. Abel (Dent '30)	
1940–41	Walter L. Bowers (Law '04)		1965–66	Charles S. Boren (LAS '29)	
1941–42	E. Earl Moody (LAS '12; Med '17)		1966–67	Winston R. Fuller (LAS '32)	
1942–43	Franklin S. Wade (Law '08)	R. Harold Smallwood (Bus '39)	1967–68	Phyllis Norton Cooper (LAS '35; Law '38)	
1943–44	J. Arthur Taylor (LAS '19)	E. Betty Donnegan (Mus '42)	1968–69	Raymond C. Sparling (Engr '66)	
1944–45	Elmer H. Howlett (Law '17)	Arnold Eddy (LAS '24)	1969–70	Stephen C. Bilheimer (Bus '26)	H. Dale Hilton (Engr '36)
1945–46	Howard L. Byram (LAS '15)		1970–71	George E. Brandow (Engr '36)	
1946–47	Clarence L. Kincaid (Law '21)		1971–72	Joseph K. Cannell (Bus '28)	
1947–48	Lloyd E. Wright Sr. (Law '15)		1972–73	Raymond J. Arbuthnot (Bus '33)	

Continued on page 226

Presidents and Directors of the USC Alumni Association, *continued*

Year	President	Executive Director
1973–74	Ashley S. Orr (PubAd '40; Law '47)	
1974–75	Ralph O. Wilcox (Bus '31)	
1975–76	Herbert G. Klein (Journ '40)	
1976–77	Eugene C. Clarke (LAS '32)	
1977–78	Richard H. Lawrence (Ed '48; MS '49)	
1978–79	Robert A. Brown Jr. (Bus '42)	
1979–80	Marshall A. Green (LAS '41)	
1980–81	Dann V. Angeloff (Bus '58; MBA '63)	
1981–82	Pascal B. Dilday (LAS '33)	Geoff Gilchrist (LAS '59)
1982–83	Lorna Young Reed (Ed '58)	Geoff Gilchrist/Shari Thorell
1983–84	Paul Kennedy Jr. (LAS '48)	Shari Thorell (LAS '65)
1984–85	Hugh H. Helm (Bus '62; Law '69)	Shari Thorell/William J. Hopkins
1985–86	David S. Atha (Bus '69)	William J. Hopkins (LAS '65)
1986–87	John P. Davis Jr. (Bus '49)	Carlos Galindo (PubAd '77)
1987–88	Ronald Orr (Bus '79)	Carlos Galindo/Rick Nordin (Bus '77)
1988–89	Richard Van Vorst (LAS '56)	Sherry May
1989–90	George Boone (Dent '46)	
1990–91	Otis Healy (Bus '50)	
1991–92	Hilton Green (Bus '52)	J. P. O'Connor-Thompson (Journ '75)
1992–93	Ralph Allman (LAS '57; Dent '62)	
1993–94	L'Cena Brunskill Rice (Ed '53; Ed '59)	
1994–95	L. Joe Enloe (LAS '57; Med '60)	
1995–96	Gerald S. Papazian (LAS '77)	Anita West (3/16/95–6/30/95) (interim) and Christopher Stoy (7/1/95–5/1/96)
1996–97	Leonard R. Fuller (PubAd '70)	Kathy Long-Phinney (Fin '87)
1997–98	Linda Dean Maudlin (Bus '61)	
1998–99	William C. Allen (Cinema '79)	
1999–2000	Richard Cook (LAS '72)	Susan Heitman (interim)

Year	President	Executive Director
2000–01	David Brubaker (Bus '67; MBA '68)	Judith Blumenthal (MBA '84; PhD '88)
2001–02	Robert Rollo (Bus '69; MBA '70)	
2002–03	Reginald Lathan (Bus '76)	
2003–04	Ann Hill (BS '71; MS 74)	
2004–05	Glenn Sonnenberg (BA '77; JD '80)	
2005–06	Gale Bensussen (BS '70; JD '74)	
2006–07	Alex Cappello (Bus '77)	Carolyn Webb de Macias (interim)

Appendix XII

University Medallion

The University Medallion is awarded very selectively to those who have made major contributions to the University.

1994
Walter Annenberg

Appendix XIII

Presidential Medallion

The Presidential Medallion is USC's top honor, awarded to those who have brought honor and distinction to the institution.

1983
Charles Heidelberger*
Zohrab A. Kaprielian*

1985
Solomon W. Golomb

1986
Sidney W. Benson

1987
Norman M. Topping

1988
Carl E. Hartnack

1989
William G. Spitzer

1990
George T. Scharffenberger

1991
Robert L. Mannes

1993
Cornelius J. Pings

1994
Leo Braudy
Alexandra M. Levine

1995
George A. Olah

1996
Carl M. Franklin
Carolyn Craig Franklin*

1997
Forrest N. Shumway
Raul Sotelo Vargas

1998
Robert P. Biller

1999
Brian E. Henderson
Barbara Solomon

2000
George A. Bekey
Leslie Bernstein

2001
Malcolm R. Currie
Warren Bennis

2002
Simon Ramo
Virginia Ramo

2003
John C. Argue*
William McClure

2004
Kenneth Leventhal
Florence A. Clark

2005
Donald G. Skinner
Kevin Starr

2006
Lloyd Armstrong Jr.

Awarded posthumously

Appendix XIV

Asa V. Call Achievement Award

*The Asa V. Call Achievement Award celebrates alumni whose outstanding accomplishments
have brought honor and recognition to themselves and to USC.*

1932
Thomas Nixon Carver
Class of 1891, LL.D. (honorary) 1928

1933
W. W. Beckett
Class of 1888, LL.D. (honorary) 1927

1934
Jesse W. Curtis
Class of 1887, LL.D. (honorary) 1924

1935
Hugh Baillie
Class of 1915, LL.D. (honorary) 1950

1936
James David McCoy
Class of 1906

1937
Harold J. Stonier
Class of 1913, D.B.A. (honorary) 1928

1938
Byron C. Hanna
Class of 1910

1939
Frank Barham
Class of 1906

1940
Capt. G. Allan Hancock
Class of 1932, D.B.A. (honorary) 1937

1941
Harry J. Bauer
Class of 1909, LL.D. (honorary) 1943

1942
Franklin S. Wade
Class of 1908, LL.D. (honorary) 1961

1943
Maj. Gen. Ira C. Eaker
Class of 1934

1944
Frank P. Doherty
Class of 1911

1945
Col. Frank H. Kurtz
Class of 1937

1946
Virgil Pinkley
Class of 1929

1947
Dean Bartlett Cromwell
M.A. (honorary) 1946

1948
C. Elvon Musick
Class of 1915, LL.D. (honorary) 1957

1949
Clarence L. Kincaid
Class of 1921

1950
Hugh Carey Wilett
Class of 1907

1951
Gordon Evans Dean
Class of 1930, LL.D. (honorary) 1951

1952
Nadine Conner Heacock
Class of 1931

1953
Lewis K. Gough
Class of 1931

1954
Thomas H. Kuchel
Class of 1932, LL.B. 1935, LL.D.
(honorary) 1963

1955
Lloyd E. Wright
Class of 1915

1956
Elmer P. Bromley
Class of 1913

1957
Patricia Ryan Nixon
Class of 1937, L.H.D. (honorary) 1961

1958
Rockwell D. Hunt
(dean of USC Graduate School)
Litt.D. (honorary) 1936

1959
Howard Payne House
M.D. 1935, LL.D.(honorary) 1974

1960
Frank H. Sparks
Class of 1937

1961
Justice Thomas P. White
Class of 1911

1962
John R. Abel
Class of 1930

1963
Norman H. Topping
Class of 1933, M.D. 1936, Sc.D.
(honorary) 1963

1964
Robert E. Brooker
Class of 1927, LL.D. (honorary) 1969

1965
Asa V. Call
Class of 1914, LL.D. (honorary) 1946

1966
Joseph A. Ball
Class of 1927

1967
Howard F. Ahmanson
Class of 1927

1968
Robert N. Dockson
Class of 1946

1969
Robert H. Finch
Class of 1951, LL.D. (honorary) 1969

1970
Neil A. Armstrong
M.S.A.E. 1970, L.H.D. (honorary) 2005

1971
Herbert G. Klein
Class of 1940

1972
Gwynn Wilson
Class of 1921, L.H.D. (honorary) 1960

1973
Roy P. Crocker
Class of 1924, LL.D. (honorary) 1968

1974
David X. Marks
L.H.D. (honorary) 1959

1975
Robert D. Wood
Class of 1949, LL.D. (honorary) 1973

1976
Robert E. Vivian
Class of 1917, A.M. 1922, Sc.D.
(honorary) 1969

1977
John Wayne
Class of 1927, D.F.A. (honorary) 1968

1978
J. Robert Fluor
Class of 1946/1943, LL.D. (honorary) 1971

1979
J. Howard Edgerton
Class of 1928, law 1930

1980
Irving Stone
Class of 1924, Litt.D. (honorary) 1965

1981
Warren M. Christopher
Class of 1945, L.H.D. (honorary) 1999

1982
Raoul M. Dedeaux
Class of 1935

1983
Kenneth T. Norris Jr.
Class of 1937, Engr.D. (honorary) 1969

1984
Albert C. Martin
Class of 1936

1985
David L. Wolper
Class of 1949, D.F.A. (honorary) 1996

1986
Virginia Ramo
Class of 1937, L.H.D. (honorary) 1978

1987
J. Douglas Pardee
Class of 1949

1988
Robert F. Erburu
Class of 1952, LL.D. (honorary) 1990

1989
Ron Stever
Class of 1926

1990
Gen. William Lyon
(military/business leader)
L.H.D. (honorary) 2002

1992
Carl E. Hartnack
LL.D. (honorary) 1981

1993
Robert K. Kerlan
Class of 1942, M.D. 1946

1994
Herb Alpert
Class of 1954

1995
Katherine Bogdanovich
Loker
Class of 1940, L.H.D. (honorary) 1997

1996
John Ferraro
Class of 1948

1997
Ray R. Irani
Ph.D. 1957

1998
John C. Argue
LL.B. 1956

2001
Patrick C. Haden
Class of 1975

2002
Edward P. Roski Jr.
Class of 1962

2003
Maj. Gen. Charles
Bolden Jr.
M.S. 1977

2004
Marilyn B. Horne
Class of 1953

2005
Gordon S. Marshall
Class of 1946

2006
Andrew J. Viterbi
Ph.D. 1962

Appendix XV

Named or Endowed Schools and Photo Gallery of Donors

(as of December 2006)

Eleven of USC's 17 professional schools are associated with farseeing donors who recognized the importance of endowment for ensuring a school's ongoing financial strength, stability, and ability to recruit and retain outstanding faculty and students and maintain state-of-the-art facilities, as well as the significance of a name in setting a school apart from its peers and elevating its reputation and stature.

THE USC GOULD SCHOOL OF LAW
Named in honor of Charles Winthrop
Gould (pictured) in recognition
of a gift from his nephew,
John W. Barnes, in 1963.
Orrin B. Evans, dean
Norman H. Topping, president

**THE USC ELAINE AND KENNETH LEVENTHAL
SCHOOL OF ACCOUNTING**
Named in recognition of a gift
from Elaine and Kenneth Leventhal in 1995.
Kenneth A. Merchant, dean
Steven B. Sample, president

**THE USC ANNENBERG
SCHOOL FOR COMMUNICATION**
Established through the support
of Walter H. Annenberg in 1971.
Frederick Williams, founding dean
John R. Hubbard, president

**THE USC GORDON S. MARSHALL
SCHOOL OF BUSINESS**
Named in recognition of a gift
from Gordon S. Marshall in 1996.
Randolph W. Westerfield, dean
Steven B. Sample, president

**THE USC LEONARD DAVIS
SCHOOL OF GERONTOLOGY**
Established through the support
of Leonard Davis in 1975.
James E. Birren, founding dean
John R. Hubbard, president

**THE USC BARBARA J. AND
ROGER W. ROSSIER SCHOOL OF EDUCATION**
Named in recognition of a gift
from Barbara J. and Roger W. Rossier in 1998.
Guilbert C. Hentschke, dean
Steven B. Sample, president

Continued on page 230

Named or Endowed Schools and Photo Gallery of Donors, *continued*

**THE USC FLORA L. THORNTON
SCHOOL OF MUSIC**
Named in recognition of a gift
from Flora Laney Thornton in 1999.
Larry J. Livingston, dean
Steven B. Sample, president

**THE USC GAYLE GARNER ROSKI
SCHOOL OF FINE ARTS**
Named in recognition of a gift
from Gayle Garner Roski and
Edward P. Roski Jr. in 2006.
Ruth E. Weisberg, dean
Steven B. Sample, president

**THE KECK SCHOOL OF MEDICINE OF THE
UNIVERSITY OF SOUTHERN CALIFORNIA**
Named in recognition of a gift
from the W. M. Keck Foundation (pictured:
Robert A. Day, chairman and president) in 1999.
Stephen J. Ryan, dean
Steven B. Sample, president

**THE USC SCHOOL
OF CINEMATIC ARTS**
Endowed by George Lucas in 2006.
Elizabeth M. Daley, dean
Steven B. Sample, President

**THE USC ANDREW AND ERNA VITERBI
SCHOOL OF ENGINEERING**
Named in recognition of a gift
from Andrew and Erna Viterbi in 2004.
C. L. Max Nikias, dean
Steven B. Sample, president

Appendix XVI

Named Buildings

(as of December 2006)

Many structures on USC's campuses are named for benefactors whose generosity has helped fund construction or otherwise had a major impact on the life of the university. Other buildings are named in recognition of the extraordinary contributions of distinguished administrators, faculty members, alumni or friends.

University Park Campus

AHMANSON CENTER FOR BIOLOGICAL RESEARCH
Erected 1962–64

DOSAN AHN CHANG HO FAMILY HOUSE
Erected before 1907
Dedicated 2006

ETHEL PERCY ANDRUS GERONTOLOGY CENTER
Erected 1971–72
Dedicated 1973

ANNENBERG SCHOOL FOR COMMUNICATION BUILDING
Erected 1974–76
Expanded 1978–82

ANNA BING ARNOLD CHILD CARE CENTER
Erected 1977
Annex erected 1988

MACDONALD BECKET CENTER
Erected 1992–93

BIEGLER HALL OF ENGINEERING
(formerly known as the College of Engineering Building)
Erected 1939–40
Rededicated 1966

BING THEATRE
Erected 1974–76

CECELE AND MICHAEL BIRNKRANT RESIDENCE HALL
Erected 1962–63

MRS. WILLIS H. BOOTH MEMORIAL HALL
Erected 1964–65

GEORGE FINLEY BOVARD ADMINISTRATION BUILDING AND KENNETH T. NORRIS JR. AUDITORIUM
Erected 1919–21
Auditorium remodeled 1979–80

BRIDGE MEMORIAL HALL
Erected 1927–28
Dedicated 1930

JOHN G. BROOKS MEMORIAL PAVILION AND DEDEAUX FIELD
Erected 1973–74

CARSON TELEVISION CENTER
Erected 1982–84

CHARLOTTE S. AND DAVRE R. DAVIDSON CONTINUING EDUCATION CONFERENCE CENTER
Erected 1975–76

CORWIN D. DENNEY RESEARCH CENTER
Erected 1977–78

EDWARD L. DOHENY JR. MEMORIAL LIBRARY
Erected 1931–32
Expanded 1967

DANA AND DAVID DORNSIFE COGNITIVE NEUROSCIENCE IMAGING CENTER
Erected 2003–04

MONTGOMERY ROSS FISHER BUILDING
Erected 1972–74

FLUOR TOWER
(formerly known as Residence West)
Erected 1971–72
Rededicated 1984

GALEN CENTER
Erected 2004–06

LOUIS J. AND HELENE GALEN ATHLETIC CENTER
(part of Heritage Hall)
Erected 1998–99

HAZEL AND STANLEY HALL FINANCIAL SERVICES BUILDING
Erected 1975–76
Dedicated 1977

ALLAN HANCOCK FOUNDATION BUILDING
Erected 1938–40
Dedicated 1941

MAY ORMEROD HARRIS HALL/ QUINN WING / ELIZABETH HOLMES FISHER GALLERY
Erected 1938–39
Dedicated 1940

MAY ORMEROD HARRIS RESIDENCE HALL
(formerly known as University Hall)
Erected 1949–51
Rededicated 1956

HEDCO NEUROSCIENCES BUILDING
Erected 1987–89

HEDCO PETROLEUM AND CHEMICAL ENGINEERING BUILDING
Erected 1981–82

H. LESLIE HOFFMAN HALL OF BUSINESS ADMINISTRATION
Erected 1965–67

JOHN R. HUBBARD HALL
(formerly known as the Women's Residence Hall, Elisabeth von KleinSmid Hall and the Student Administrative Services Building)
Erected 1924–25
Rededicated 2003

HUGHES AIRCRAFT ELECTRICAL ENGINEERING CENTER
Erected 1989–91

RAY R. IRANI HALL
Erected 2003–05
To be rededicated 2007

KAPRIELIAN HALL
Erected 1988–90

KENNEDY FAMILY AQUATICS BUILDING
Erected 1987–88

FRANK L. KING OLYMPIC HALL OF CHAMPIONS
Erected 1982–84

THOMAS AND DOROTHY LEAVEY LIBRARY
Erected 1992–94

ELAINE AND KENNETH LEVENTHAL SCHOOL OF ACCOUNTING
(formerly known as the Law Building)
Erected 1925–26
Rededicated 1995

Continued on page 232

University Park Campus, *cont.*

RALPH AND GOLDY LEWIS HALL
Erected 1998–99

HAROLD LLOYD MOTION PICTURE SCORING STAGE
Erected 1982–84

DONALD P. AND KATHERINE B. LOKER HYDROCARBON RESEARCH INSTITUTE
Erected 1978–79
Expanded 1994–95

KATHERINE B. LOKER TRACK STADIUM
Erected 2000–02

GEORGE LUCAS INSTRUCTIONAL BUILDING
Erected 1982–84

MARCIA LUCAS POST PRODUCTION BUILDING
Erected 1982–84

GENERAL WILLIAM LYON UNIVERSITY CENTER
Erected 1987–89

DAVID X. MARKS RESIDENCE HALL
Erected 1953

DAVID X. MARKS TENNIS STADIUM
Erected 1971–72

DAVID X. MARKS TOWER
(formerly known as Sarah Marks Residence Hall)
Erected 1962–63

McDONALD'S OLYMPIC SWIM STADIUM
Erected 1981–83

HAROLD E. AND LILLIAN M. MOULTON ORGANIC CHEMISTRY WING
(formerly known as the Organic Chemistry Wing)
Erected 1950–51
Rededicated 1985

SEELEY G. MUDD BUILDING
Erected 1980–82
Dedicated 1983

SEELEY WINTERSMITH MUDD MEMORIAL HALL OF PHILOSOPHY
Erected 1929
Dedicated 1930

ELVON AND MABEL MUSICK LAW BUILDING
Erected 1969–70
Expanded 1987–89

JERRY AND NANCY NEELY PETROLEUM AND CHEMICAL ENGINEERING BUILDING
(formerly known as the Petroleum and Chemical Engineering Building)
Erected 1955–58
Rededicated 1985

EILEEN AND KENNETH T. NORRIS DENTAL SCIENCE CENTER
(formerly known as the School of Dentistry Building)
Erected 1951–52
Expanded and rededicated 1969

EILEEN L. NORRIS CINEMA THEATRE
Erected 1974–76

OLIN HALL OF ENGINEERING
Erected 1962–63

MARIANNE AND J. DOUGLAS PARDEE TOWER
(formerly known as Parkside Hall)
Erected 1981–82
Rededicated 1984

PERTUSATI UNIVERSITY BOOKSTORE
(formerly known as the University Bookstore)
Erected 1987–89
Rededicated 1993

WAITE PHILLIPS HALL OF EDUCATION
Erected 1966–68

JANE HOFFMAN POPOVICH AND J. KRISTOFFER POPOVICH HALL
Erected 1998–99

CHARLES LEE POWELL HALL
(formerly known as Powell Hall for Information Sciences and Systems Engineering)
Erected 1971–73

VIRGINIA RAMO HALL OF MUSIC
Erected 1973–74

ROBERT GLENN RAPP ENGINEERING RESEARCH LABORATORY
(formerly known as the Applied Physics Laboratory)
Erected 1957–58
Rededicated 1987

ALBERT S. RAUBENHEIMER MUSIC FACULTY MEMORIAL BUILDING
(formerly known as the Music Faculty Memorial Building)
Erected 1973–75
Rededicated 1980

GRACE FORD SALVATORI HALL OF LETTERS, ARTS AND SCIENCES
Erected 1978–80

HENRY SALVATORI COMPUTER SCIENCE CENTER
Erected 1975–76
Dedicated 1977

CLAIRE ZELLERBACH SARONI STUDENT HEALTH CENTER
(formerly known as the Student Health Center)
Erected 1950–51
Rededicated 1971

ARNOLD SCHOENBERG INSTITUTE BUILDING
Erected 1975–77

FRANK R. SEAVER SCIENCE CENTER AND SEAVER SCIENCE LIBRARY
Erected 1968–69
Dedicated 1970

STEVEN SPIELBERG MUSIC SCORING STAGE
Erected 1982–84

LAIRD J. STABLER MEMORIAL HALL
Erected 1962–64

STAUFFER HALL OF SCIENCE
Erected 1964–65
Dedicated 1966

JOHN STAUFFER SCIENCE LECTURE HALL
Erected 1965
Dedicated 1966

STONIER HALL
(formerly known as Aeneas Hall)
Erected 1926–27
Acquired by USC 1955
Rededicated 1956

EMERY STOOPS AND JOYCE KING STOOPS EDUCATION LIBRARY
(formerly known as the University Branch of the Los Angeles Public Library, beginning in 1999 as the East Asian Library)
Erected 1922–23
Acquired by USC 1965

MARK TAPER HALL OF HUMANITIES
(formerly known as Founders Hall)
Erected 1949–50
Expanded 1980–81
Rededicated 1982

NORMAN TOPPING STUDENT ACTIVITIES CENTER
(formerly known as the Student Activities Center)
Erected 1966–68
Renamed and rededicated 1970–71

RONALD TUTOR HALL OF ENGINEERING
Erected 2003–05

VIVIAN HALL OF ENGINEERING
(formerly known as Robert E. Vivian Hall of Engineering and Materials Science)
Erected 1965–66
Dedicated 1967

University Park Campus, *cont.*

BELLE D. VIVIAN YWCA BUILDING
(formerly known as the YWCA Hospitality House)
Erected 1950–51
Acquired by USC in 1966
Rededicated 1979

VON KLEINSMID CENTER FOR INTERNATIONAL AND PUBLIC AFFAIRS
Erected 1964–65
Dedicated 1966

ELISABETH VON KLEINSMID MEMORIAL RESIDENCE HALL
Erected 1949–51

RAY AND NADINE WATT HALL OF ARCHITECTURE AND FINE ARTS
Erected 1971–73
Dedicated 1974

WEBB TOWER
(formerly known as Apartment Tower)
Erected 1970–72
Rededicated 1974

WIDNEY ALUMNI HOUSE
(originally known as the University Building)
Erected 1880
Rededicated 1977

GWYNN WILSON STUDENT UNION
(formerly known as the Student Union)
Erected 1927–28
Rededicated 1971

ROBERT ZEMECKIS CENTER FOR DIGITAL ARTS
Dedicated 2001

JAMES H. AND MARILYN E. ZUMBERGE HALL
(formerly known as Science Hall)
Erected 1924–28
Rededicated 2003

Health Sciences Campus

JOHN E. BISHOP MEDICAL TEACHING AND RESEARCH BUILDING
Erected 1967–69

DOROTHY AND HUGH EDMONDSON RESEARCH BUILDING
Erected 1971–73

RENETTE AND MARSHALL EZRALOW FAMILY RESEARCH TOWER
Erected circa 1982
Rededicated 2005

ELAINE STEVELY HOFFMAN MEDICAL RESEARCH CENTER
Erected 1966–68

WILLARD KEITH ADMINISTRATION AND MEDICAL FORUM BUILDING / LOUIS B. MAYER MEDICAL TEACHING CENTER
(formerly known as the Willard W. Keith Administration and Postgraduate Forum Building)
Erected 1969–70
Dedicated 1971

PAUL S. McKIBBEN HALL
Erected 1958–61

MUDD MEMORIAL RESEARCH BUILDING
(formerly known as the Seeley Wintersmith Mudd Memorial Laboratory of the Medical Sciences)
Erected 1958–61

EILEEN AND KENNETH T. NORRIS MEDICAL LIBRARY
Erected 1967–68

HARLYNE J. NORRIS CANCER RESEARCH TOWER
Erected 2003–07 (estimated)

KENNETH NORRIS JR. CANCER HOSPITAL AND RESEARCH INSTITUTE
Erected 1979–82
Dedicated 1983

BURRELL O. RAULSTON MEMORIAL RESEARCH BUILDING
(formerly known as the Medical Research Building)
Erected 1950–52
Rededicated 1960s

BLANCHE AND FRANK R. SEAVER STUDENT RESIDENCE
Erected 1962–63

JOHN STAUFFER PHARMACEUTICAL SCIENCES CENTER
Erected 1973–74

DR. NORMAN TOPPING TOWER
Erected 1993–96

ZILKHA NEUROGENETIC INSTITUTE
Erected 2000–03

Other Locations

GEORGE AND MARYLOU BOONE CENTER FOR SCIENCE AND ENVIRONMENTAL LEADERSHIP
(Santa Catalina Island)
Groundbreaking 2006

BOONE HOUSE
(Santa Catalina Island)
Erected 2002

DEWEY HOUSE
(Santa Catalina Island)
Erected 2002

FREEMAN HOUSE
(Hollywood Hills)
Erected 1924
Deeded to USC 1986

THE GAMBLE HOUSE
(Pasadena)
Erected 1908–09
Deeded to USC and the City of Pasadena 1966

MAX KADE CENTER
(South Hoover Street)
Erected circa 1920
Acquired for USC 1975

KERCKHOFF HALL
(Adams Boulevard, formerly known as Louise E. Kerckhoff House)
Erected 1908
Acquired by USC 1948

McCULLOCH TOWNHOMES
(30th and Hoover, named for Irene McCulloch)
Erected 1990–91

PEREGRINE FOUNDATION HOUSE
(Santa Catalina Island)
Erected 2002

PLUMLEIGH HOUSE
(Santa Catalina Island)
Erected 2002

ROSE HILLS FOUNDATION HOUSE
(Santa Catalina Island)
Erected 2002

JOHN AND ALICE TYLER BUILDING
(South Flower Street)
Acquired by USC and dedicated 1970

PHILIP K. WRIGLEY MARINE SCIENCE CENTER
(Santa Catalina Island, formerly known as the Marine Science Center)
Erected 1966–68
Rededicated 1990

Appendix XVII

Named Centers, Institutes and Departments

(as of December 2006)

The USC Catherine and Joseph Aresty Department of Urology

The USC Ethel Percy Andrus Gerontology Center

The USC Annenberg Center for Communication

The USC Judith and John Bedrosian Center on Governance and the Public Enterprise

The USC Boeckmann Center for Iberian and Latin American Studies

The USC George and MaryLou Boone Center for Science and Environmental Leadership

The USC George and MaryLou Boone Parkinson's Disease and Movement Disorders Research Center

The USC Mary J. and Thoms C. Bowles Center for Alzheimer's Disease

The Broad Institute for Integrative Biology and Stem Cell Research at the Keck School of Medicine of USC

The USC Casden Institute for the Study of the Jewish Role in American Life

The USC Casden Real Estate Economics Forecast

The Doheny Eye Institute at the University of Southern California

The Doheny Retina Institute and Microsurgical Advanced Design Laboratory

The USC Electronic Arts Game Innovation Lab

The USC Daniel J. Epstein Department of Industrial and Systems Engineering

The USC Merwyn C. Gill Foundation Composites Center

The Jane Goodall Research Center at the University of Southern California

The USC Lloyd Greif Center for Entrepreneurial Studies

The USC Hamovitch Center for Science in the Human Services

The USC John C. Hench Division of Animation and Digital Arts

The USC Ming Hsieh Department of Electrical Engineering

The USC Keck Photonics Laboratory

The USC Fred V. Keenan MBA Career Resource Center

The USC Keston Institute for Infrastructure

The USC Klein Institute for Undergraduate Engineering Life

The USC Norman Lear Center

The USC Chase L. Leavitt Building Science Program

The USC Harold E. and Henrietta C. Lee Breast Center

The USC Henrietta C. Lee and Harold E. Lee Women's Health Center

The USC Donald P. and Katherine B. Loker Hydrocarbon Research Institute

The USC Lusk Center for Real Estate

The Alfred E. Mann Institute for Biomedical Engineering at the University of Southern California

The USC Mork Family Department of Chemical and Materials Science

The USC/Norris Comprehensive Cancer Center

The USC Gregor Piatigorsky Seminar for Cellists

The USC Pratt & Whitney Institute for Collaborative Engineering

The Tomás Rivera Policy Institute at the University of Southern California

The USC Ross Minority Program in Real Estate

The USC Edward R. Roybal Institute for Applied Gerontology (effective March 2007)

The Saban Research Institute at Childrens Hospital Los Angeles

The USC Shoah Foundation Institute for Visual History and Education

The USC Peter Stark Producing Program

The USC Mark and Mary Stevens Institute for Technology Commercialization

The USC Tingstad Older Adult Counseling Center

The USC Titus Family Department of Pharmacy

The USC Jesse M. Unruh Institute of Politics

The USC Charles Annenberg Weingarten Program on Online Communities

The USC David L. Wolper Center for the Study of the Documentary

The USC Wrigley Institute for Environmental Studies

The USC Robert Zemeckis Center for Digital Arts

The USC Zilkha Neurogenetic Institute

Appendix XVIII

Endowed Faculty Positions

(as of October 2006)

The excellence of any university is directly related to the quality of its faculty, and one of the most powerful tools for recruiting and retaining world-class scholars—who, in turn, attract other distinguished faculty and the most promising students—is an endowed chair. Over the years, many far-seeing donors have established endowed faculty positions at USC, generating funds to support outstanding teaching and research in perpetuity.

Chairs

1885
John R. Tansey Chair in Christian Ethics

1923
Bishop James W. Bashford Chair
in Oriental Religions

1961
Leo S. Bing Chair in English and
American Literature

1967
Fred Champion Chair in Civil Engineering

Lloyd F. Hunt Chair in Electrical
Power Engineering

Harold Quinton Chair in Business Policy

1970
Robert E. Brooker Chair in Marketing

1971
Grace and Emery Beardsley Chair
in Ophthalmology

Bernard J. Hanley Chair in Medicine

James Irvine Chair in Urban and
Regional Planning

1972
David Packard Chair in Manufacturing
Engineering

UPS Foundation Chair in Gerontology

1974
Jascha Heifetz Chair in Music

IBM Chair in Engineering Management

Irving R. Melbo Chair in Education

Omar B. Milligan Chair
in Petroleum Engineering

1974, *continued*
N.I.O.C. Chair in Petroleum Engineering

George T. and Harriet E. Pfleger Chair in Law

Robert E. Vivian Chair in Energy Resources

1975
Gregor Piatigorsky Chair in Violoncello

1976
Aerol Arnold Chair in English

King Faisal Chair in Islamic Thought
and Culture

John Robert Fluor Chair in Chemical
Engineering

George C. Griffith Chair in Cardiology

Northrop Chair in Engineering

George T. Pfleger Chair in Electrical
Engineering

Henry Salvatori Chair in Computer Science

1977
Ralph Edgington Chair in Medicine

Don and Sybil Harrington Foundation Chair
in Esthetic Dentistry

Fletcher Jones Chair in Computer Science

Della Martin Chair in Psychiatry

Charles Lee Powell Chair in Electrical
Engineering and Computer Science

1978
Rex Ingraham Chair in Restorative Dentistry

1979
USC Associates Chair in Humanities

1979, *continued*
USC Associates/Thomas H. Brem Chair
in Medicine

Joseph A. DeBell Chair in Business
Administration

Captain Allan Hancock/USCA Chair
in Marine Science

Emery Evans Olson Chair in Nonprofit
Entrepreneurship and Public Policy

1980
USC Associates Chair in Business
Administration

John R. Hubbard Chair in History

1982
W. M. Keck Foundation Chair
in Geological Sciences

Leon J. Tiber and David S. Alpert Chair
in Medicine

1983
Carl Mason Franklin Dean's Chair in Law

Donald P. and Katherine B. Loker Chair
in Organic Chemistry

Gordon S. Marshall Chair in Engineering

1984
George and MaryLou Boone Chair
in Craniofacial Molecular Biology

Chester F. Dolley Chair
in Petroleum Engineering

Zohrab A. Kaprielian Dean's Chair in
Engineering

Emery Stoops and Joyce King-Stoops
Dean's Chair in Education

Continued on page 236

Chairs, *continued*

1985
ARCO/William F. Kieschnick Chair
in the Neurobiology of Aging

Sidney R. Garfield Chair in Health Sciences

1986
James E. Birren Chair in Gerontology

Carolyn Craig Franklin Chair in Law
and Religion

M.C. Gill Chair in Composite Materials

Richard Angus Grant, Sr., Chair in Neurology

William M. Keck Chair in Biological Sciences
(Office of the Provost)

William M. Keck Chair in Cognitive Neuroscience
(Office of the Provost)

G. Donald and Marian James Montgomery
Dean's Chair in Dentistry

Robert A. Naslund Chair in Curriculum Theory

Capt. Henry W. Simonsen Chair
in Strategic Entrepreneurship

Ervin and Florine Yoder Chair in Real Estate Law

Wilford and Daris Zinsmeyer Chair
in Marine Studies

1987
Charles E. Cook/Community Bank Chair
in Banking

Robert R. Dockson Dean's Chair
in Business Administration

H. Leslie Hoffman and Elaine S. Hoffman
Chair in Cancer Research

Lusk Chair in Real Estate

Fred W. O'Green Chair in Engineering

Kenneth King Stonier Chair
in Business Administration

1988
AARP University Chair in Gerontology

William M. Keck Chair in Biochemistry
(Office of the Provost)

William M. Keck Chair in Engineering
(Office of the Provost)

1988, *continued*
Jerry and Nancy Neely Chair
in American Enterprise

John Stauffer Dean's Chair
in Pharmaceutical Sciences

UPS Foundation Chair in Law and Gerontology

1989
William and Sylvia Kugel Dean's Chair
in Gerontology

Ruth and Albert McKinlay Chair in Theatre

Paul A. Miller Chair in Letters, Arts
and Sciences

John and Trish O'Donnell Chair in Real Estate
and Urban Economics

Charles Lee Powell Chair in Engineering

Charles F. Sexton Chair in American Enterprise

Norman Topping/National Medical Enterprises
Chair in Medicine and Public Policy

1990
Mary D. Allen Chair in Vision Research
(Doheny Eye Institute)

Dave and Jeanne Tappan Chair in Marketing

1991
Judge Edward J. and Ruey L. Guirado
Endowed Chair in Law

John A. McCone Chair in International
Relations

McCulloch-Crosby Chair in Marine Biology

Harold and Lillian Moulton Chair
in Organic/Polymer Chemistry

Wilbur N. & Ruth Van Zile Chair
in Oral and Maxillofacial Surgery

1992
Richard and Jarda Hurd Chair
in Distribution Management

George and Louise Kawamoto Chair
in Biological Sciences

1993
USC Associates Chair in Natural Sciences

USC Associates Chair in Social Science

1993, *continued*
Steven J. Ross/Time Warner Endowed Dean's
Chair in Cinema-Television

E. Morgan Stanley Chair
in Business Administration

1994
Blue Cross of California Chair
in Health Care Finance

Flora L. Thornton Chair in Preventive Medicine

1995
Catherine and Joseph Aresty Chair
in Urologic Research

Robert R. and Katheryn A. Dockson Chair
in Economics and International Relations

Judy and Larry Freeman Chair
in Basic Science Research

Hanson-White Chair in Medical Research

May S. and John Hooval Dean's Chair in Medicine

Ray R. Irani, Chairman of Occidental
Petroleum Corp., Chair in Chemistry

Jeffrey J. Miller Chair in Government, Business
and the Economy

George A. and Judith A. Olah Nobel Laureate
Chair in Hydrocarbon Chemistry

Robert C. Packard President's Chair

Mary Pickford Foundation Endowed Chair
(USC School of Cinematic Arts)

C. Erwin and Ione L. Piper Dean's Chair
(USC School of Policy, Planning, and Development)

Stuart E. Siegel Chair in Pediatric Oncology

Kenneth L. Trefftzs Chair in Finance

William and Julie Wrigley Chair
in Environmental Studies

1996
Fahmy Attallah, Ph.D. and Donna Attallah
Chair in Humanistic Psychology

Ted Banks Chair for the Director of Track and
Field Program

Deloitte & Touche LLP Chair in Accountancy

Chairs, *continued*

1996, *continued*
Ester Dornsife Chair in Biological Sciences

Harold Dornsife Neurosciences Chair

Hugh M. Hefner Chair for the Study
of American Film

Fred V. Keenan Chair in Finance

Vincent and Julia Meyer Chair
in Orthopaedic Surgery

Kenneth T. Norris Jr. Chair in Epidemiology

Kenneth T. Norris Jr. Chair in Medicine

Martin H. Weiss Chair in Neurosurgery

1997
AFLAC Chair in Cancer Research

Margaret and John Ferraro Chair
in Effective Local Government

The Golden Age Association/Frances Wu Chair
in Chinese Elderly

Alma and Alfred Hitchcock Chair
(USC School of Cinematic Arts)

Sydney M. Irmas Chair in Public Interest Law
and Legal Ethics

Della and Harry MacDonald Dean's Chair
in Architecture

Raymond and Betty McCarron Chair
in Neurology

Rita and Edward Polusky Chair
in Basic Cancer Research

The Katherine and Frank Price Endowed Chair
for the Study of Race and Popular Culture

Donald G. Skinner Chair in Urology

Fran and Ray Stark Endowed Chair
(USC School of Cinematic Arts)

Wrigley Chair in Environmental Studies

1998
Berle and Lucy Adams Chair in Cancer Research

Dwight C. and Hildagarde E. Baum Chair
in Biomedical Engineering

J. Harold and Edna L. LaBriola Chair
in Genetic Orthopaedic Research

1998, *continued*
Harold E. Lee Chair in Cancer Research

Henrietta C. Lee Chair in Cancer Research

McAlister Chair in Business Administration

J. Thomas McCarthy Trustee Chair in Law

Orfalea Director's Chair in Entrepreneurship

Verna R. Richter Chair in Cancer Research

Walter A. Richter Chair in Cancer Research

Rupert and Gertrude Stieger Vision Research
Chair (Doheny Eye Institute)

1999
Anna H. Bing Dean's Chair in the College
of Letters, Arts and Sciences

Charles W. and Carolyn Costello Chair
in Colorectal Diseases

John Elliott Chair in Economics

James E. Goerz Chair in Management

Edna M. Jones Chair in Gerontology

Rita and Edward Polusky Chair
in Education and Aging

Jeffrey P. Smith Chair in Surgery

Joseph P. Van Der Meulen, M.D., Chair
in Parkinson's Disease Research in Honor
of Robert J. Pasarow

Andrew and Erna Viterbi Chair in Communications
(USC Viterbi School of Engineering)

Charles S. and Hildegard Warren Chair
in Vision Research (Doheny Eye Institute)

2000
Lloyd Armstrong Jr. Chair for Science
and Engineering (Office of the Provost)

Warren Bennis Chair in Leadership

Alan Casden Dean's Chair at the Leventhal
School of Accounting

Richard T. Cooper and Mary Catherine Cooper
Chair in Public School Administration

A. Ray Irvine Chair in Clinical Ophthalmology
(Doheny Eye Institute)

2000, *continued*
Jon Adams Jerde, FAIA, Chair in Architecture

Joan J. Michael and William B. Michael Chair
in Measurement, Evaluation and
Accountability

Roger and Lilah Stangeland Chair
in Interventional Cardiology

Flora L. Thornton Chair in Vision Research
(Doheny Eye Institute)

Leslie P. Weiner Chair in Neurology

James and Dorothy Williams Chair in Neurology

2001
Wallis Annenberg Chair in Communication
and Journalism

Wallis Annenberg Chair in Communication
Technology and Society

Bloom Family Chair in Lymphoma Research

George Bozanic and Holman G. Hurt Chair
in Sports and Entertainment Business

Veronica P. Budnick, M.D., Chair in Liver Disease

Marion and Harry Keiper Chair
in Cancer Research

Gordon L. MacDonald Chair in History

Robert C. Packard Trustee Chair in Law (1)

Robert C. Packard Trustee Chair in Law (2)

2002
Chonette Chair in Biomedical Technology

Gabilan Chair (Office of the Provost)

William A. Heeres and Josephine A. Heeres
Chair in Community Pharmacy

Hygeia Centennial Chair in Clinical Pharmacy

Knight Chair in Media and Religion

David Packard Chair in Engineering

Kay Rose Endowed Chair in the Art of Sound
and Dialogue Editing

Nathan and Lilly Shapell Chair in Law

Shapell-Guerin Chair in Jewish Studies

Continued on page 238

Chairs, *continued*

2002, *continued*
Audrey Skirball-Kenis Chair
for Colorectal Diseases

Audrey Skirball-Kenis Chair
in Plastic and Reconstructive Surgery

Ken Wannberg Endowed Chair
in Music Editing

2003
Jeanne Cox Brady Chair to Research Arthritis
in Young People

W. M. Keck Chair in Medicine
(Office of the Provost)

2004
Judith and John Bedrosian Chair
on Governance and Public Enterprise

Electronic Arts Endowed Chair
in Interactive Entertainment

Daniel J. Epstein Chair (USC Viterbi School
of Engineering)

Linda MacDonald Hilf Chair in Philosophy

Bowen H. "Buzz" McCoy and Barbara M.
McCoy Endowed Chair in Jazz

Presidential Chair (USC Viterbi School
of Engineering)

Viterbi Early Career Chair in Engineering

Ziegler Chair in Culture, Faith and History

2005
Scott H. Bice Chair in Healthcare Law, Policy
and Ethics

Corfman Family Chair (USC College of Letters,
Arts and Sciences)

Dana Dornsife Chair in the College of Letters,
Arts and Sciences

David Dornsife Chair in the College of Letters,
Arts and Sciences

Robert F. Erburu Chair in Ethics, Globalization
and Development

Renette and Marshall Ezralow Family Chair
in Cancer Therapeutics

Flores (Rene Sr., Connie, Rene Jr., Jeffery
and Brandon) Chair in Health Services Research

2005, *continued*
Conrad Hall Chair in Cinematography
and Color Timing

Robert G. Kirby Chair in Behavioral Finance

Robert G. & Mary G. Lane Early Career Chair
(USC Viterbi School of Engineering)

Philip & Cayley MacDonald Early Career Chair
(USC Viterbi School of Engineering)

A. N. Mosich Chair in Accounting

Stephen K. Nenno Endowed Chair
in Television Production

Stephen K. Nenno Endowed Chair
in Television Studies

Leonard Silverman Chair
(USC Viterbi School of Engineering)

2006
Annenberg Family Chair in Communication
Leadership

The Dr. Robert C. and Veronica Atkins Chair
in Childhood Obesity and Diabetes

The Larry Auerbach Endowed Chair
(USC School of Cinematic Arts)

Ming Hsieh Chair in Electrical Engineering –
Electrophysics

Ming Hsieh Chair in Electrical Engineering –
Systems

Lear Chair in Entertainment, Media and
Society

Daniel Mishell Chair in OB/GYN

Jack Munushian Early Career Chair
(USC Viterbi School of Engineering)

Jerry and Nancy Neely Chair
in Business Administration

James McN. Stancill Chair
in Business Administration

Professorships

1945
Lyle G. McNeile Professorship in Obstetrics

1952
Henry W. Bruce Professorship in Equity

1955
William C. DeMille Professorship in Drama

1957
Robert H. and Nellie V. H. Dutton Professorship
in Forensic Medicine

1961
Hastings Professorship in Medicine

1964
Franz Alexander Professorship in Psychiatry

1970
Colin Rhys Lovell Professorship in History

Seeley G. Mudd Professorship in Engineering

1972
Ernst & Young Professorship in Accounting

Leonard K. Firestone Professorship in Religion

Industry Visiting Professorship in Electrical
Engineering

Mendel B. Silberberg Professorship
in Social Psychology

1973
Arthur B. Freeman Professorship in Engineering

Kenneth T. Norris Professorship in Engineering

Florence R. Scott Professorship in English

Grace Whisler Professorship in Medicine

1974
Richard Crutcher Professorship
in Letters, Arts and Sciences

Andrew W. Mellon Professorship in Humanities

John B. and Alice Sharp Professorship in Law

1976
Alton M. Brooks Professorship in Religion

Smith International Professorship
in Mechanical Engineering

Charles B. Thornton Professorship in Finance

TRW Professorship in Software Engineering

Professorships, *continued*

1977
Roy P. Crocker Professorship in Law

QSAD Centurion Professorship
in Pharmaceutical Science

1978
Joseph A. DeBell Professorship
in Business Administration

Gavin S. Herbert Professorship
in Pharmaceutical Science

KPMG Foundation Professorship in Accounting

Charles Krown/Pharmacy Alumni Professorship
in Pharmaceutical Sciences

John Milner Professorship in Child Welfare

Albert Soiland Professorship
in Radiation Biology

Torrey H. Webb Professorship in Law, Emeritus

1979
Frances R. and John J. Duggan Distinguished
Professorship in Law

William M. Hogue Professorship in Electrical
Engineering

1980
John A. Biles Professorship
in Pharmaceutical Sciences

Justin Dart Professorship in Finance

Justin Dart Professorship
in Operations Management

Maurice Jones, Jr., Professorship in Law

1981
Richard Crutcher Professorship in Law

Frances R. and John J. Duggan Distinguished
Professorship in Public Administration

Study of Women and Men in Society
Professorship in Media and Sex Roles

1982
Accounting Circle Professorship in Accounting

Arthur Andersen & Co. Alumni Professorship
in Accounting

USC Associates Assistant Professorship in Dentistry

1982, *continued*
USC Associates Professorship in Cinema-TV

Robert Kingsley Professorship in Law

Dorothy W. Nelson Professorship in Law

1983
Leon Benwell Professorship in Law

Orrin B. Evans Professorship in Law

1984
Walter H. Annenberg Professorship
in Communication

George and Miriam Jacobson Professorship
in Radiology

Barbra Streisand Professorship
in Contemporary Gender Studies

1985
Herbert W. Armstrong Professorship
in Constitutional Law

William T. Dalessi Professorship in Law

William E. Leonhard Professorship
in Engineering

1986
Ernest Hahn Professorship in Marketing

Ramona and Charles Hilliard Professorship in Law

Ivadelle and Theodore Johnson Professorship
in Banking and Finance

John B. Milliken Professorship in Taxation

1987
USC Accounting Associates Professorship
in Accounting

Stephen Crocker Professorship in Education

Stephen Crocker Professorship in Music

Florence Everline Professorship in Sociology

1988
Harry J. Bauer and Dorothy Bauer Rawlins
Professorship in Cardiology

Boyd P. and Elsie D. Welin Professorship
in Pharmaceutical Sciences

1989
Robert C. Packard Professorship in Law

1990
Merle H. Bensinger Professorship
in Gerontology

Albert L. and Madelyne G. Hanson Family Trust
Assistant Professorship (USC Davis School
of Gerontology)

Ivadelle and Theodore Johnson Professorship
in Law and Business

Phillip Maurer Tennis Professorship
in Clinical Dentistry

1991
Virginia S. and Fred H. Bice Professorship in Law

Judge Edward J. and Ruey L. Guirado
Professorship in Law

Charles F. and Helen Ann Langmade
Professorship in Obstetrics and Gynecology

Todd-Wells Professorship in Neurosurgery

1992
USC Associates Professorship in Art History

Marion Frances Chevalier Professorship in French

1993
C. C. Crawford Professorship
in Productivity Improvement

Charles L. and Ramona I. Hilliard Professorship
in Business Administration

1995
Milo Don and Lucille Appleman Professorship
in Biological Sciences

Dennis F. and Brooks Holt Professorship
in Public Policy and Communications Technology

Helen N. & Emmett H. Jones Professorship
in Engineering

1996
Richard B. Newton Professorship
in Constitutional Law

Tatter Professorship in Medicine

Continued on page 240

Professorships, *continued*

1997
Ralph W. and Jean L. Bleak Professorship
in Restorative Dentistry

George Burns Distinguished Visiting Professorship
in Performance (USC School of Theatre)

Maria B. Crutcher Professorship
in Citizenship and Democratic Values

Driscoll/Clevenger Professorship
in Social Policy and Administration

Richard L. and Antoinette Schamoi Kirtland
Professorship in Law

G. Donald Montgomery Professorship
in Dentistry

Robert Grandford Wright Professorship
in Psychology

1998
Lt. Col. Earle and Patricia M. Smith
Professorship in Neurogenetic Research

Chief Information Officer and John Stauffer
Professorship in Law

David Lawrence Stein/Violet Goldberg Sachs
Professorship (USC School of Social Work)

Leslie Wilbur and Norma Lash Wilbur–Evelyn
Kieffer Professorship in Higher Education

1999
A. C. Martin Visiting Professorship
in Architectural Design

Moss Foundation Professorship in Sports
Medicine in Memory of Dr. Robert K. Kerlan

Vascular Surgery Endowed Professorship

Kenneth and Bette Volk Professorship
in Neurology

2000
MacDonald and Diane Rusling Becket
Professorship in Community Design

Diane and MacDonald Becket Professorship
in Educational Policy

Timothy M. Chan Professorship
in Complementary Therapeutics

Nancy M. and Edward D. Fox Urban Design
Critic

2000, *continued*
Gavin S. Herbert Professorship in Vision
Research (Doheny Eye Institute)

Mary Pickford Foundation Professorship
in Gerontology

2001
Clifford H. and Betty C. Allen Professorship
in Urban Leadership

Wayne G. and Margaret L. Bemis Professorship
in Endodontics

Violet S. Bonney Professorship
in Dental Hygiene

Fred H. Cole Professorship
in Electrical Engineering

Ernest P. Larson Professorship
in Health, Ethnicity and Poverty

Frances G. Larson Professorship
in Social Work Research

2002
Paxson H. Offield Professorship
in Fisheries Ecology

2003
Gabilan Assistant Professorship in Biological
Sciences (Office of the Provost)

Gabilan Assistant Professorship in Chemistry
(Office of the Provost)

Gabilan Assistant Professorship in Computer
Science (Office of the Provost)

Charles M. Goldstein Professorship
in Community Dentistry

2004
Delmar & Nina and Lonnie & Pam Laster
Professorship in Neurology

Edward L. Schneider/Michael and Susan
Lombardi Professorship in Gerontology

Lenore Stein-Wood and William S. Wood
Professorship in Social Work and Business
in a Global Society

Richard M. and Ann L. Thor Endowed
Professorship in Urban Social Development

Viterbi Professorship in Engineering

2005
George N. and MaryLou Boone Professorship
in Medical Excellence

Herbert and Ruth Busemann Visiting Assistant
Professorship in Mathematics

2006
Fred Champion Professorship in Civil and
Environmental Engineering

Stephen and Etta Varra Professorship (USC
Viterbi School of Engineering)

Robert E. Vivian Professorship in Energy
Resources

Other Faculty Positions

1988
Charles E. and Janet R. Elerding Head Coach
Position for the Cardinal Team

1998
James N. Gamble Directorship
of the Gamble House

2000
Myron and Marian Casden Directorship of the
Casden Institute for the Study of the Jewish
Role in American Life

July 2001
Arthur C. Bartner Trojan Marching Band
Director's Chair

Appendix XIX

Gifts of $10 Million or More*

(as of December 2006)

$175 million – From George Lucas and the Lucasfilm Foundation to endow USC's School of Cinematic Arts and to fund a new building for the school (2006)

$163 million – From Alfred E. Mann, including an initial gift of $113 million to create the Alfred E. Mann Institute for Biomedical Engineering at USC and a subsequent gift of $50 million (1998, 2005)

$120 million – From the Annenberg Foundation to establish the USC Annenberg Center for Communication (1993)

$110 million – From the W. M. Keck Foundation to name the Keck School of Medicine of the University of Southern California (1999)

$100 million – From the Annenberg Foundation to support key activities of the USC Annenberg School for Communication (2002)

$52 million – From Andrew J. and Erna Viterbi to endow and name the USC Andrew and Erna Viterbi School of Engineering (2004)

$50 million – From Louis and Helene Galen to support and name USC's Galen Center (2003, 2006)

$35 million – From Ming Hsieh to name the USC Ming Hsieh Department of Electrical Engineering (2006)

$35 million – From Gordon S. Marshall to endow and name the USC Gordon S. Marshall School of Business (1996)

$27 million – From an anonymous donor to support USC's Women in Science and Engineering (WiSE) program and fund capital improvements for the USC School of Social Work (2000)

$25 million – From the Eli and Edythe Broad Foundation to create the Broad Institute for Integrative Biology and Stem Cell Research at the Keck School of Medicine of USC (2006)

$25 million – From Elaine and Kenneth Leventhal to endow and name the USC Elaine and Kenneth Leventhal School of Accountaing (1995, 2002)

$25 million – From Flora Laney Thornton to endow and name the USC Flora L. Thornton School of Music (1999)

$23 million – From Gayle Garner Roski and Edward P. Roski Jr. to endow and name the USC Gayle Garner Roski School of Fine Arts (2006)

$22 million – From Mark A. and Mary Stevens to create the USC Mark and Mary Stevens Institute for Technology Commercialization (2004)

$21 million – From Catherine and Joseph Aresty to support urologic cancer research programs and facilities at the USC/Norris Comprehensive Cancer Center and Hospital (1995, 1998, 2001, 2003)

$20 million – From Barbara J. and Roger W. Rossier to endow and name the USC Barbara J. and Roger W. Rossier School of Education (1998)

$20 million – From Selim K. Zilkha to complete construction of and name the Zilkha Neurogenetic Institute on USC's Health Sciences campus (2002)

$18 million – From the Wrigley Family Estates to support USC's Philip K. Wrigley Marine Science Center on Santa Catalina Island (1978, 1995)

$17 million – From Katherine B. Loker to augment USC's Donald P. and Katherine B. Loker Hydrocarbon Research Institute and build the Katherine B. Loker Track Stadium (1998)

$15 million – From Henrietta C. Lee to establish the Henrietta C. Lee and Harold E. Lee Women's Health Center at the USC/Norris Comprehensive Cancer Center (2005)

$15 million – From John, Julie, Kyle and Alison Mork to endow and name the USC Mork Family Department of Chemical Engineering and Materials Science (2005)

$15 million – From the Kenneth T. and Eileen L. Norris Foundation to support construction of and name the Harlyne J. Norris Cancer Research Tower (2000)

$15 million – From an anonymous donor to establish the USC-CHLA Institute for Pediatric Clinical Research at Childrens Hospital Los Angeles (2004)

$14 million – In property from May Department Stores Inc. to provide university parking facilities (1990)

Included here are single gifts as well as multiple gifts, pledges and other intended gifts to a single program.

Continued on page 242

Gifts of $10 Million or More*, *continued*

$13 million – From Synopsys to support engineering (2005)

$12 million – From the Annenberg Foundation to endow graduate and faculty positions at the Annenberg School for Communication and to support studies on topics affecting women and children in fields ranging from psychology and literature to education and economics, USC's Summer Seminars and the USC Mobile Dental Clinic (2001)

$12 million – From Oracle Corporation to supply computers throughout the university (2002)

$12 million – From the Thomas Lord Estate for university endowment (1989)

$11 million – From Alan Casden to endow and name the Casden Institute for the Study of the Jewish Role in American Life, create the Casden Real Estate Economics Forecast and endow the Alan Casden Dean's Chair in the USC Elaine and Kenneth Leventhal School of Accounting (2000)

$11 million – From Computer Associates to support engineering (2004)

$11 million – From Daniel J. Epstein to endow and name the USC Daniel J. Epstein Department of Industrial and Systems Engineering (2002)

$11 million – From the estate of Augustus Russell to support scholarships at the university (1998)

$10 million – From Judith and John Bedrosian to create the Judith and John Bedrosian Center on Governance and the Public Enterprise in the USC School of Policy, Planning, and Development (2004)

$10 million – From Janice Bryant Howroyd to create the Janice Bryant Howroyd Fund for Student Aid in the USC College of Letters, Arts and Sciences (2005)

$10 million – From Pratt & Whitney, UTC, to create the USC Pratt & Whitney UTC Institute for Collaborative Engineering (2002)

$10 million – From James E. and Beverly Rogers to support the USC Gould School of Law (2005)

$10 million – From Ronald Tutor to name Ronald Tutor Hall of Engineering (1997)

$10 million – From an anonymous donor to support construction of the Galen Center (1996)

Included here are single gifts as well as multiple gifts, pledges and other intended gifts to a single program.

Appendix XX

Olympic Athletes

(as of December 2005)

USC's participation in the Olympics dates to 1904, when Emil Breitkreutz became the first USC student to compete in the Olympic games, bringing home a bronze medal in the 800 meters. Since then, there have been 361 athletes who attended USC before, during, or after their Olympic appearance. They have collected 234 medals—including 112 golds, 64 silvers and 58 bronzes—and have won at least one gold medal in every Summer Olympics since 1912.

Name (Country)	Year (Location)	Sport	Event	Medal/Place
Ablowich, Edgar (U.S.A.)	1932 (Los Angeles)	Track	1600m Relay	Gold
Abrahams, Guy (Panama)	1976 (Montreal)	Track	100m	5th
Akins, Sid (U.S.A.)	1984 (Los Angeles)	Baseball		Silver
Alade'fa, Kehinde (Nigeria)	1996 (Atlanta)	Track	400m Hurdles	
Al-Kudmani, Ahmad (Saudi Arabia)	2000 (Sydney) / 2004 (Athens)	Swimming / Swimming	100m Breaststroke / 100m Breaststroke	56th / 47th
Allan, Scott (U.S.A.)	1972 (Munich)	Yachting	Flying Dutchman	
Althin, Nils (Sweden)	1932 (Los Angeles)	Boxing	Welterweight	
Amend, Eric (U.S.A.)	1984 (Los Angeles)	Tennis	Singles	
Anderson, Gary (Canada)	1988 (Seoul) / 1992 (Barcelona)	Swimming / Swimming	200m IM / 200m IM	8th / 8th
Anderson, Norman (U.S.A.)	1924 (Paris)	Track	Shotput	5th
Anderson, Otto (U.S.A.)	1920 (Antwerp) / 1924 (Paris)	Track / Track	110m Hurdles / Decathlon	
Anderson, Wayne (U.S.A.)	1964 (Tokyo)	Swimming	200m Breaststroke	7th
Argue, Clifford (U.S.A.)	1924 (Paris)	Track	Pentathlon	10th
Arnarson, Orn (Iceland)	2000 (Sydney)	Swimming	200m Backstroke / 200m Freestyle	4th / 15th
Ayuso, Elias (Puerto Rico)	2004 (Athens)	Basketball		6th
Babka, Rink (U.S.A.)	1960 (Rome)	Track	Discus	Silver
Barak, Ron (U.S.A.)	1964 (Tokyo)	Gymnastics	All Around	39th
Barakat, Mohammed (U.S.A.)	1984 (Los Angeles)	Field Hockey		
Barber, Richard (U.S.A.)	1932 (Los Angeles	Track	Long Jump	5th
Barberic, Bret (U.S.A.)	1988 (Seoul)	Baseball		Gold
Barnard, Arthur (U.S.A.)	1952 (Helsinki)	Track	110m Hurdles	Bronze
Barnes, Lee U.S.A.)	1924 (Paris) / 1928 (Amsterdam)	Track / Track	Pole Vault / Pole Vault	Gold / 5th
Barrett, Casey (Canada)	1996 (Atlanta)	Swimming	200m Butterfly	11th

Continued on page 244

Name (Country)	Year (Location)	Sport	Event	Medal/Place
Bayer, Herwig (Austria)	1980 (Moscow)	Swimming	100m Freestyle 100m Backstroke	22nd 20th
Beaton, Rayfield (Guyana)	1976 (Montreal)	Track	800m	
Beck, Kenneth (U.S.A.)	1936 (Berlin) 1948 (London)	Water Polo Water Polo		
Becker, Carolyn (U.S.A.)	1980 (Moscow) 1984 (Los Angeles)	Volleyball Volleyball		 Silver
Becker, Nick (U.S.A.)	1992 (Barcelona)	Volleyball		Bronze
Beckner, John "Jack " (U.S.A.)	1952 (Helsinki) 1956 (Melbourne) 1960 (Rome)	Gymnastics Gymnastics Gymnastics	All Around Team All Around Team All Around Team	8th 6th 5th
Benko, Lindsay (U.S.A.)	2000 (Sydney) 2004 (Athens)	Swimming Swimming	200m Freestyle 800m Free Relay 200m Backstroke 200m Freestyle 400m Free Relay 800m Free Relay	12th Gold 10th 14th Silver Gold
Bennett, Robert (U.S.A.)	1960 (Rome) 1964 (Tokyo)	Swimming Swimming	100m Backstroke 200m Backstroke	Bronze Bronze
Benyarku, Esi (Canada)	2000 (Sydney)	Track	100m 400 relay	1st Round 1st Round
Billings, Brook (U.S.A.)	2004 (Athens)	Volleyball		4th
Bisbey, Harry (U.S.A.)	1952 (Helsinki)	Water Polo		4th
Bittick, Charles (U.S.A.)	1960 (Rome)	Water Polo		7th
Black, Byron (Zimbabwe)	1996 (Atlanta)	Tennis	Singles Doubles	2nd Round 2nd Round
Black, Kim (U.S.A.)	2000 (Sydney)	Swimming	800m Free Relay	Gold
Black, Wayne (Zimbabwe)	1996 (Atlanta) 2000 (Sydney) 2004 (Athens)	Tennis Tennis Tennis	Singles Doubles Singles Doubles Doubles	2nd Round 2nd Round 1st Round 1st Round 5th Tie
Bodrogi, Viktor (Hungary)	2000 (Sydney) 2004 (Athens)	Swimming Swimming	200m Butterfly 200m Backstroke	24th 24th
Borah, Charles (U.S.A.)	1928 (Amsterdam)	Track	400m Relay	Gold
Bottom, Joe (U.S.A.)	1976 (Montreal)	Swimming	100m Butterfly 100m Freestyle 400m Medley Relay	Silver 6th
Bottom, Mike (U.S.A.)	1980 (Moscow)*	Swimming	100m Butterfly	
Bourland, Clifford (U.S.A.)	1948 (London)	Track	1600m Relay 200m	Gold 5th
Bradford, Colin (Jamaica)	1976 (Montreal) 1984 (Los Angeles)	Track Track	400m 1600m Relay (did not compete)	 5th

Name (Country)	Year (Location)	Sport	Event	Medal/Place
Breitkreutz, Emil (U.S.A.)	1904 (St. Louis)	Track	800m	Bronze
Bridgewater, Brad (U.S.A.)	1996 (Atlanta)	Swimming	200m Backstroke	Gold
Bright, Patty Lucas (U.S.A.)	1964 (Tokyo)	Volleyball		5th
	1968 (Mexico City)	Volleyball		8th
Brown, Terrezene (U.S.A.)	1964 (Tokyo)	Track	High Jump	14th
Brown, Wendy (U.S.A.)	1988 (Seoul)	Track	Heptathlon	17th
Bruwier, Jean-Paul (Belgium)	1992 (Barcelona)	Track	400m Hurdles	
	1996 (Atlanta)	Track	400m Hurdles	
Bryggare, Arto (Finland)	1980 (Moscow)	Track	110m Hurdles	6th
	1984 (Los Angeles)	Track	110m Hurdles	Bronze
	1992 (Barcelona)	Track	110m Hurdles	
Burns, Marvin (U.S.A.)	1952 (Helsinki)	Water Polo		4th
	1960 (Rome)	Water Polo		7th
Calvert, Sherry (U.S.A.)	1972 (Munich)	Track	Javelin	15th
	1976 (Montreal)	Track	Javelin	
Campbell, Tonie (U.S.A.)	1980 (Moscow)*	Track	110m Hurdles	
	1984 (Los Angeles)	Track	110m Hurdles	5th
	1988 (Seoul)	Track	110m Hurdles	Bronze
Caperonis, Pano (Switzerland)	1964 (Tokyo)	Swimming	100m Freestyle	
			400m Freestyle	
	1968 (Mexico City)	Swimming	100m Freestyle	
			200m Freestyle	
Carden, John (U.S.A.)	1956 (Melbourne)	Soccer		
Careaga, Javier (Mexico)	1988 (Seoul)	Swimming	100m Breast	
			200m Breast	
			200m Ind'l Medley	
			400m Ind'l Medley	
	1992 (Barcelona)	Swimming	100m Breast	20th
Carfagno, Edward (U.S.A.)	1940 (cancelled)	Fencing Foil		
Carlsen, Gary (U.S.A.)	1968 (Mexico City)	Track	Discus	6th
Carpenter, Ken (U.S.A.)	1936 (Berlin)	Track	Discus	Gold
Case, Lee (U.S.A.)	1948 (London)	Water Polo		
Castro, Rodrigo (Brazil)	2000 (Sydney)	Swimming	200m Freestyle	33th
			800m Free Relay	13th
	2004 (Athens)	Swimming	200m Freestyle	20th
			400m Free Relay	12th
			800m Free Relay	9th
Cater, Mojca (Canada)	1988 (Seoul)	Swimming	200m Butterfly	9th
Cavanaugh, Chris (U.S.A.)	1980 (Moscow)*	Swimming	100m Freestyle	
	1984 (Los Angeles)	Swimming	400m Free Relay	Gold

Continued on page 246

Name (Country)	Year (Location)	Sport	Event	Medal/Place
Cawley, Rex (U.S.A.)	1964 (Tokyo)	Track	400m Hurdles	Gold
Chalmers, Chris (Canada)	1988 (Seoul)	Swimming	1500m Freestyle	
Chambers, Robert (U.S.A.)	1948 (London)	Track	800m	6th
Chan, Sau Ying (Hong Kong)	1992 (Barcelona) 1996 (Atlanta)	Track Track	100m Hurdles 100m Hurdles	
Chatfield , Mark (U.S.A.)	1972 (Munich)	Swimming	100m Breaststroke	4th
Chikina, Natalya "Natasha" (Kazakhstan)	1996 (Atlanta) 2000 (Sydney)	Diving Diving	Platform Platform	Semifinals 9th
Chowen, Wesley (U.S.A.)	1960 (Rome)	Cycling	Individual Road Team Road	57th 11th
Clayton, Wellesley (Jamaica)	1964 (Tokyo) 1968 (Mexico City)	Track Track	Long Jump Long Jump	
Clentzos, Peter (Greece)	1932 (Los Angeles)	Track	Pole Vault	7th
Cockburn, Murray (Canada)	1956 (Melbourne)	Track	400m 1600m Relay	5th
Cochran, Roy (U.S.A.)	1948 (London)	Track	400m Hurdles 1600m Relay	Gold Gold
Coffman, Bob (U.S.A.)	1980 (Moscow)*	Track	Decathlon	
Collins, Luci (U.S.A.)	1980 (Moscow)*	Gymnastics		
Connor, Richard (U.S.A.)	1956 (Melbourne)	Diving	Platform	Bronze
Cooper, Cynthia (U.S.A.)	1988 (Seoul) 1992 (Barcelona)	Basketball Basketball		Gold Bronze
Copeland, Lillian (U.S.A.)	1928 (Amsterdam) 1932 (Los Angeles)	Track Track	Discus Discus	Silver Gold
Cornell Douty, Sheila (U.S.A.)	1996 (Atlanta) 2000 (Sydney)	Softball Softball		Gold Gold
Corsiglia, Robin (Canada)	1976 (Montreal)	Swimming	100m Breaststroke 400m Medley Relay	9th Bronze
Corson, James Hunt (U.S.A.)	1928 (Amsterdam)	Track	Discus	Bronze
Costa, Leonardo (Brazil)	2000 (Sydney)	Swimming	800m Free Relay 200m Backstroke	13th 14th
Courtney, J. Ira (U.S.A.)	1912 (Stockholm)	Track	100m, 200m 400m Relay	
Crabbe, Clarence "Buster" (U.S.A.)	1928 (Amsterdam) 1932 (Los Angeles)	Swimming Swimming	1500m Freestyle 400m Freestyle 400m Freestyle 1500m Freestyle	Bronze 4th Gold 5th
Craig, Bill (U.S.A.)	1964 (Tokyo)	Swimming	400m Medley Relay	Gold
Crear, Mark (U.S.A.)	1996 (Atlanta) 2000 (Sydney)	Track Track	110m Hurdles 110m Hurdles	Silver Bronze
Cummings Critchell, Iris (U.S.A.)	1936 (Berlin)	Swimming	200m Breaststroke	

Name (Country)	Year (Location)	Sport	Event	Medal/Place
Danvers, Natasha (Great Britain)	2000 (Sydney)	Track	400m Hurdles 1600 Relay	8th 6th
Davis, David (U.S.A.)	1960 (Rome)	Track	Shotput	
Davis, Jack (U.S.A.)	1952 (Helsinki) 1956 (Melbourne)	Track Track	110m Hurdles 110m Hurdles	Silver Silver
De La Riva, Sandra (U.S.A.)	1988 Seoul)	Team Handball		7th
Deutsch Devaney, Joseph (Romania)	1956 (Melbourne)	Water Polo		8th
Draper, Foy (U.S.A.)	1936 (Berlin)	Track	400m Relay	Gold
Drew, Howard (U.S.A.)	1912 (Stockholm)	Track	100m	
Drown, Dan (U.S.A.)	1964 (Tokyo)	Water Polo		9th
Dumais, Justin (U.S.A.)	2004 (Athens)	Diving	3m Synchronized	6th
Dumas, Charles (U.S.A.)	1956 (Melbourne) 1960 (Rome)	Track Track	High Jump High Jump	Gold 6th
Dvorak, Dusty (U.S.A.)	1984 (Los Angeles)	Volleyball		Gold
Dye, Leighton (U.S.A.)	1928 (Amsterdam)	Track	110m Hurdles	4th
Edwards, Torri (U.S.A.)	2000 (Sydney)	Track	100m 200m 400 Relay	2nd Round Semifinals Bronze
Ekpenyong, Udeme (Nigeria)	1992 (Barcelona) 1996 (Atlanta)	Track Track	1600m Relay 1600m Relay	 Finals (dns)
Erese, William (Nigeria)	1996 (Atlanta)	Track	110m Hurdles	
Evans, Janet (U.S.A.)	1988 (Seoul) 1992 (Barcelona) 1996 (Atlanta)	Swimming Swimming Swimming	400m IM 400m Freestyle 800m Freestyle 400m Freestyle 800m Freestyle 400m Freestyle 800m Freestyle	Gold Gold Gold Silver Gold 6th
Evans, Roy (U.S.A.)	1920 (Antwerp)	Track	Discus	
Fahrner, Thomas (West Germany)	1984 (Los Angeles) 1988 (Seoul)	Swimming Swimming	200m Freestyle 400m Freestyle 800m Free Relay 200m Freestyle 100m Freestyle 800m Free Relay 400m Free Relay	Bronze 9th Silver 8th Bronze 6th
Fargus, Joanna (Great Britain)	2000 (Sydney)	Swimming	200m Backstroke	9th
Faust, Joseph (U.S.A.)	1960 (Rome)	Track	High Jump	17th
Felix, Allyson (U.S.A.)	2004 (Athens)	Track	200m	Silver
Findlay, Conn (U.S.A.)	1956 (Melbourne) 1960 (Rome) 1964 (Tokyo) 1976 (Montreal)	Rowing Rowing Rowing Yachting	Pair Oars w/Cox. Pair Oars w/Cox. Pair Oars w/Cox. Tempest	Gold Bronze Gold Bronze

Continued on page 248

Name (Country)	Year (Location)	Sport	Event	Medal/Place
Finneran Rittenhouse, Sharon (U.S.A.)	1964 (Tokyo)	Swimming	400m Indv'l Medley	Silver
Fitch, Al (U.S.A.)	1936 (Berlin)	Track	1600m Relay	Silver
Fitzpatrick, Ken (Canada)	1984 (Los Angeles)	Swimming	200m Breaststroke	5th
Float, Jeff (U.S.A.)	1980 (Moscow)*	Swimming	400m Freestyle	
	1984 (Los Angeles)	Swimming	800m Free Relay	Gold
			200m Free	4th
Ford, Michelle (Australia)	1976 (Montreal)	Swimming	200m Freestyle	16th
			200m Butterfly	16th
	1980 (Moscow)	Swimming	800m Freestyle	Gold
			400m Freestyle	4th
			200m Butterfly	Bronze
Fredriksson, Anette (Sweden)	1976 (Montreal)	Swimming	100m Breaststroke	21st
			200m Breaststroke	24th
			400m Medley Relay	10th
Frischknecht, Paulo (Portugal)	1976 (Montreal)	Swimming	200m Freestyle	51st
			100m Butterfly	41st
			200m Butterfly	37th
			800m Free Relay	17th
			400m Medley Relay	14th
	1980 (Moscow)	Swimming	200m Freestyle	21st
			400m Freestyle	
			100m Butterfly	23rd
Furniss, Bruce (U.S.A.)	1976 (Montreal)	Swimming	200m Freestyle	Gold
			800m Free Relay	Gold
Furniss, Steve (U.S.A.)	1972 (Munich)	Swimming	200m Indv'l Medley	Bronze
			400m Indv'l Medley	4th
	1976 (Montreal)	Swimming	400m Indv'l Medley	6th
Galitzen, Michael "Mickey Riley" (U.S.A.)	1928 (Amsterdam)	Diving	Springboard	Silver
			Platform	Bronze
	1932 (Los Angeles)	Diving	Springboard	Gold
			Platform	Silver
Garapick, Nancy (Canada)	1976 (Montreal)	Swimming	100m Backstroke	Bronze
			200m Backstroke	Bronze
	1980 (Moscow)	Swimming	200m Freestyle	
			400m Indv'l Medley	
Gardner, Gabe (U.S.A.)	2004 (Athens)	Volleyball		4th
Gardner, Randy (U.S.A.)	1976 (Innsbruck)	Figure Skating	Pairs w/Tai Babilonia	5th
	1980 (Lake Placid)	Figure Skating	Pairs w/Tai Babilonia	
Gilchrist, Allan (Canada)	1948 (London)	Swimming	400m Free	
			1500m Free	
			800m Free Relay	
	1952 (Helsinki)	Swimming	400m Free	
			1500m Free	
			800m Free Relay	

Name (Country)	Year (Location)	Sport	Event	Medal/Place
Gilchrist, John "Sandy" (Canada)	1964 (Tokyo)	Swimming	400m Indv'l Medley	5th
			100m Freestyle	
			400m Freestyle	
			1500m Freestyle	
			400m Free Relay	
			800m Free Relay	
			400m Medley Relay	
	1968 (Mexico City)	Swimming	200m Indv'l Medley	6th
			400m Indv'l Medley	5th
			100m Freestyle	
			200m Freestyle	
			400m Free Relay	7th
			800m Free Relay	4th
			400m Medley Relay	7th
Gilhula, James (U.S.A.)	1932 (Los Angeles)	Swimming	400m Freestyle	
Gilkes, James (Guyana)	1976 (Montreal)	Track	100m	
Gingsjo, Bengt (Sweden)	1972 (Munich)	Swimming	400m Freestyle	6th
			1500m Freestyle	4th
			400m Indv'l Medley	6th
			800m Free Relay	4th
	1976 (Montreal)	Swimming	200m Freestyle	27th
			400m Freestyle	28th
			800m Free Relay	7th
Gleie, Katrin (Denmark)	2000 (Sydney)	Rowing	Quadruple Sculls	6th
Gonzales, Mike (Puerto Rico)	1998 (Nagano)	Bobsled	4-Man Bobsled	
Gordien, Fortune (U.S.A.)	1948 (London)	Track	Discus	Bronze
	1952 (Helsinki)	Track	Discus	4th
	1956 (Melbourne)	Track	Discus	Silver
Graber, William Sr. (U.S.A.)	1932 (Los Angeles)	Track	Pole Vault	4th
	1936 (Berlin)	Track	Pole Vault	5th
Green, Bill (U.S.A.)	1980 (Moscow)*	Track	400m	
Green Vargas, Debbie (U.S.A.)	1980 (Moscow)*	Volleyball		
	1984 (Los Angeles)	Volleyball		Silver
Greenbaum, Dan (U.S.A.)	1992 (Barcelona)	Volleyball		Bronze
Greene, Paul (Australia)	1996 (Atlanta)	Track	400m	Quarterfinals
			400m Relay	Semifinals
			1600m Relay	Semifinals
Griffin, Kenneth (U.S.A.)	1936 (Berlin)	Gymnastics	Team	10th
Haaf, Dietmar (Germany	1992 (Barcelona)	Track	Long Jump	
Hallock, Jeanne (U.S.A.)	1964 (Tokyo)	Swimming	100m Freestyle	9th
Hammer, Richard (U.S.A.)	1964 (Tokyo)	Volleyball		9th
Handelsman, Mark (Israel)	1984 (Los Angeles)	Track	400m	
			800m	
Haney Neville, Jeannie (U.S.A.)	1976 (Montreal)	Swimming	400m Indv'l Medley	9th
Harris, Charles (U.S.A.)	1992 (Barcelona)	Water Polo		4th

Continued on page 250

Name (Country)	Year (Location)	Sport	Event	Medal/Place
Harrison, Reginald (U.S.A.)	1928 (Amsterdam)	Water Polo		
Hartley, Blythe (Canada)	2000 (Sydney)	Diving	3m Springboard	10th
			3m Synchronized	5th
	2004 (Athens)	Diving	3m Springboard	5th
			3m Synchronized	7th
			10m Synchronized	Bronze
Heck, Kathryn Ann (U.S.A.)	1968 (Mexico City)	Volleyball		8th
Henricks, Jon (Australia)	1956 (Melbourne	Swimming	100m Freestyle	Gold
			800m Free Relay	Gold
	1960 (Rome)	Swimming	100m Freestyle	
Hernandez de Belmar, Claudia (Mexico)	1988 (Seoul)	Tennis		
Hogholm, Vagn (Denmark)	1988 (Seoul)	Swimming	400m Free Relay	
Horton Racker, Joyce (U.S.A.)	1952 (Helsinki)	Yachting	Dragon	11th
Horton, William Sr. (U.S.A.)	1952 (Helsinki)	Yachting	Dragon	11th
House Helmath, Carolyn (U.S.A.)	1960 (Rome)	Swimming	400m Freestyle	
Houser, Clarence "Bud" (U.S.A.)	1924 (Paris)	Track	Discus	Gold
			Shotput	Gold
	1928 (Amsterdam)	Track	Discus	Gold
Hughes, Robert (U.S.A.)	1952 (Helsinki)	Water Polo		4th
	1956 (Melbourne)	Water Polo		5th
		Swimming	200m Breaststroke	
Hume, Sylvia (New Zealand)	1988 (Seoul)	Swimming	100m Backstroke	
			200m Backstroke	
Ilika, Josh (Mexico)	2000 (Sydney)	Swimming	100m Butterfly	33rd
	2004 (Athens)	Swimming	200m Freestyle	28th
			100m Butterfly	33rd
Iness, Sim (U.S.A.)	1952 (Helsinki)	Track	Discus	Gold
Ivie, Bryan (U.S.A.)	1992 (Barcelona)	Volleyball		Bronze
	1996 (Atlanta)	Volleyball		9th
Jacquin, Lisa (U.S.A.)	1988 (Seoul)	Equestrian	Show Jumping	Silver/Team
	1992 (Barcelona)	Equestrian	Show Jumping	5th
				17th/Team
Jeffrey, Rhi (U.S.A.)	2004 (Athens)	Swimming	800m Free Relay	Gold
Jensen, Larsen (U.S.A.)	2004 (Athens)	Swimming	400m Freestyle	4th
			1500m Freestyle	Silver
Jewell, William (U.S.A.)	1964 (Tokyo)	Canoeing	Kayak-4	
	1968 (Mexico City)	Canoeing	Kayak-4	
Johnson, William (U.S.A.)	1968 (Mexico City)	Swimming	800m Free Relay	
Jones, Jacque (U.S.A.)	1996 (Atlanta)	Baseball		Bronze
Jones, Sue (U.S.A.)	1968 (Mexico City)	Swimming	100m Breaststroke	
			400m Medley Relay	
Jorgensen, Dan (U.S.A.)	1988 (Seoul)	Swimming	400m Freestyle	12th
			800m Free Relay	Gold
	1992 (Barcelona)	Swimming	400m Freestyle	13th
			800m Free Relay	Bronze

Name (Country)	Year (Location)	Sport	Event	Medal/Place
Jorgensen, Lars (U.S.A.)	1988 (Seoul)	Swimming	1500m Freestyle	
Jorgensen, Ninja (U.S.A.)	1968 (Mexico City)	Volleyball		8th
Kaer, Morton (U.S.A.)	1924 (Paris)	Track	Pentathlon	5th
Kalache, Celso (Brazil)	1972 (Munich)	Volleyball		10th
	1976 (Montreal)	Volleyball		7th
Kapek, Julien (France)	2004 (Athens)	Track	Triple Jump	10th
Keller, Kalyn (U.S.A.)	2004 (Athens)	Swimming	400m Freestyle	10th
			800m Freestyle	8th
Keller, Klete (U.S.A.)	2000 (Sydney)	Swimming	400m Freestyle	Bronze
			800m Free Relay	Silver
	2004 (Athens)	Swimming	200m Freestyle	4th
			400m Freestyle	Bronze
			800m Free Relay	Gold
Kelly, Fred (U.S.A.)	1912 (Stockholm)	Track	110m Hurdles	Gold
Ker, Mike (Canada)	1976 (Montreal)	Swimming	1500m Freestyle	18th
Kerekjarto, Tamas (Hungary)	1996 (Atlanta)	Swimming	50m Freestyle	55th
	2004 (Athens)	Swimming	200 IM	13th
			800m Free Relay	16th
Kimura, Eri (Japan)	1992 (Barcelona)	Swimming	400 IM	7th
Kirkwood, David (U.S.A.)	1964 Tokyo)	Modern Pentathlon	Team	Silver
Kiss, Balazs (Hungary)	1996 (Atlanta)	Track	Hammer	Gold
Klapkarek, Nicolai (West Germany)	1984 (Los Angeles)	Swimming	200m Backstroke	6th
			200m Indv'l Medley	7th
			100m Backstroke	15th
Klein, Hans (West Germany)	1960 (Rome)	Swimming	800m Free Relay	7th
	1964 (Tokyo)	Swimming	100m Freestyle	Bronze
			800m Free Relay	Silver
			400m Medley Relay	Silver
Koch, Desmond (U.S.A.)	1956 (Melbourne)	Track	Discus	Bronze
Koh, Desmond (Singapore)	1992 (Barcelona)	Swimming	200m Indv'l Medley	31st
			400m Indv'l Medley	21st
			200m Breaststroke	32nd
	1996 (Atlanta)	Swimming	200m Breaststroke	
			200m Indv'l Medley	
			400m Indv'l Medley	
			400m Medley Relay	
			800m Free Relay	
Konoukh, Sofia (Russia)	2000 (Sydney)	Water Polo		Bronze
	2004 (Athens)	Water Polo		5th
Konrads, John (Australia)	1960 (Rome)	Swimming	1500m Freestyle	Gold
			400m Freestyle	Bronze
			800m Free Relay	Bronze
	1964 (Tokyo)	Swimming	1500m Freestyle	
Krayzelburg, Lenny (U.S.A.)	2000 (Sydney)	Swimming	100m Backstroke	Gold
			200m Backstroke	Gold
			400m Medley Relay	Gold
	2004 (Athens)	Swimming	100m Backstroke	4th
			400m Medley Relay	Gold

Continued on page 252

Name (Country)	Year (Location)	Sport	Event	Medal/Place
Krempel, Paul (U.S.A.)	1920 (Antwerp)	Gymnastics		
	1924 (Paris)	Gymnastics	Rings	7th
	1928 (Amsterdam)	Gymnastics	Rings	7th
				7th/Team
Kurtz, Frank (U.S.A.)	1932 (Los Angeles))	Diving	Platform	Bronze
	1936 (Berlin)	Diving	Platform	5th
Kwok, Mark (Hong Kong)	1996 (Atlanta)	Swimming	200m Butterfly	
			200m Indv'l Medley	
			400m Freestyle	
			400m Indv'l Medley	
	2000 (Sydney)	Swimming	400m Freestyle	30th
			200m Freestyle	26th
			200m Butterfly	32nd
LaBerge, Karen (U.S.A.)	1980 (Moscow)*	Swimming	800m Freestyle	
Landreth Brown, Debbie (U.S.A.)	1980 (Moscow)*	Volleyball		
Lang, Ronald (U.S.A.)	1964 (Tokyo)	Volleyball		9th
Langerholc, Brigita (Slovenia)	2000 (Tokyo)	Track	800m	4th
			1600 relay	1st Round
Larrabee, Michael (U.S.A.)	1964 (Tokyo)	Track	400m	Gold
			1600m Relay	Gold
Larson, Lance (U.S.A.)	1960 (Rome)	Swimming	100m Freestyle	Silver
			400m Medley Relay	Gold
Lea, James (U.S.A.)	1956 (Melbourne)	Track	400m	
Lee, Sammy (U.S.A.)	1948 (London)	Diving	Platform	Gold
			Springboard	Bronze
	1952 (Helsinki)	Diving	Platform	Gold
Lenard, Michael (U.S.A.)	1984 (Los Angeles)	Team Handball		
Leslie, Lisa (U.S.A.)	1996 (Atlanta)	Basketball		Gold
	2000 (Sydney)	Basketball		Gold
	2004 (Athens)	Basketball		Gold
Li, Arthur (Hong Kong)	1988 (Seoul)	Swimming	100m Freestyle	
			200m Freestyle	
	1992 (Barcelona)	Swimming	100m Freestyle	42nd
			200m Freestyle	30th
			100m Butterfly	38th
			200m Indv'l Medley	37th
	1996 (Atlanta)	Swimming	50m Freestyle	
			100m Freestyle	
			100m Butterfly	
Lindberg, Per Ola (Sweden)	1960 (Rome)	Swimming	100m Freestyle	8th
			800m Free Relay	6th
	1964 (Tokyo)	Swimming	100m Freestyle	
			400m Medley Relay	
			400m Free Relay	5th
Lindner, Dorte (Germany)	2000 (Sydney)	Diving	Syncho. Springboard	7th
			Springboard	Bronze
Long, Dallas (U.S.A.)	1960 (Rome)	Track	Shotput	Bronze
	1(yo)	Track	Shotput	Gold

Name (Country)	Year (Location)	Sport	Event	Medal/Place
Luna, Jashia (Mexico)	2000 (Sydney)	Diving	3m Synchronized 3m Springboard	6th 19th
	2004 (Athens)	Diving	10m Synchronized 10m Platform 3m Springboard	5th 13th 20th
Lynn, Robert (U.S.A.)	2000 (Sydney)	Water Polo		6th
Martin, Miklos "Nick" (Hungary)	1952 (Helsinki) 1956 (Melbourne)	Water Polo Water Polo		Gold Gold
Mason, Mike (Canada)	1992 (Barcelona)	Swimming	200m Breaststroke	23rd
Maxie, Leslie (U.S.A.)	1988 (Seoul)	Track	400m Hurdles	
Mayberry, Myra (Puerto Rico)	1992 (Barcelona)	Track	100m 400m	
	1996 (Atlanta)	Track	100m 200m	Quarterfinals 2nd Round
Mayer, Helene (Germany)	1928 (Amsterdam) 1932 (Los Angeles) 1936 (Berlin)	Fencing Fencing Fencing	Foil Foil Foil	Gold 5th Silver
Mayers, Natasha (St. Vincent and the Grenadines)	2000 (Sydney) 2004 (Athens)	Track Track	100m 100m	 31st
McBreen, Tom (U.S.A.)	1972 (Munich)	Swimming	400m Freestyle	Bronze
McCormack, John (U.S.A.)	1952 (Helsinki)	Diving	Platform	4th
McFadden Briggs, Miki (U.S.A.)	1968 (Mexico City)	Volleyball		8th
McGeagh, Rich (U.S.A.)	1964 (Tokyo)	Swimming	400m Medley Relay	
McGee, Pam (U.S.A.)	1984 (Los Angeles)	Basketball		Gold
McGwire, Mark (U.S.A.)	1984 (Los Angeles)	Baseball		Silver
McIlroy, Ned (U.S.A.)	1964 (Tokyo)	Water Polo		9th
McNaughton, Duncan (Canada)	1932 (Los Angeles)	Track	High Jump	Gold
Meadows, Earle (U.S.A.)	1936 (Berlin)	Track	Pole Vault	Gold
Mellon, Muriel (U.S.A.)	1948 (London)	Swimming	100m Backstroke	7th
Mellouli, Ous (Tunisia)	2000 (Sydney) 2004 (Athens)	Swimming Swimming	400m IM 200m IM 400m IM 1500m Freestyle	43rd 9th 5th 14th
Mendel, Ingo (West Germany)	1984 (Los Angeles)	Basketball		
Meszaros, Gergerly (Hungary)	2004 (Athens)	Swimming	800m Free Relay	DNS
Metcalf, Malcolm (U.S.A.)	1932 (Los Angeles) 1936 (Berlin)	Track Track	Javelin Javelin	7th
Miller, Cheryl (U.S.A.)	1984 (Los Angeles)	Basketball		Gold
Miller, Inger (U.S.A.)	1996 (Atlanta)	Track	200m 400m Relay	4th Gold
	2000 (Sydney)	Track	(did not compete)	

Continued on page 254

Name (Country)	Year (Location)	Sport	Event	Medal/Place
Miller, Lennox (Jamaica)	1968 (Mexico City)	Track	100m	Silver
			400m Relay	4th
	1972 (Munich)	Track	100m	Bronze
			400m Relay	
Morales, Luis (Puerto Rico)	1984 (Los Angeles)	Track	100m	Semis
			200m	Semis
Morris, Ron (U.S.A.)	1960 (Rome)	Track	Pole Vault	Silver
Motridge, Edith (U.S.A.)	1936 (Berlin)	Swimming	100m Backstroke	4th
Muglia, Pat (U.S.A.)	1988 (Seoul)	Yachting	Tornado	
Munk, Annemarie (Hong Kong)	1988 (Seoul)	Swimming	100m Breaststroke	
			200m Breaststroke	
Naber, John (U.S.A.)	1976 (Montreal)	Swimming	100m Backstroke	Gold
			200m Backstroke	Gold
			200m Freestyle	Silver
			800m Free Relay	Gold
			400m Medley Relay	Gold
Nakano, Ayako (Japan)	1992 (Barcelona)	Swimming	100m Freestyle	22nd
			400m Free Relay	
Nagy, Gabor (Romania)	1952 (Helsinki)	Water Polo		
	1956 (Melbourne)	Water Polo		8th
Nagy, George (Canada)	1976 (Montreal)	Swimming	200m Butterfly	10th
	1980 (Moscow)	Swimming	200m Butterfly	
Nelson, Lyle Barber (U.S.A.)	1976 (Innsbruck)	Biathlon		
	1980 (Lake Placid)	Biathlon		
	1984 (Sarajevo)	Biathlon		
	1988 (Calgary)	Biathlon		
Norris, James (U.S.A.)	1952 (Helsinki)	Water Polo		4th
Novelo, Lupita (Mexico)	1992 (Barcelona)	Tennis	Singles	
			Doubles	
Numano, Mimi (Japan)	1980 (Moscow)	Swimming	100m Freestyle	
O'Brien, Michael (U.S.A.)	1984 (Los Angeles)	Swimming	1500m Freestyle	Gold
O'Brien, Parry (U.S.A.)	1952 (Helsinki)	Track	Shotput	Gold
	1956 (Melbourne)	Track	Shotput	Gold
	1960 (Rome)	Track	Shotput	Silver
	1964 (Tokyo)	Track	Shotput	4th
O'Hara, Michael (U.S.A.)	1964 (Tokyo)	Volleyball		9th
Okash, Ibrahim (Somalia)	1984 (Los Angeles)	Track	400m	
	1988 (Seoul)	Track	800m	
Olivan, Jesus (Spain)	1992 (Barcelona)	Track	Long Jump	
	1996 (Atlanta)	Track	Long Jump	
Omwansa, David (Kenya)	1972 (Munich)	Track	800m	
	1976 (Montreal)	Track	800m	
Ong, Jeffrey (Malaysia)	1988 (Seoul)	Swimming	400m Freestyle	
			1500m Freestyle	
	1992 (Barcelona)	Swimming	200m Freestyle	33rd
			400m Freestyle	39th
			1500m Freestyle	20th

Name (Country)	Year (Location)	Sport	Event	Medal/Place
Orban, Eva (Hungary)	2004 (Athens)	Track	Hammer Throw	
Orwig, Bernice (U.S.A.)	2000 (Sydney)	Water Polo		Silver
Osuna, Rafael (Mexico)	1968 (Mexico City)	Tennis	Doubles	Gold
Ottenbrite, Anne (Canada)	1984 (Los Angeles)	Swimming	100m Breaststroke	Silver
			200m Breaststroke	Gold
			400m Medley Relay	Bronze
Paddock, Charles (U.S.A.)	1920 (Antwerp)	Track	100m	Gold
			200m	Silver
			400m Relay	Gold
	1924 (Paris)	Track	100m	5th
			200m	Silver
	1928 (Amsterdam)	Track	200m	
Patton, Mel (U.S.A.)	1948 (London)	Track	100m	5th
			200m	Gold
			400m Relay	Gold
Paulsen, John (U.S.A.)	1932 (Los Angeles)	Swimming	200m Breaststroke	
Pelle, Aniko (Hungary)	2004 (Athens)	Water Polo		6th
Pedder, Margie (Great Britain)	2000 (Sydney)	Swimming	200m Butterfly	11th
Pederson, Ivan (Denmark)	1968 (Mexico City)	Swimming	100m Backstroke	
			200m Backstroke	
Phuangthong, Dulyarit "Goh" (Thailand)	1996 (Atlanta)	Swimming	100m Backstroke	
			200m Backstroke	
			400m Medley Relay	
	2000 (Sydney)	Swimming	100m Backstroke	43rd
			200m Butterfly	38th
Pickell, Steve	1976 (Montreal)	Swimming	100m Backstroke	10th
			200m Butterfly	10th
			400m Medley Relay	Silver
			800m Free Relay	
	1980 (Moscow)	Swimming	100m Backstroke	
Pielen, Silke (West Germany)	1972 (Munich)	Swimming	100m Backstroke	8th
			400m Medley Relay	Bronze
Ping, Li Hong (China)	1980 (Moscow)**	Diving		
	1984 (Los Angeles)	Diving	Springboard	4th
Place Brandel, Terry (U.S.A.) (West Germany)	1980 (Moscow)*	Volleyball		
	1984 (Los Angeles)	Volleyball		
Ploessel, Velma Dunn (U.S.A.)	1936 (Berlin)	Diving	Platform	Silver
Poindexter, James (U.S.A.)	1972 (Munich)	Shooting	Trap	6th
Pope-Irwin, Paula Jean Myers (U.S.A.)	1952 (Helsinki)	Diving	Platform	Silver
	1956 (Melbourne)	Diving	Platform	Bronze
	1960 (Rome)	Diving	Platform	Silver
			Springboard	Silver
Powers, Pat (U.S.A.)	1984 (Los Angeles)	Volleyball		Gold
Quance, Kristine (U.S.A.)	1996 (Atlanta)	Swimming	100m breaststroke	
			200m Indv'l Medley	9th
			400m Medley Relay	Gold

Continued on page 256

Name (Country)	Year (Location)	Sport	Event	Medal/Place
Quarrie, Don (Jamaica)	1968 (Mexico City)	Track	200m	
	1972 (Munich)	Track	200m	
			400m Relay	
	1976 (Montreal)	Track	100m	Silver
			200m	Gold
			1600m Relay	5th
	1980 (Moscow)	Track	100m	
			400m Relay	
			200m	Bronze
	1984 (Los Angeles)	Track	200m	Semis
			400m Relay	Silver
Questad, Larry (U.S.A.)	1968 (Mexico City)	Track	200m	6th
Ralphs, Tony (U.S.A.)	1964 (Tokyo)	Canoeing	Kayak 2 and 4	
	1972 (Munich)	Canoeing	Kayak 4	
Ratanachote, Vicha (Thailand)	2000 (Sydney)	Swimming	200m Freestyle	43rd
Richards, Alma (U.S.A.)	1912 (Stockholm)	Track	High Jump	Gold
Richardson, Dorothy "Dot" (U.S.A.)	1996 (Atlanta)	Softball		Gold
	2000 (Sydney)	Softball		Gold
Ris, Wally (U.S.A.)	1948 (London)	Swimming	100m Freestyle	Gold
			800m Free Relay	Gold
Rodrigues, Pedro (Portugal)	1992 (Barcelona)	Track	400m Hurdles	
	2000 (Sydney)	Track	400m Hurdles	Semifinals
Romary, Janice Lee York (U.S.A.)	1948 (London)	Fencing	Foil	
	1952 (Helsinki)	Fencing	Foil	4th
	1956 (Melbourne)	Fencing	Foil	4th
	1960 (Rome)	Fencing	Foil	
	1964 (Tokyo)	Fencing	Foil	
	1968 (Mexico City)	Fencing	Foil	
Romero, Maria Elena (Mexico)	1992 (Barcelona)	Diving	Platform	16th
	1996 (Atlanta)	Diving	3m Springboard	Semifinals
Roney, Brian (U.S.A.)	1980 (Moscow)*	Swimming	400m Freestyle	
Ronson, Peter (Iceland)	1960 (Rome)	Track	110m Hurdles	
Rose, Murray (Australia)	1956 (Melbourne)	Swimming	400m Freestyle	Gold
			1500m Freestyle	Gold
			800m Free Relay	Gold
	1960 (Rome)	Swimming	400m Freestyle	Gold
			1500m Freestyle	Silver
			800m Free Relay	Bronze
Ross, William (U.S.A.)	1956 (Melbourne)	Water Polo		5th
Roth, George (U.S.A.)	1932 (Los Angeles)	Gymnastics	Club Swinging	Gold
Rothhammer Weisbly, Keena (U.S.A.)	1972 (Munich)	Swimming	200m Freestyle	Bronze
			400m Freestyle	6th
			800m Freestyle	Gold
Rudd, Debbie (Great Britain)	1976 (Montreal)	Swimming	200m Breast	8th
	1980 (Moscow)	Swimming	200m Breast	11th
Ruddins, Kim (U.S.A.)	1984 (Los Angeles)	Volleyball		Silver
	1988 (Seoul)	Volleyball		7th
Saari, Roy (U.S.A.)	1964 (Tokyo)	Swimming	400m Indv'l Medley	Silver
			400m Freestyle	4th
			1500m Freestyle	7th
			800m Free Relay	Gold
Sakamoto, Makoto (U.S.A.)	1964 (Tokyo)	Gymnastics	All Around Team	7th
	1972 (Munich)	Gymnastics	All Around Team	10th
Salcedo, Hugo (U.S.A.)	1972 (Munich)	Soccer		

Name (Country)	Year (Location)	Sport	Event	Medal/Place
Sanchez, Felix (Dominican Republic)	2000 (Sydney) 2004 (Athens)	Track Track	400m Hurdles 400m Hurdles	Semifinals Gold
Sandeno, Kaitlin (U.S.A.)	2000 (Sydney) 2004 (Athens)	Swimming Swimming	800m Freestyle 400m Indv'l Medley 200m Butterfly 400m IM 400m Freestyle 200m Butterfly 800m Free Relay	Bronze 4th 5th Silver Bronze 4th Gold
Sandlund, Asa (Sweden)	1996 (Atlanta)	Swimming	800m Free Relay	9th
Sayner, Daniel (U.S.A.)	1980 (Moscow)*	Rowing		
Schiller, George (U.S.A.)	1920 (Antwerp)	Track	400m	
Seagren, Bob (U.S.A.)	1968 (Mexico City) 1972 (Munich)	Track Track	Pole Vault Pole Vault	Gold Silver
Sefton, William (U.S.A.)	1936 (Berlin)	Track	Pole Vault	4th
Seko, Toshihiko (Japan)	1984 (Los Angeles) 1988 (Seoul)	Track Track	Marathon Marathon	14th 9th
Serpas, Edgardo "Tony" (El Salvador)	2000 (Sydney)	Track	100m	1st Round
Severa, Ronald (U.S.A.)	1956 (Melbourne) 1960 (Rome)	Water Polo Water Polo		5th 7th
Shadden, John (U.S.A.)	1988 (Seoul)	Yachting	470m	Bronze
Shelton, Jason (Jamaica)	1996 (Atlanta)	Track	400m	Semifinals
Shrader Butler, Dana (U.S.A.)	1972 (Munich)	Swimming	100m Butterfly	5th
Shriver, Marley Lynn (U.S.A.)	1956 (Melbourne)	Swimming	400m Freestyle	4th
Siering, Laura (U.S.A.)	1976 (Montreal)	Swimming	100m Breaststroke 400m Medley Relay	11th Silver
Silvestri, Russ (U.S.A.)	2000 (Sydney)	Sailing	Finn	6th
Simms, Charles (U.S.A.)	1952 (Helsinki) 1956 (Melbourne)	Gymnastics Gymnastics	All Around All Around	89th 8th/Team 32nd 6th/Team
Sink, Roland (U.S.A.)	1948 (London)	Track	1500m	
Smallwood, Robert (U.S.A.)	1936 (Berlin)	Track	400m	
Smith, Miriam (U.S.A.)	1976 (Montreal)	Swimming	200m Backstroke	13th
Spencer, Jeffrey (U.S.A.)	1972 (Munich)	Cycling		
Spencer, Kyle (Great Britain)	2000 (Sydney)	Tennis	Doubles	1st Round
Staley, Roy (U.S.A.)	1936 (Berlin)	Track	110m Hurdles	
Steel, John (New Zealand)	1992 (Barcelona) 1996 (Atlanta)	Swimming Swimming	100m Freestyle 200m Freestyle 400m Free Relay 800m Free Relay 100m Freestyle 400m Free Relay 800m Free Relay	13th 16th
Stewart, James (U.S.A.)	1928 (Amsterdam)	Track	Decathlon	4th
Strachan, Rodney (U.S.A.)	1976 (Montreal)	Swimming	400m Indv'l Medley	Gold

Continued on page 258

Name (Country)	Year (Location)	Sport	Event	Medal/Place
Strenk, Andrew (U.S.A.)	1968 (Mexico City)	Swimming	800m Free Relay	
Suxho, Donald (U.S.A.)	2004 (Athens)	Volleyball		4th
Sveinsson, Jakob (Iceland)	2000 (Sydney)	Swimming	200m Breaststroke	25th
Szabados, Bela (Hungary)	1996 (Atlanta)	Swimming	100m Freestyle 400m Freestye	
	2000 (Sydney)	Swimming	200m Freestyle 800m Free Relay	11th 10th
Takacs, Attila (Hungary)	1956 (Melbourne)	Gymnastics	All Around	24th
Thompson, Tina (U.S.A.)	2004 (Athens)	Basketball		Gold
Thompson, Wilbur (U.S.A.)	1948 (London)	Track	Shotput	Gold
Thomson, Earl (Canada)	1920 (Antwerp)	Track	110m Hurdles	Gold
Thurber, Delos (U.S.A.)	1936 (Berlin)	Track	High Jump	Bronze
Timmons, Steve (U.S.A.)	1984 (Los Angeles) 1988 (Seoul) 1992 (Barcelona)	Volleyball Volleyball Volleyball		Gold Gold Bronze
Tisue, Fred (U.S.A.)	1960 (Rome)	Water Polo		7th
Tobian, Gary (U.S.A.)	1956 (Melbourne) 1960 (Rome)	Diving Diving	Platform Springboard Platform	Silver Gold Silver
Toribio, Simeon (Philippines)	1928 (Amsterdam) 1932 (Los Angeles)	Track Track	High Jump High Jump	4th Bronze
Truex, Max (U.S.A.)	1956 (Melbourne)	Track	5,000m 10,000m	
	1960 (Rome)	Track	10,000m	6th
Tudja, Julianna	2004 (Athens)	Track	Hammer	18th
Van der Maath, Carlos (Argentina)	1964 (Tokyo) 1968 (Mexico City)	Water Polo Swimming	100m Backstroke 200m Backstroke 400m Medley Relay	
Vanderstock, Geoffrey (U.S.A.)	1968 (Mexico City)	Track	400m Hurdles	4th
Vandeweghe, Tauna (U.S.A.)	1976 (Montreal)	Swimming	100m Backstroke	14th
Van Osdel, Robert (U.S.A.)	1932 (Los Angeles)	Track	High Jump	Silver
Van Wolvelaere-Johnson, Patty (U.S.A.)	1968 (Mexico City) 1972 (Munich)	Track Track	100m Hurdles 100m Hurdles	4th
Vasconcellos, Cito (Ecuador)	1996 (Atlanta)	Swimming	200m Butterfly 800m Free Relay	
Vendt, Erik (U.S.A.)	2000 (Sydney)	Swimming	400m Ind'l Medley 1500m Freestyle	Silver 6th
	2004 (Athens)	Swimming	400m Ind'l Medley 1500m Freestyle	Silver 16th
Walton, Frank (U.S.A.)	1948 (London)	Water Polo		
Watts, Quincy (U.S.A.)	1992 (Barcelona)	Track	400m 1600m Relay	Gold Gold
Weishoff, Paula (U.S.A.)	1984 (Los Angeles) 1992 (Barcelona) 1996 Atlanta)	Volleyball Volleyball Volleyball		Silver Bronze 11th

Name (Country)	Year (Location)	Sport	Event	Medal/Place
Wen, Lisa (Taiwan)	1984 (Los Angeles)	Swimming	400m Freestyle 800m Freestyle	15th 17th
Wharton, Dave (U.S.A.)	1988 (Seoul) 1992 (Barcelona)	Swimming Swimming	400m Indv'l Medley 200m Indv'l Medley 400m Indv'l Medley 200m Butterfly	Silver 9th 4th 10th
Wijesekara, Manjula (Sri Lanka)	2004 (Athens)	Track	High Jump	
Willeford, Dean (U.S.A.)	1968 (Mexico City)	Water Polo		5th
Williams, Angela (U.S.A.)	2004 (Athens)	Track	400m Relay	DNF
Williams, Randy (U.S.A.)	1972 (Munich) 1976 (Montreal) 1980 (Moscow)*	Track Track Track	Long Jump Long Jump Long Jump	Gold Silver
Wilson, R. Earle (U.S.A.)	1924 (Paris)	Track	Triple Jump	7th
Winters, Tom (U.S.A.)	1960 (Rome)	Swimming	800m Free Relay	
Wolf, Paul (U.S.A.)	1936 (Berlin)	Swimming	800m Free Relay	Silver
Wolf, Wallace (U.S.A.)	1948 (London) 1952 (Helsinki) 1956 (Melbourne) 1960 (Rome)	Swimming Swimming Water Polo Water Polo	800m Free Relay 800m Free Relay	Gold 5th 7th
Wollthan, Tim (Germany)	2004 (Athens)	Water Polo		6th
Woodhead Kantzer, Cynthia "Sippy" (U.S.A.)	1980 (Moscow)* 1984 (Los Angeles)	Swimming Swimming	200m Freestyle 100m Freestyle 400m Freestyle 800m Freestyle 200m Freestyle	 Silver
Woodstra, Sue (U.S.A.)	1980 (Moscow)* 1984 (Los Angeles)	Volleyball Volleyball		 Silver
Woodward, Gabe (U.S.A.)	2004 (Athens)	Swimming	400m Free Relay	Bronze
Wykoff, Frank (U.S.A.)	1928 (Amsterdam) 1932 (Los Angeles) 1936 (Berlin)	Track Track Track	100m 400m Relay 400m Relay 100m 400m Relay	4th Gold Gold 4th Gold
Wyland, Wendy (U.S.A.)	1984 (Los Angeles)	Diving	Platform	Bronze
Yamanaka, Tsuyoshi (Japan)	1956 (Melbourne) 1960 (Rome) 1964 (Tokyo)	Swimming Swimming Swimming	400m Freestyle 1500m Freestyle 800m Free Relay 400m Freestyle 1500m Freestyle 800m Free Relay 400m Freestyle	Silver Silver 4th Silver 4th Silver 6th
Zamperini, Louis (U.S.A.)	1936 (Berlin)	Track	5000m	8th
Zatovic, Juraj (Slovakia)	2000 (Sydney)	Water Polo		12th
Zikarsky, Bjorn (West Germany) (Germany)	1988 (Seoul) 1996 (Atlanta)	Swimming Swimming	400m Medley Relay 400m Free Relay 100m Freestyle 400m Free Relay 400m Medley Relay	4th 6th 11th Bronze 4th

* U.S.A. Boycott   ** China Boycott

(Note: This list includes all Olympic non-coaching competitors who attended at least one class at USC before, during or after their Olympic appearance.)

Appendix XXI

National Championships

(as of December 2005)

USC has long dominated the world of intercollegiate athletics. In fact, it could be argued that Troy was **the** *collegiate athletic program of the 20th century. The following list includes the names of the coaches of the winning teams.*

USC MEN'S TEAM TITLES (86)

Football (11)

1928	Howard Jones
1931	Howard Jones
1932	Howard Jones
1939	Howard Jones
1962	John McKay
1967	John McKay
1972	John McKay
1974	John McKay
1978	John Robinson
2003	Pete Carroll
2004	Pete Carroll

Baseball (12)

1948	Sam Barry and Rod Dedeaux
1958	Rod Dedeaux
1961	Rod Dedeaux
1963	Rod Dedeaux
1968	Rod Dedeaux
1970	Rod Dedeaux
1971	Rod Dedeaux
1972	Rod Dedeaux
1973	Rod Dedeaux
1974	Rod Dedeaux
1978	Rod Dedeaux
1998	Mike Gillespie

Gymnastics (1)

1962	Jack Beckner

Indoor Track and Field (2)

1967	Vern Wolfe
1972	Vern Wolfe

Swimming and Diving (9)

1960	Peter Daland
1963	Peter Daland
1964	Peter Daland
1965	Peter Daland
1966	Peter Daland
1974	Peter Daland
1975	Peter Daland
1976	Peter Daland
1977	Peter Daland

Tennis (16)

1946	William Moyle
1951	Louis Wheeler
1955	George Toley
1958	George Toley
1962	George Toley
1963	George Toley
1964	George Toley
1966	George Toley
1967	George Toley
1968	George Toley
1969	George Toley
1976	George Toley *(tie)*
1991	Dick Leach
1993	Dick Leach
1994	Dick Leach
2002	Dick Leach

Track and Field (26)

1926	Dean Cromwell
1930	Dean Cromwell
1931	Dean Cromwell
1935	Dean Cromwell
1936	Dean Cromwell
1937	Dean Cromwell
1938	Dean Cromwell
1939	Dean Cromwell
1940	Dean Cromwell
1941	Dean Cromwell
1942	Dean Cromwell
1943	Dean Cromwell
1949	Jess Hill
1950	Jess Hill
1951	Jess Mortensen
1952	Jess Mortensen
1953	Jess Mortensen
1954	Jess Mortensen
1955	Jess Mortensen
1958	Jess Mortensen
1961	Jess Mortensen
1963	Vern Wolfe
1965	Vern Wolfe *(tie)*
1967	Vern Wolfe
1968	Vern Wolfe
1976	Vern Wolfe

Volleyball (6)

1949	Hans Vogel (USVBA)
1950	Hans Vogel (USVBA)
1977	Ernie Hix
1980	Ernie Hix
1988	Bob Yoder
1990	Jim McLaughlin

Water Polo (3)

1998	John Williams and Jovan Vavic
2003	Jovan Vavic
2005	Jovan Vavic

USC WOMEN'S TEAM TITLES (20)

Basketball (2)

1983	Linda Sharp
1984	Linda Sharp

Golf (1)

2003	Andrea Gaston

Swimming and Diving (1)

1997	Mark Schubert

Tennis (7)

1977	Dave Borelli (AIAW)
1977	Dave Borelli (USTA)
1978	Dave Borelli (USTA)
1979	Dave Borelli (AIAW)
1980	Dave Borelli (AIAW)
1983	Dave Borelli
1985	Dave Borelli

Track and Field (1)

2001	Ron Allice

Volleyball (6)

1976	Chuck Erbe (AIAW)
1977	Chuck Erbe (AIAW)
1980	Chuck Erbe (AIAW)
1981	Chuck Erbe
2002	Mick Haley
2003	Mick Haley

Water Polo (2)

1999	Jovan Vavic (NCWWP)
2004	Jovan Vavic

Acknowledgments

This book has its foundations in the generous contributions of ideas, insights and historical materials from many, many people.

First, the authors would like to thank USC President Steven B. Sample, who conceived the notion of publishing a history to commemorate the university's first 125 years. We are also deeply indebted to Martha Harris, senior vice president for university relations, and Susan Heitman, associate vice president for public relations, whose vision and support helped carry the project to fruition.

Thanks are due as well to George Abdo, James Appleton, Robert P. Biller, Malcolm R. Currie, Dennis F. Dougherty, Stanley P. Gold, John R. Hubbard, Herbert G. Klein, Alan Kreditor, Anthony B. "Tony" Lazzaro, Kenneth Leventhal, Sylvia Manning, C. L. Max Nikias, George A. Olah, Roger F. Olson, Forrest N. Shumway, William G. Spitzer, Robert E. Tranquada, Joseph P. Van Der Meulen and Leonard Wines, who graciously gave of their time, memories and perspectives for questions and interviews. Others who provided invaluable assistance in collecting facts and figures include Noel Aguilar, Steve Arbuckle, Holly Bridges, Jean Crampon, Carolyn Webb de Macias, Michael Duffy, Frances L. Feldman, Paul Hadley, Robert S. Harris, Anne D. Katz, Martin L. Levine, Karin Ryan, Christine E. Shade, Christopher Stoy, Ramesh N. Swamy, Tim Tessalone, John G. "Tom" Tomlinson Jr., Anne Westfall and USC's "unofficial historian," Gerald "Jerry" Papazian.

A very special debt of gratitude is owed to Claude Zachary and Susan Hikida in the USC University Archives for their partnership in conducting the photo research for this book and for helping the authors access countless original source materials. Also instrumental in securing and captioning images were Alexis Bergen, Katie Blatter, Bob Calverley, Dennis Cornell, Katharine A. Díaz, Carol Dougherty, Melissa Gaeke, LouAnne Greenwald, Michael Ned Holte, Jennifer Jaskowiak, Michael Kloss, Dennis J. Martinez, Nicole McAllister, Nancy McHose, Cynthia Monticue, Sarah Oesterle, Sherri Sammon, Norm Schneider, Richard Stone, Dace Taube, Jon Weiner, John Windler, Karen Newell Young and John Zollinger.

The authors also would like to express appreciation to Evelyn Alva, Tamara Baringer, Geoffrey Baum, Erik Brink, Michelle R. Clark, Todd R. Dickey, Cheryl Dionaldo, Eva Emerson, Mickie Faris, Elsa Goay, Randolph Hall, Nancy Hodges, Robert Jenkins, Bob Kiddoo, Lydia Lee, Martin Levine, Sam Martinuzzi, Anthony Michaels, Dottie O'Carroll, Ron Orr, Darren Schenck, Justin Scupine, Michael Seymour, Jon Soffa, Margo Steurbaut, Marlene Wagner, Bill Watson and others for their help in compiling a set of appendices that should serve as a valuable reference for years to come.

Deepest thanks are extended to Betsey Binét and Elizabeth Bailey of 2B Communications as well, whose impeccable design, organizational and editorial skills helped shape the rough manuscript into a polished whole, and to Janet Klein of Delta Graphics for her care in bringing forth a high-quality product. Finally, we also would like to acknowledge Sonsie Carbonara Conroy of Catalyst Communication Arts for her patience and skill in producing the index.

Selected Bibliography

Alderman, Pauline. *We Build a School of Music: The Commissioned History of Music at the University of Southern California*. Los Angeles, CA: The Alderman Book Committee, 1989.

Boaz, Martha Terosse. *USC School of Library Science: History of the School of Library Science, University of Southern California*. Los Angeles, CA: University of Southern California, 1976.

Bogardus, Emory Stephen. *A History of Sociology at the University of Southern California*. Los Angeles, CA: University of Southern California, 1972.

Braun, Eric. *Fight On! The USC Trojans Story*. Mankato, MN: Creative Education/The Creative Company, 1999.

Feldman, Frances Lomas, with Maurice Hamovitch, Helen Northern, Rino Patti, and others. *The Evolution of Professional Social Work Education, Scholarship, and Community Service at the University of Southern California*. Los Angeles, CA: School of Social Work, University of Southern California, 1996.

Gaw, Allison. *A Sketch of the Development of Graduate Work in the University of Southern California, 1910–1935*. Los Angeles, CA: University of Southern California, 1935.

Henley, W. Ballentine & Arthur E. Neelley. *Cardinal and Gold: A Pictorial and Factual Record of the Highlights of Sixty Years of Progress on the Southern California Campus with Views and News of some of the 70,000 students who played their part in the growth of a great university, 1880–1940*. Los Angeles, CA: General Alumni Association, 1939.

Holmes, Robert (photographer), with William Butler and William Strode (executive editors). *The University of Southern California*. Prospect, Kentucky: Harmony House, 1987.

Hunt, Rockwell D. *The First Half-Century*. Los Angeles, CA: University of Southern California, 1930.

Hunt, Rockwell D. *Mr. California*. San Francisco, CA: Fearon Publishers, 1956.

Lane, Mary C. *The Melbo Years: A History of the School Education of the University of Southern California 1953–1973*. Los Angeles, CA: University of Southern California Press, 1974.

Lifton, Sarah. *Keck School of Medicine of the University of Southern California: Trials and Transformation*. Los Angeles, CA: Keck School of Medicine of the University of Southern California, 2004.

Lifton, Sarah. *University of Southern California: Glimpses of History 1880–1995*. Los Angeles, CA: University of Southern California/The USC History Project, 1995.

Moore, Annette. *USC's First Book of Lists and Urban Legends*. Los Angeles, CA: Figueroa Press, 2005.

Moore, Annette, with additional text by Elizabeth Sample. *USC's First Ladies: A Trojan Family Album*. Los Angeles, CA: Figueroa Press, 2005.

Nyiri, Alan (photographer), with Jerry Wingate (executive editor). *The Heritage of USC*. Poultney, VT: University of Southern California Bookstore in association with I.R.I. Studios, 1999.

Reynolds, John H. *The Trojan Gallery: A Pictorial History of the University of Southern California 1880–1980*. Los Angeles, CA: University of Southern California, 1980.

Servìn, Manuel Patricio, and Iris Higbie Wilson. *Southern California and its University: A History of USC 1880–1964*. Los Angeles, CA: The Ward Ritchie Press, 1969.

Somerville, J. Alexander. *Man of Color*. Los Angeles, CA: Lorrin L. Morrison, 1949.

Topping, Norman, with Gordon Cohn. *Recollections*. Los Angeles, CA: University of Southern California, 1990.

Vivian, Robert E. *The USC Engineering Story*. Los Angeles, CA: University of Southern California Press, 1975.

Index

Page numbers in *italics* indicate photos or information in captions.